# SAVAGE ANXIETIES

## THE INVENTION OF
## WESTERN CIVILIZATION

ROBERT A. WILLIAMS, JR.

palgrave
macmillan

First published in 2012 by PALGRAVE MACMILLAN® in the United
States—a division of St. Martin's Press LLC, 175 Fifth Avenue, New York, NY
10010.

Where this book is distributed in the UK, Europe and the rest of the world,
this is by Palgrave Macmillan, a division of Macmillan Publishers Limited,
registered in England, company number 785998, of Houndmills, Basingstoke,
Hampshire RG21 6XS.

Palgrave Macmillan is the global academic imprint of the above companies and
has companies and representatives throughout the world.

Palgrave® and Macmillan® are registered trademarks in the United States, the
United Kingdom, Europe and other countries.

ISBN 978-0-230-33876-0


Library of Congress Cataloging-in-Publication Data

Williams, Robert A., 1955–
    Savage anxieties : the invention of western civilization / by Robert A.
Williams, Jr.
       p.   cm.
    ISBN 978-0-230-33876-0
    1. Indigenous peoples. 2. Noble savage. 3. Tribes. 4. Primitive societies.
I. Title.
GN380.W549   2012
305.8—dc23

                                                            2012011360

A catalogue record of the book is available from the British Library.

Design by Letra Libre, Inc.

First edition: August 2012

P   1

Printed in the United States of America.

# CONTENTS

*For Joy*

# ACKNOWLEDGMENTS

Many friends, colleagues, and students generously helped me in writing this book over the course of the past decade. My wife, Joy Fischer Williams, to whom the book is dedicated, deserves special thanks. I also wish to thank my agent at Trident Media Group, Don Fehr, for his enthusiasm and support for the project from the start. I am also grateful to Luba Ostashevsky at Palgrave Macmillan who provided me with invaluable advice and assistance in the early stages of turning my book proposal into an actual manuscript, and Karen Wolny, Editorial Director at Palgrave Macmillan, who came up with the title and also encouraged me to write the book that was always inside my head. I want to especially acknowledge Akilah Kinnison, who helped me to edit, proofread, and cite-check the entire manuscript several times over. I've delivered many talks over the years in developing the ideas in the book, but I particularly remember the formative exchanges with students and faculty at the School of Oriental and African Studies at the University of London, organized by Professor Catriona Drew; at the Critical Race Studies program at the University of California, Los Angeles, organized by Professor Addie Rolnick; at the National Centre for Indigenous Studies at Australian National University, organized by Professor Mick Dodson; at the Native American Studies Institute at the University of Georgia, organized by Professor Jace Weaver; and at American Indian Studies at the University of Illinois Urbana-Champaign, organized by Professors Robert Warrior and Fred Hoxie. My deans at the University of Arizona Rogers College of Law, Toni Massaro and Larry Ponoroff, have provided me with invaluable institutional support and encouragement. My colleagues and students at the Indigenous Peoples Law and Policy Program have been a continuing source of inspiration and knowledge. Thanks to all.

# INTRODUCTION

*We are all Greeks. Our laws, our literature, our religion, our arts have their roots in Greece. But for Greece—Rome, the instructor, the conqueror, or the metropolis of our ancestors, would have spread no illumination with her arms, and we might still have been savages and idolaters; or, what is worse, might have arrived at such a stagnant and miserable state of social institution as China and Japan possess.*

—Percy Bysshe Shelley, "Preface" to *Hellas* (1821)

From its very beginnings in ancient Greece, Western civilization has sought to invent itself through the idea of the savage. We are all familiar with the basic elements of the idea: The savage is a distant, alien, uncivilized being, unaware of either the benefits or burdens of modernity. Lacking in sophisticated institutions of government and religion, ignorant of property and laws, without complex social bonds or familial ties, living in a state of untamed nature, fierce and ennobled at the same time, the savage has always represented an anxious, negating presence in the world, standing perpetually opposed to Western civilization. As I argue in this book, without the idea of the savage to understand what it is, what it was, and what it could be, Western civilization, as we know it, would never have been able to invent itself.

Throughout the book, I tell the story of the West's three-thousand-year obsession with the idea of the savage by looking at influential examples, enduring works, and great thinkers and writers who have used this construct to reflect on the essential differences between their own seemingly more advanced, Westernized form of civilization and the rest of the world. Along the way, I hope to show how the ancient notion of an irreconcilable difference between civilization and savagery has helped to shape and direct the West's response and actions toward the non-Western world from its earliest beginnings in ancient Greece.

I begin the story with the ancient Greeks because that is where the identifying markers and iconic imagery associated with the idea of the savage in the West were invented. Although certainly not racists, as we understand that term today in the twenty-first century, the ancient Greeks did give birth to Western civilization's first and most influential stereotypes of non-Westernized peoples. As modern social science research teaches us, this type of stereotyping and categorizing of peoples we regard as different from ourselves can be a trigger for what we recognize today as racist behaviors and attitudes.[1]

The term "stereotype" is derived from ancient Greek *stereos*, meaning "solid, firm," and *tupos*, meaning "blow, impression, engraved mark." Thus comes our English word "stereotype," or solid impression. The Greek neologism does a nice job of capturing the durability of the mental image left on the imagination once introduced to such iconic stereotypes as the fierce or ennobled savage. But the Greeks cannot claim credit beyond these roots for inventing the word. "Stereotype" is an early-nineteenth-century coinage from the world of printing, borrowed and made famous by the Pulitzer Prize–winning journalist Walter Lippmann. Lippmann featured the term prominently in his influential 1922 book, *Public Opinion,* calling stereotypes "pictures in our heads."[2]

A generation after Lippmann popularized the term, Western social scientists were demonstrating how stereotypes could serve as root generating causes of racial and ethnic prejudice in a democratic, pluralistic society like the United States. Gordon Allport, an American pioneer in the field of racial stereotyping, defined "prejudice" in his classic 1954 book, *The Nature of Prejudice,* as an "avertive or hostile attitude toward a person who belongs to a group, simply because he belongs to that group, and is therefore presumed to have the objectionable qualities ascribed to the group."[3] Stereotypes, as Allport and other influential scholars at the beginnings of the post–World War II civil rights era showed in their groundbreaking research, play an important role in rationalizing individual prejudice and bias in attitudes and behaviors toward certain ethnic and racial groups in our society. They are much more, in other words, than just mere pictures in our heads. They shape the way we see the world and react to others in it.

The year 1954 was the same year in which attorneys for the National Association for the Advancement of Colored People argued the landmark US Supreme Court case of *Brown v. Board of Education*.[4] In that case, the attorneys successfully relied on research produced by psychologists Kenneth Bancroft Clark and Mamie Phipps Clark regarding the harmful effects of racial stereotypes and prejudice on young children. The Clarks' ground-breaking investigations, first published in 1950, demonstrated the injurious psychological effects of racial discrimination and forced segregation on black children through observations of how they played with baby dolls of different colors. The children, influenced by the pervasive negative racial stereotypes of African Americans in the United States, consistently chose to play with the "nice" white baby dolls rather than the "bad" black baby dolls.

Following the end of the civil rights era of the 1960s and 1970s, researchers continued to investigate the ongoing persistence of racist attitudes and behaviors in US society. This important body of research on the psychological and sociological processes behind racism continues to affirm the powerful role of stereotypes in the ways that minorities are perceived and the ways they perceive themselves. This research indicates that long-held stereotypes tracing back centuries in our history are powerful forces that leave lasting impressions on the ways that we see and perceive others in our world who seem different and strange.[5] Think, for example, of just a few of the common images and stereotypes that are widely associated with American Indians today in US society and in many other parts of the Western world; they really do not have "red skins," few if any live in teepees, they tend to leave their bows and arrows at home when they go to the supermarket, and when they speak their native tongue, they never use the words "ugh" and "how."

In fact, studies by cognitive psychologists and other social scientists over the past several decades have shown that these types of clichéd and demeaning images insinuate themselves into our minds at a very young age. Long before we possess the cognitive ability to decide whether this way of talking and thinking about others is rational or personally acceptable, a good number of ethnic and racial stereotypes and caricatured, clichéd images still prevalent in our society have become nearly ineradicable features of the way we see the world. Through this absorptive, insidious process, these identifying markers of strangeness and divergence from what we are used to seeing and experiencing become embedded as essential truths deep within the recesses of our developing cognitive worldview as we grow older and mature. Told and retold, repackaged and rebooted in innumerable stories, books, movies, video games, and other modes of expression, they become a kind of habitual response to certain events and chance encounters we have every day with those we regard as being different or strange. The psychologist Phyllis Katz produced one of the most compelling examples of the perniciousness and deeply entrenched nature of the stereotyping process at work in a young child's mind in her groundbreaking research published in 1976, more than two decades after *Brown v. Board of Education*. Katz tells the story of observing a three-year-old white child who, seeing a black infant for the first time, says to her mother, "Look, Mom, a baby maid."[6]

What is abundantly clear from even a brief survey of their surviving literature, art, philosophy, and even their great public monuments and buildings is that the ancient Greeks frequently engaged in the use of what we today can easily recognize as stereotypes and stereotyping behaviors to describe those they considered alien, exotic, and strange in their world. These stereotypes and clichéd notions helped the Greeks define collectively who they were as a people and what separated and distinguished them apart from those peoples who inhabited the distant, uncharted parts of the world. To the ancient Greeks, the rest of the world was inhabited for the most part by tribes of savage, uncivilized "barbarians."

Much as today's social science literature teaches, this type of stereotyping behavior toward foreigners was not something the Greeks thought much about. They called all foreigners "barbarians," without distinction. "Barbarian" was an onomatopoeic term that basically translated as "babblers." It was used generally to refer to people who could not speak the Greek language or who could not speak it very well. The term almost always held negative connotations and was deployed mostly as an unconscious, uncontrolled response by Greeks to all things foreign and strange. A modern-day cognitive psychologist might call it a kind of bad habit—"an action that has been done many times and has become automatic."[7]

If it is true that the Greeks of this critical founding period in the history of the West commonly engaged in what we would today call stereotyping attitudes and behaviors, the implications for our present-day inability to escape the hold of certain habitual ways of thinking about certain types of non-Westernized peoples are profound and, I hope, disturbing to readers of this book. Much like the three-year-old girl seeing a black baby for the first time, Western civilization, as I try to show, learned its stereotyping behaviors toward non-Westernized tribal peoples at a relatively youthful and impressionable stage in its development.

The stories and myths told by the Greeks about the irreconcilable differences between the barbarian and their highly urbanized, imperially minded *polis* (city-state) form of civilization left an enduring and profound imprint, a "solid impression," as it were, on the West's growth and development and its relations and responses to the non-Western world. Stereotyping and categorizing distant, strange peoples as irreconcilable primitive savages was deeply embedded in the very roots of Western civilization, from its beginning point of emergence in Classical Greece. The poet Shelley's list therefore was only partially complete[8]; our laws, our literature, our religion, our arts, and, as I show in this book, our racial stereotypes of non-Westernized tribal peoples as irreconcilable savages all have their roots in Greece.

I begin the story of the emergence and development of the idea of the savage in the West by focusing on the ancient Greek bard Homer and his two epic poems, the *Iliad* and the *Odyssey*. Homer's immortal poems of the legendary events and figures of the Trojan War incorporate and reinvent a number of ancient mythic tales and legends of Greek warrior-heroes defeating man-eating Cyclopean monsters, Lestrygonian giants, drunken rampaging centaurs, and other hybrid beasts and subhuman creatures on the uncharted edges (*eschatiai*) of the world. The two poems, which have been called the "bible of the Greeks,"[9] draw on an ancient mythic language of familiar cultural markers and iconic imagery that identify and isolate the savage as a primitive, uncivilized, lawless force, violently encountered on the frontiers of an expansion-minded civilization.

The Homeric epics introduce the foundational stereotypes and identifying categories that the West will continue to use in telling and retelling its myths, stories, and legends of immortal warrior-heroes and their violent encounters with lawless savages in distant lands for the next three thousand years. This dark-sided savage, however, is not the only version of the idea invented by the Greeks that has been perpetuated by Western civilization. With their noted affinity for dualistic forms of thought and dialectical argument, the Greeks created another important way of imagining the savage that continues to resonate throughout the storytelling traditions of the Western world. In chapter 2, I show how many, if not all, of the basic elements of the theme of the noble savage in the protest literature of Western civilization can be traced all the way back to the ancient Greeks' Legend of the Golden Age, written down for the first time by Homer's contemporary, Hesiod, in his famous poem *Works and Days*. The idea of the savage as rendered in this poetic ode to the hardscrabble life of a simple Boeotian dirt farmer tells of an irretrievably lost-in-time Golden Age, when the first humans lived a blessed life of utopian simplicity and ennobled virtue in wild, untamed nature.

The flourishing, happy life reflected by this stripped-down version of humanity (literally speaking, for nakedness was one of the key identifying markers of both the dark-sided and the ennobled savage's way of life) was drawn on and alluded to by countless Greek poets, writers, playwrights, artists, sculptors, and philosophers. The theme of the noble savage in fact becomes a favored storytelling device of stressed-out and anxiety-ridden critics of contemporary civilization from this point forward in the West's contrarian literary traditions. Whenever Western civilization's discontents, cynics, and utopian critics are looking for a subversive or ironically intended counterexample of the corruption, decadence, and decline of their own troubled times, they turn to a notion that traces to the ancient Greek Legend of the Golden Age and its anxiety-producing theme of the noble savage to shame their contemporaries into changing their ways or face the wrath of the gods.

In chapter 3, I explore the myriad, diverse, and divergent uses of the idea of the savage by the Greeks of the celebrated Classical Age (fifth and fourth centuries B.C.). I focus particularly on the story of how the West's first great imperial civilization in fifth-century B.C. Athens used the idea of the savage as handed down from the ancient myths and legends as a way of imagining, reflecting on, and representing the "barbarian" (meaning anyone who did not speak Greek). The Greeks of the so-called Athenian Golden Age, as I show, used the construct to reveal the polar opposite of everything that was grand and glorious about their own imperially minded form of civilization. The distant tribal savage became the most extreme form of the barbarian's radical difference from the Greeks' civilized norms and values that could be imagined.

Chapter 4 tells how Socrates, Plato, Aristotle, and other important Greek philosophers of the Classical Age utilized the idea of the savage in their founding contributions to Western philosophy. As I show, the idea of the savage was an agreed-on starting point for Greek philosophers pursuing the answer to a central question that has consumed Western speculative thought ever since the Classical Age: What constitutes the good life for humanity, according to our own true nature?

In chapters 5 and 6, I explore the genius of the Romans for cultural appropriation, as evidenced by the influential and enduring ways they used the idea of the savage as handed down from the Greeks. As I show, the Romans deployed the concept to generate insights and understanding into the rise and fall of empires and the fate of their own unique form of imperial civilization. Influential poets such as Virgil and Ovid, masters of Latin prose and oratory such as Cicero and Julius Caesar, and the great satirists of the post-Augustan Age, Juvenal and Lucian, reveal the Romans' skill in applying and adapting the idea of the savage as an ethical ideal as they reflected on the challenges and problems confronting their empire.

In chapters 7 and 8, I show how the idea of the savage, as represented by the biblically inspired image of the Wild Man, emerged out of the darkness of the medieval Christian era in Western history (fifth through fifteenth centuries). As depicted by Christian dogmatists and theologians, the Wild Man absorbed the most fearsome, accursed elements and negative stereotypes associated with the Classical idea of the savage while thoroughly rejecting all discordant pagan myths and legends. The Golden Age legend's contrarian themes of ennobled primitives living contented and virtuous lives in bounteous nature, without knowledge of the true Christian faith or God, were anathema to the Church hierarchy. Such benign, subversively intended images of humanity living free and happy without the benefits of Christianity were suppressed throughout the Middle Ages while Crusades against the infidel were launched to the Holy Lands, witches and heretics were burned at the stake by the Inquisition, and the pope in Rome sought to impose the Church's divine law on the entire world. The idea of the savage as embodied in medieval Christianity's biblical Wild Man, as I show, was central to these and other significant developments that helped to shape the subsequent history of the Western world and its relations with non-Westernized peoples.

In chapters 9 and 10, I explain how a group of pious Italian Renaissance scholars and the early travel literature of New World voyages of discovery reinvigorated the full scope of the Classical idea of the savage. The result was the invention of the American Indian as the embodiment of the rehabilitated Classical ideal. Many of the familiar stereotypical images of the Indians of the New World—images still associated with indigenous tribal peoples around the world—were first perpetuated by Renaissance-era writers' borrowings and adaptations from Classical Greek and Roman sources, many of which had been suppressed by the Catholic Church for centuries.

In chapter 11, I explain how influential European Enlightenment–era philosophers such as Jean-Jacques Rousseau, Thomas Hobbes, John Locke, and Adam Smith used the idea of the savage to transform the American Indian into a "living model" of savage humanity in a primitive state of nature as part of a new science of society that emerged in Western Europe in the eighteenth century. As I show, the Founding Fathers of the United States embraced this Enlightenment-era construct as an organizing principle of their new nation's first Indian policy. Assuming that the Indians on the western frontier were destined to be surpassed by the inevitable progress of a superior agrarian civilization, the Founders signed treaties and established reservations that were intended to facilitate the ultimate extinguishment of Indian tribalism as a way of life on the North American continent.

In the final chapter, I explore the continued vitality and resonance of the idea of the savage's presumed fundamental irreconcilability with Western civilization in the contemporary human rights struggles of indigenous peoples around the world today. As I show, even in the twenty-first century, the Western world's most advanced nation-states continue to perpetuate the stereotypes and clichéd images of human savagery that were first invented by the ancient Greeks to justify their ongoing violations of the most basic human rights of cultural survival belonging to indigenous tribal peoples.

Alien and exotic, threatening and subversive, the savage has long been imagined as a familiar, diametrically opposed figure throughout the history of the West, helping to define by counterexample and antithesis a distinctive form of Western civilization. Today that highly urbanized, expansion-minded, resource-consuming way of life and its antiquated, atavistic notions of the savage constitute a grave and most dangerous threat to the continuing cultural survival of the world's indigenous tribal peoples.

The pre-eminent Native American scholar of the twentieth century, Vine Deloria, Jr., once wrote that for indigenous peoples, the "burning question" of our time is "where the complex of ideas that constitute Western civilization originated, how they originated, and whether they have any realistic correspondence to what we can observe and experience in nature."[10] My hope in writing this book is that the anxious concerns produced by reflecting on the persistence and pervasiveness of the idea of the savage in the history of the West's relations with the non-Westernized world might lead to a serious reassessment of the way we think and talk about the human rights and the continued survival of the world's indigenous tribal peoples. The "burning question" for the West will then be how to reinvent itself, once again, but this time without using the idea of the savage.

# ONE

# HOMER AND THE IDEA OF THE SAVAGE

## *First Impressions*

The idea of the savage is first encountered in Western civilization's first great written works of literature, the *Iliad* and the *Odyssey* by Homer. In Book I of the *Iliad,* assumed by scholars to be the earlier of Homer's two epics, the aged Greek warlord Nestor, king of Pylos, attempts to unite the feuding Greeks in the darkest days of the Trojan War. Here, at the very beginnings of written civilization in the West, in the first book of the *Iliad,* Nestor invokes the names of the immortal Greek warrior-heroes who defeated the savage tribes of half-human, half-horse creatures, the centaurs, in the legendary battle of the Centauromachy. "Such warriors have I never since seen, nor shall I see, as Peirithous was and Dryas, shepherd of the people, and Caeneus and Exadius and godlike Polyphemus, and Theseus, son of Aegeus, a man like the immortals. Mightiest were these of men reared upon the earth; mightiest were they, and with the mightiest they fought, the mountain-dwelling centaurs, and they destroyed them terribly."[1]

The Centauromachy was one of the Greeks' favorite and most oft-told stories of mythic warrior-heroes defeating a fierce tribe of savage, monstrous beings. The epic contest took place between the Lapiths of Thessaly, on the northern frontiers of ancient Greek civilization, and the mythical centaurs. Relief sculptures of the legendary battle were chiseled onto the south metopes of the Parthenon in Athens under the supervision of the greatest sculptor and architect of Greek antiquity, Pheidias (ca. 480–430 B.C.), in the fifth century B.C., following the Greeks' civilization-shaping victory over the Persian Empire in the Persian Wars. Western scholars have interpreted Pheidias's intent in featuring the Centauromachy atop the Parthenon as an effort to symbolize the Greeks' triumph over the Persians and their barbarian hordes. What survives of the sculptures can be seen today in the Elgin Marble Room in the British Museum in London.

Fierce, savage monsters are encountered by Homer's most famous mythic hero, Odysseus, in several anxiety-producing scenes in the epic companion piece to the *Iliad,* the *Odyssey.* The Lestrygonians, a rock-heaving tribe of giants, are featured in Book X. These savage monsters spear and devour all the men on eleven of Odysseus's twelve ships that had survived the battle at Troy, before our hero escapes with his life in his lone surviving ship along with its crew. In Book XII, Odysseus loses six of those crew members

*Metope from the Parthenon, British Museum, London (photograph by R. Williams)*

as he sails through the deadly straits guarded by the hideous sea monsters Scylla and Charybdis.

Homer's most enduring and influential tale of a mythic Greek warrior-hero engaged in life-and-death struggle (what the Greeks called *agon*) against a fierce, savage monster is found in Book IX, where Odysseus battles the giant, one-eyed, man-eating Cyclops, Polyphemus. The *Odyssey's* vivid description of the Cyclopes' primitive way of life indelibly inscribes the idea of the savage as a remote, lawless, and primitive enemy to civilized humanity on the West's written storytelling traditions at their earliest point of emergence in Homer's two epic poems. As noted by modern scholars,[2] Odysseus's description of the land of the Cyclopes uses virtually the same stereotypes, images, and identifying markers of the savage that Christopher Columbus and other Renaissance-era discoverers later would use to describe their first anxious encounters with the Indians of the New World (see chapter 10).

> Thence we sailed on, grieved at heart, and we came to the land of the Cyclopes, an overweening and lawless folk, who, trusting in the immortal gods, plant nothing with their hands nor plough; but all these things spring up for them without sowing or ploughing, wheat, and barley, and vines, which bear the rich clusters of wine, and the rain of Zeus gives them increase. Neither assemblies for council have they, nor appointed laws, but they dwell on the peaks of lofty mountains in hollow caves, and each one is lawgiver to his children and his wives, and they reck nothing one of another.[3]

Homer's *Iliad* and *Odyssey* have long been regarded as important literary beginning points for the emergence of civilization in the West. The ancient Greeks' conception of the savage as a fierce, lawless, irreconcilable enemy to civilization traces its earliest written point of emergence to Homer's two epic poems as well.

## WHO WAS HOMER?

Homer, of course, did not invent the notion of the savage for the Greeks. It had been around for a long time. The savage emerges out of ancient myths and legends dating back centuries prior to the appearance of Homer's epics, when the Greeks themselves were living as primitive, preliterate tribal peoples dispersed over their homeland on the Balkan Peninsula. The two poems bearing Homer's name are regarded by most Western scholars as the written end products of an ancient oral tradition, preserving the sacred myths and tribal legends of the Greeks from primeval times.

The *Iliad* and *Odyssey* are generally believed to have been set down in writing for the first time in the early part of what have been called the Greek "Renaissance" centuries (800–600 B.C.), perhaps around 750 to 700 B.C.[4] That time period is probably not too long after writing was reintroduced to the Greeks by the Phoenicians. In any case, the poems were apparently written down long after the supposed occurrence of the events surrounding the Trojan War described by Homer. Scholars believe that event to have taken place, if it took place at all, perhaps in the twelfth or eleventh centuries B.C.

Most modern scholars tend to follow some version of Milman Parry's early-twentieth-century thesis that there was no single historic personality named Homer who authored the *Iliad* and *Odyssey* in their entirety.[5] Rather, according to Parry's theory, the two poems were the result of a largely Ionian oral tradition.

The Ionians, according to Greek legends, were the ancient tribe descended from Ion, son of the god Apollo. They believed themselves to have been originally from Attica, on the Greek mainland, but were forced by a legendary invasion of Dorian tribes from the north (another group of fierce tribal savages as far as the Ionian Greeks were concerned) to migrate across the Aegean Sea. The Ionians went on to establish scores of colonies in Asia Minor on the Anatolian coast in modern-day Turkey. Many of these colonies, nourished by their extensive commercial contacts and close cultural connections with the great trading civilizations of Asia Minor and Egypt, became prosperous metropolitan urban centers. Greek learning, culture, and religious traditions flourished in Anatolia. So too did the art of storytelling.

According to Parry's theory, Homer's two poems are surviving examples of oral formulaic poetry, representing the collective inheritance of many generations of singing Ionian poet-bards, called *aoidoi* in Greek. Accompanied usually by a stringed instrument like the lyre, a skillful aoidos could make an honorable living entertaining the *aristoi* of the town—the nobles and aristocratic families, along with their frequent table guests, hangers-on, and retainers.

Collecting stories and songs from travelers and traders, going from town to town to ply his trade, a well-versed aoidos could draw from a large and diverse archive of myths, legends, and folktales that circulated throughout the ancient Greek world. As a professional storyteller, the skilled aoidos could seamlessly combine and reinvent such useful tropes and narrative snippets into fresh new stories or twists on an old theme as the occasion or audience demanded. The Greeks believed that the truly gifted aoidos was divinely inspired by the Muses, the goddesses of ancient Greek mythology who were the secret sources of the sacred knowledge contained in the poems and stories sung by the aoidos. The term "aoidos" in fact is used to describe one such honored bard, Demodocus, in Book VIII of Homer's *Odyssey:* "to him above all others has the god granted skill in song, to give delight in whatever way his spirit prompts him to sing."

Following Parry's thesis, with the reintroduction of writing and literacy among the Greeks in the early Renaissance period, the *Iliad* and the *Odyssey* were likely narrated to a scribe or scribes by some particularly well-regarded aoidos, perhaps eponymously named Homer. From this "Homeric" recitation of the two poems, Western civilization's first best-sellers were born, copied down on papyrus, and then recited word for word, book for book, at festivals and religious celebrations. Homer's beloved poems became the bible of the Greeks, closely read, studied, and memorized as sacred texts, often in their entirety.

Through such ancient methods of written transmission of varied snippets and pieces of mythic stories and songs, the two poems bearing Homer's name introduced the West's literary traditions to the idea of the savage as a fierce, irreconcilable enemy to an expansion-minded form of civilization. We can see that for Homer, the savage was a great storytelling device, used in antagonistic, scene-setting fashion to prove his heroes' virtues. But from these rather prosaic Homeric beginnings, we can begin to trace the origins of many of the identifying behaviors, clichés, and categorical markers that will be applied and adapted down through the ages to stereotype and imagine distant, strange lands inhabited by fierce savage races, irreconcilably opposed to Western civilization.

## THE STORY OF THE TROJAN WAR AND
## THE GREEKS' SACRED LAW OF *XENIA*

Homer's epic poem the *Iliad* focuses on the decade-long war between two such expansion-minded imperial civilizations, the Mycenaean Empire of the ancient Greeks (Homer calls them the Achaeans) and the Trojan Empire (Ilium). The war's legendary origins trace to the actions of the Trojan prince, Paris, who kidnapped the most beautiful woman in the world, Helen, wife of Menelaus, king of Sparta. Menelaus also happened to be the brother of Agamemnon, king of the Mycenaean Greeks and their empire on the Peloponnese. The greedy Agamemnon had long desired to invade and plunder the imperial city of Troy across the Aegean Sea. With help from the Greek goddess of love, Aphrodite, Paris cuckolded Menelaus while a guest at his palace in Sparta. Compounding the offense, Paris seduced and absconded with Helen while Menelaus was away from his kingdom attending his grandfather's funeral.

For the ancient Greeks, such acts violated the sacred law of *xenia*, a form of higher law based on the sacred relationship of reciprocal respect and courtesy owed between guests and hosts. The god Zeus was specifically referred to as Zeus Xenios in the ancient genealogies, the divine protector of travelers and strangers (including singing bards like Homer).

Seeking to avenge his brother for Paris's crime in violating xenia, and further lured by the prospect of plundering the great imperial city of Troy, Agamemnon called on the other kings and warlords of Greece to defend the marriage of Helen to Menelaus. Launching a legendary force of more than a thousand Greek ships, immortally cataloged by Homer in Book II of the *Iliad*, Agamemnon leads the invasion across the Aegean Sea to conquer the Trojan Empire and take Helen back to Sparta, along with all the booty the Greeks could carry home with them following their anticipated victory.

After a near-decade long, failed siege of Troy's famed impenetrable walls, the Greeks finally win the war thanks to a cunning ploy devised by Odysseus. The "man of many ways" in Homer's epics has the Greeks pretend retreat and board their ships for home. Before this seeming departure, they leave the equestrian-loving Trojans a parting gift of seeming homage: a large wooden horse.

The horse was closely associated with notions savagery and wildness in ancient Greek mythology: an unruly beast of nature, roaming free and unrestrained. Pegasus, the winged white horse of divine origins, bringer of lightning and thunder from Olympus, was captured and ridden by the hero Bellerophon, who killed the Chimera, a savage fire-breathing monster with a lion's head, goat's body, and serpent's tail as described by Homer in the *Iliad*. Characteristic of Homer's method as a storyteller, the Trojan horse device quite effectively ties the Trojans' primitivistic fetish for a wild and savage beast of nature to their ultimate downfall at the hands of the civilized Greeks.

Led by brave Odysseus, the Greek soldiers inside the horse escape at night while the city is asleep and open the gates for their comrades in arms, now stealthily reassembled outside the city walls. The Trojans are quickly routed and the famed imperial city is sacked, pillaged, and burned to the ground by Agamemnon's marauding army. The rest is history, as they say in the West.

## THE FIRST RECORDED SAVAGES IN THE HISTORY OF THE WEST

All of this is background material to the main story line of the *Iliad*. As the Roman poet Horace once famously noted, Homer jumps *in media res*, at a relatively late point in the war, to commence his story. It is the ninth year of the Greeks' siege of Troy, and Achilles, king of the fiercely loyal Myrmidon warriors, is furious at Agamemnon for claiming his captive slave girl, Briseis. Achilles vows that he will no longer fight against the Trojans and threatens to take his Myrmidon warriors with him and go home. Such a loss of Achilles and the Myrmidons would have been devastating for the Greeks' morale in continuing their fight against the Trojans.

Making a last desperate plea for Achilles and Agamemnon to reconcile their differences, Nestor, the aged Pylian king, invokes the names of the immortal heroes and demigods who fought by his side in defeating the savage tribes of centaurs in the great mythic battle called the Centauromachy by the Greeks:

Listen to me, for you are both younger than I. In earlier times I moved among men more warlike than you, and never did they despise me. Such warriors have I never since seen, nor shall I see, as Peirithous was and Dryas, shepherd of the people, and Caeneus and Exadius and godlike Polyphemus,[6] and Theseus, son of Aegeus, a man like the immortals. Mightiest were these of men reared upon the earth; mightiest were they, and with the mightiest they fought, the mountain-dwelling centaurs, and they destroyed them terribly.

Nestor's invocation of the "mightiest" men ever "reared upon the earth" refers to the immortal roster of Greek warrior-heroes invited to the wedding feast of Peirithous, one of the great Lapith warrior-kings, and the horse-woman Hippodamia, "Tamer of horses" (*hippos* meaning "horse"; *damazo*, "to tame"). The centaurs,[7] distant cousins to the Lapiths, proved to be most inhospitable guests, as they were unable to control the libertine effects of wine on their bestial natures. When Hippodamia is presented as the king's bride, the centaur Eurytion tries to rape her. The other centaurs then commence to mount and straddle the women and young boys in attendance at the royal celebration. The wedding feast erupts in riot over this most heinous offense against xenia, the Greeks' sacred law of ritualized guest-friendship.

Nestor and the other Greeks in attendance at the wedding respond by coming to the aid of the Lapiths. A great battle ensues, and the centaurs are roundly defeated. The victors cut off the ears and nose of Eurytion, the initial offender, as part of his sentence. To the Greeks, such mutilations were one of the most severe and humiliating forms of punishment imaginable for a crime, short of death. Eurytion and the rest of the centaurs then are expelled from Thessaly to the distant regions of the Eurasian steppe by the great mythic warrior-heroes of the Centauromachy, who have secured their immortal fame by enforcing a superior civilization's higher form of law against the monstrous savage.

## THE SACRED LAW OF *XENIA* AND THE IDEA OF THE SAVAGE

To the Greeks, xenia was a universally binding law that made civilized existence possible. Savage creatures like the centaurs, by virtue of their irrational, unconstrained nature, could neither understand nor abide by this form of sacred, higher law. In the ancient myths and legends of the Greeks, unpardonable violations of xenia typically are what mark the savage as an irredeemable enemy of the warrior-hero of a superior civilization.

Professor Victor Alonso stresses the role of xenia as an overarching, transcending form of universally binding law in ancient Greece.[8] He writes that the Greeks employed the institution of xenia, or guest-friendship, as a fundamental instrument and precept of international law. For the Greeks, xenia is what makes civilized existence possible. The concept traces back to ancient customary law on the creation of relations of friendship and reciprocity within and without the local familial groupings, particularly among members of the aristocratic ruling elite.

Guest-friendship among leading families could help to create any number of beneficial relationships within the extensive network of Greek trading communities spread out throughout the Aegean and Mediterranean world. Xenia's many benefits could include, as just one example, valuable military alliances in times of war and defense of homeland.

In the Homeric epics, the binding force of xenia exists at the highest levels of society between nobles from different Greek ruling families and even from different countries. Book VI of the *Iliad* provides one of the most memorable scenes in Homer's epics testifying to the force of xenia as a form of fundamental, universally binding law: the display of aristocratic virtue on the field of battle shown by Glaucus of Lycia, an ally of Troy, and Diomedes of Argos, a Greek warrior-king. When they recognize each other at the walls of Troy, they put down their arms and shake hands as xenoi, then declare their refusal to fight each other. Instead, they exchange gifts in the middle of the battle in ritual renewal of their sacred obligations of guest-friendship. Notably, Glaucus and Diomedes inherited xenia from their parents; the two had not created xenia between themselves. But the rule of law enforced by this sacred regime of ritualized guest-friendship still had binding force in defining the appropriate norms and conduct of future generations of xenoi, Greek and non-Greek alike. Respect for xenia was what distinguished the higher forms of civilization from savagery.

## THE CENTAURS' STORY

Centaurs were long represented in Greek mythology as mountain-dwelling, lawless, hypersexualized creatures, paradigm examples of savage beings, driven by their bestial passions and irrational urges to violate the most sacred laws of civilized humanity. According to one ancient Greek myth on their origins, the centaurs and Lapiths were kindred races. Lapithes, the eponymous ancestor of the Lapith race, was a valiant warrior, whose descendants included a great line of warrior-kings and heroes. Centaurus, his twin, who was born deformed, mated with the wild mares of Thessaly to produce the half-man, half-horse race of the centaurs.

In alluding to the xenia-defiling centaurs defeated by the warrior-heroes of the Centauromachy, Nestor's speech for Greek unity in the *Iliad* reveals the first intimations of the motivating power and force of the ancient Homeric stereotype of the fierce, irreconcilable savage in the literary *and* legal traditions of the West. To Nestor, the respected elder statesman, vanquishing the savage tribes of centaurs in battle is inarguable proof of the heroes' incontestable claim to virtue, honor, and therefore authority. The defeat of the centaurs by these immortal heroes validates the wisdom of following Nestor's advice, for "they listened to my counsel, and obeyed my words. So also should you obey, since to obey is better." Agamemnon and Achilles should stop their feud and unite their armies in order to defeat the Trojans for their detestable violations of the Greeks' sacred law of xenia.

Dropped as an aside by Homer in his larger tale of the central conflict between Agamemnon and Achilles, Nestor's reference to the Centauromachy introduces the Western world to its first mythic stereotype of a fierce, lawless savage. A subhuman beast, irreconcilably opposed to the higher law of a superior form of civilization, this Homerically inspired image will now be repeated, adapted, and extended by countless Greek poets, dramatists, prose writers, and artists. From this point forward, Homer's defining categories of lawlessness, remoteness, habitual intemperance, primitive bestiality, and sexual licentiousness will become foundational elements of the idea of the savage, applied to non-Westernized peoples by Western civilization for the next three thousand years.

## MYTHIC WARRIOR-HEROES AND FIERCE SAVAGE ENEMIES ON THE EDGES OF THE EARTH

The centaurs, of course, are just one of the innumerable forms of lawless, chaotic savagery that proliferate on the far edges of the unknown world in

ancient Greek myths and legends. The mythic image of the savage as a distant, fierce, xenia-defiling enemy to the warrior-heroes of a superior form of
civilization reflects the Greeks' pervasive sense of fear regarding the "edges
of the earth."[9]

At the time of the written appearance of Homer's poems, the widely
dispersed Aeolic-, Ionic-, and Dorian-speaking tribes of Greeks had developed a rich and varied archive of myths, fables, legends, and folktales
of great heroes and demigods defeating various forms of human, subhuman, and nonhuman savages on the edges of the earth. Hybrid beasts, fierce
primitive tribes, and giant man-eating monsters proliferate and propagate
themselves in abundant, countless ways throughout the boundless waste-
lands of Greek myth and legend.

Typically, the hero encounters the most threatening, strange, and alien-
seeming forms of savagery venturing on the most distant, chaotic, uncharted
fringes of the known world, the *eschatiai* in Greek. The eschatiai represented
the uncultivated periphery in ancient Greek cosmology: an indeterminate,
terrifying, primordial space ruled by untamed beasts, man-eating monsters,
and the savage forces of nature. According to ancient cosmographic myths
and creation stories, the lands, waters, peoples, and other beings encountered in that threatening, alien, hybrid-prone zone at the periphery would be
radically divergent from what the Greeks knew at the more familiar, orienting center of their own world.

This orienting worldview of disorder, chaos, and savagery on the periphery and the anxieties it created with respect to the unknown, uncharted
regions of the earth is reflected in the earliest surviving Greek maps. The
oldest, dating to the sixth century B.C., represents the earth as an island, surrounded by a circular Ocean, stretching unbounded and undefined toward a
distant horizon. The Greeks' use of the term *apeiron,* or "boundless," to mark
off the limits of land and sea from the formless expanse of Ocean surrounding it also underscores the sense of anxiety and intense fear of the vast and
unknown edges of the world.[10]

Homer's poems consistently affirm and even extend this basic orienting cosmographic view of Greek civilization at the center, surrounded by
a strange, alien, and threatening expanse that stretched beyond the watery
frontiers and chaos at the edges of the world. In Book X of the *Odyssey,*
Homer draws on this Greek sense of dread and anxiety in the famous scene

where Odysseus visits Hades, the underworld. To reach this nether region of the dead, Odysseus is told by the goddess Circe to "set up thy mast, and spread the white sail, and sit thee down; and the breath of the North Wind will bear her onward." Once having crossed the stream of "deep eddying Oceanus," Odysseus is instructed to beach his ship and "go thyself to the dank house of Hades."

The dread-inducing aspects of the ocean's boundlessness were heightened by the association in Greek cosmographic discourse of Ocean as a form of "primordial water." Ocean was thought to be full of primeval savage monsters and giants to be overcome before the universe can be properly ordered. The comforting "boundaries" separating earth, water, and air all seemed to break down within "the infinitude of Ocean."[11]

Western scholars have long recognized that the Greeks of the Renaissance era were transforming themselves into a rapidly urbanizing, expansion-minded form of civilization, made prosperous and bold by seaborne trade, colonizing entrepreneurs, and maritime adventurers. At the same time, the Greeks were terrified of being on the open seas associated with distant Ocean for too long. The waters and lands at the edges of the earth, far from the known civilized world, were the dwelling places of mythic sea monsters and other strange, unknown, savage creatures. In Greek mythology, the abodes of the gods and immortals and murky morasses of cosmic disorder and chaos were all associated with distant Ocean.

For the Greeks, the mythic creatures and beings that inhabited Ocean were either terrifyingly strange or mystically irrational in their own unique, dread-inspiring, anxiety-producing ways. They all confirmed the generalized belief and worldview, held from primeval times, that the farther one moved from the local waters and shores known to the Greeks, the more alien and different would be everything encountered.

Some of the best-known myths and legends of the Greeks, which long predate Homer's time, tell of great warrior-heroes traveling to distant, strange places and confronting savagery in all its undifferentiated, violent, and chaotic forms. To the Greeks, it did not matter what type of savage enemy, demonic beast, or untamed aspect of wild nature the hero overcame in his struggles. The more muddled and strange the better; the giant monsters, man-eating beasts, strange hybrid creatures, and fierce, warlike primitive tribes of ancient Greek mythology were all just storytelling props anyway, designed so that the warrior-hero invading distant lands could prove his *arête*—his excellence in virtue and valor—in distant uncharted regions of the world.

Nestor himself, for instance, makes several appearances in well-known legends about monstrous beasts and hybrid creatures fought by famous Greek warrior-heroes in distant tribal lands. He was one of Jason's famed Argonauts on the quest for the Golden Fleece, the fabled treasure guarded by a sleepless, man-eating dragon, in faraway Colchis, a barbarian kingdom at the edges of the Baltic Sea.

Theseus, mentioned prominently by Nestor in his speech in Book I of the *Iliad* ("son of Aegeus, a man like the immortals"), was celebrated in Greek mythology for slaying the savage half-bull, half-man Minotaur in the

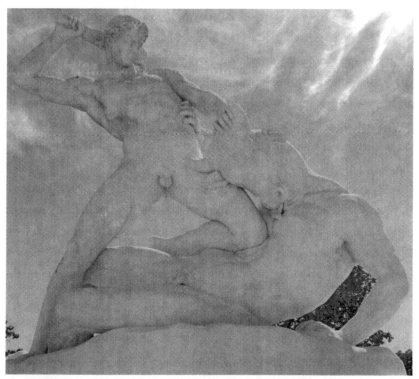

*Theseus Battles the Minotaur, Jean-Etienne Ramey (1826), Tuileries Gardens, Paris (photograph by R. Williams)*

Labyrinth on Crete. The legendary king of Athens was the paradigmatic liberating warrior-hero who overthrew an oppressive, archaic social order represented by the early Bronze Age Minoan civilization.

The most famous warrior-hero of Greek mythology of course was Herakles, or Hercules as the Romans would later call him. The twelve labors of Herakles, as sculpted on the metopes of the Temple of Zeus at Olympia, depict a series of superhuman contests taken on in distant lands by the great Dorian founder-hero and bastard son of Zeus. In this famous series of great mythic challenges, Herakles plays the role of the invading hero, securing his immortality and fame by his victorious battles over wild beasts, Amazon warrior-women, and hybrid, man-eating monsters like the multiheaded Hydra and Cerberus, the savage, multiheaded hound that guarded the gates of hell in Greek mythology.[12]

These mythic stories of life-and-death struggles with savagery in its many different, chaotic forms, dispersed across distant and strange lands on the edges of the earth, revealed the true, virtuous character of Herakles. The Greek demigod unified and consolidated in one package all the many meanings of the archetypal hero for the Greeks. He was a civilizing force, liberator of the oppressed, subduer of monsters and hybrid man-eating beasts, and vanquisher of fierce primitive tribes. The definitive conquering warrior-hero of ancient Greek mythology and Western civilization, Herakles imposed order on chaos, defeated the forces of savagery in all their threatening, diverse forms, and brought civilization to the distant frontier boundaries of the world.

To the ancient Greeks, the hero's choice to take on such struggles with the savage, chaotic forces of untamed nature, in and of itself, justly merited glory, fame, and immortality. It did not really matter what kind of fierce savage enemy the hero encountered on his quest for fame and honor—merely choosing to strive against this untamed force of wild, savage nature makes him the *agonistes*, literally "someone who struggles for a cause." In this ancient storytelling tradition, introduced to the West's literary traditions for the first time by Homer's epic poems, the archetypal hero is the fearless warrior who proves his arête in life-and-death battles against the violent, chaotic forces of savagery encountered in far-off lands on the edges of the earth. Without this dark-sided version of the idea of the savage, the mythic warrior-hero, as imagined by the West since the time of Homer and the ancient Greeks, might never have been invented.

## THE STORY OF ODYSSEUS'S LIFE-AND-DEATH STRUGGLE WITH THE CYCLOPS MONSTER

Homer's most famous and influential account of a Greek warrior-hero who proves his arête in life-and-death struggle against a xenia-defying tribal savage in a far-off land occurs in Book IX of the *Odyssey*. There Odysseus encounters the one-eyed, man-eating Cyclops monster Polyphemus.

Believed by classical scholars as a later and perhaps unfinished composition by Homer, the *Odyssey* is twenty-four books long like the *Iliad*, its epic companion piece, but three thousand words shorter. The first great road tale in the West's literary traditions, Homer's epic tells the story of Odysseus's decade-long, much-delayed homecoming journey following the Trojan War. The poem is full of divine sex, death-defying escapes, meddling gods, and tawdry palace freeloaders seeking to bed Odysseus's loyal wife, Penelope, spinning away at her loom. There is also a plot by those same suitors to murder his son, Telemachus, who has grown to manhood during his father's absence.

Unlike the demigod and warrior-hero Achilles in the *Iliad*, Odysseus is not famous for any feats of great strength. He is the archetypal *anthropos polytropos*, the "man of many ways" and "many devices" (*polymechanos*): the mastermind behind the cunning ploy of the Trojan Horse in the *Iliad*.[13]

The *Odyssey* begins with Odysseus delayed for ten years in his homecoming to Ithaca to reunite with his loyal but suitor-besieged wife, Penelope. For most of that time, Homer's hero has been marooned on an island having divine sex with the nymph-goddess Calypso. Madly in love with the man of many devices, Calypso offers Odysseus immortality to stay with her forever. Our homesick hero, however, persuades the gods to command Calypso to release him. He returns to Ithaca, kills off the disloyal suitors pursuing his wife, and resumes his rightful place as king.

Some of the most memorable and oft-appropriated parts of the *Odyssey* occur when Homer lets Odysseus tell his own stories of the trials and tribulations that have delayed him on his journey home. His escape from the rock-heaving tribe of Lestrygonian giants and his harrowing tale of surviving the narrow straits guarded by the man-eating sea monsters Scylla and Charybdis are classic examples of the Homeric hero prevailing over fierce, savage enemies and demonic forces of nature on the edges of the earth.

Of all his tales, Odysseus's vivid description of his encounter with the one-eyed, man-eating Cyclops monster, Polyphemus, has exercised a particularly enduring and powerful effect on the ways that the Western world has stereotyped and depicted non-Westernized tribal peoples as fierce, lawless, irrational enemies to civilization. As I show in later chapters of the book, Julius Caesar, Christopher Columbus, George Washington, and the US Supreme Court have all described non-Westernized tribal peoples according to the same basic set of cultural markers, clichéd stereotypes, and identifying categories that Homer first introduced to Western civilization nearly three thousand years ago in his mythical tale of the one-eyed Cyclops monster.

As told in Odysseus's own words, the Cyclopes are a fierce, primitive race of savages. They "plant nothing with their hands nor plough," but trust in what nature provides, living on the fruits of the earth that "spring up for them" without labor on their part. They are without laws or assemblies, live in caves in the mountains, and are ignorant of social bonds, treating their womenfolk and children harshly.

Odysseus's account of the Cyclopes' primitive way of life establishes the basic stereotypes and categories that will come to be closely associated with the idea of the savage from this point forward in the Western world. Like the centaurs, the Cyclopes live distant and apart from civilization and its benefits, without laws or religion or close ties to others, like wild and brutish beasts.

Further demonstrating the Cyclopes' uncivilized, backward way of life, Odysseus tells us that they "have at hand no ships" or craftsmen who could build them. Because they have no ships, the Cyclopes have no trade or commerce and are therefore unaware of the colonizing potential represented by a nearby "wooded" and fertile island. Odysseus describes the island as overrun with "wild goats innumerable, for the tread of men scares them not away." It is a wilderness "unsown and untilled all the days it knows." But it is well watered and full of grass meadows. Grapes, he notes, would do excellently on this type of soil and topography. There is level land for plowing with rich topsoil that would yield abundant harvests.

With a perfectly fine island to colonize right off their coast, the Cyclopes are the first group of primitive tribal savages in the literary traditions of the West whose distant underutilized lands and resources are identified as ripe for exploitation by an expansion-minded form of civilization. Stereotypical savages, they will now provide the perfect plot device for our hero Odysseus to prove his virtues.

## THE CYCLOPES' MAN CAVE

Having come upon the land of the Cyclopes, Odysseus decides to embark on a reconnaissance mission. He goes ashore with members of his crew and spies a cave on the face of a cliff high above, with many goats and sheep about. The cave is the abode of Polyphemus, the hybrid spawn of the god Poseidon and water-nymph goddess of swift currents Thoosa. He is "a monstrous man" who shepherded his flocks "and mingled not with others, but lived apart, with his heart set on lawlessness," as described by Odysseus.

Odysseus takes twelve of his crewmen up to the cave of Polyphemus. They feast on the cheeses they find in the giant's cave. The Greeks build a fire to warm themselves while waiting for the Cyclops to return. As the unwitting Polyphemus enters his cave with his sheep and covers the entrance with a boulder, Odysseus announces himself and explains that the Greeks, as visitors, are traveling under the protection of the gods. But instead of offering hospitality and gifts according to xenia, an angry Polyphemus declares his contempt for the gods. In one of the *Odyssey*'s most terrifying scenes of xenia-defiling behavior, the monster snatches two of Odysseus's crewmen and devours them whole, like a "mountain-nurtured lion, leaving naught."

Trapped in the cave for nearly two full days, Odysseus loses four more men to the pitiless, man-eating savage. Desperate, Odysseus devises a plan of escape. The "man of many ways" had brought along a goatskin full of strong wine—just in case, he says, he was forced to deal with "a savage man that knew naught of justice or of law."

Even at this very early point in the literary traditions of the West, we have already seen this tired stereotype of the drunken savage; recall that in the story of the Centauromachy, cited by Nestor in the *Iliad*, the centaurs were also unable to control their bestial, primitive urges and were punished for violating xenia after imbibing too much wine at the wedding of Peirithous and Hippodamia.

The Greeks were known to prefer their wine mixed with water, never drinking it "neat" and unadulterated as uncivilized peoples were wont to do. The savage's habitual intemperance as a cause of criminal deviancy from xenia is a recurring theme in the ancient myths. According to legend, Herakles himself once slew a tribe of centaurs on Mount Pholoe after they went on a drunken rampage.

The legendary image of the drunken savage, reinforced and extended by Homer's use of this already-clichéd stereotype in his epic poems, was appropriated and adapted by innumerable subsequent Greek writers, dramatists, and artisans. From this point forward in the history of the West, the abuse of alcohol serves as a readily apprehended, telltale categorical marker of the savage's cultural inferiority and brutishness in comparison with a more temperate and refined civilization, such as that of the Greeks.

As Homer tells the tale, Odysseus proceeds to get Polyphemus drunk on the undiluted wine. When the giant passes out, Odysseus blinds him with a heat-sharpened pike (another form of maiming used by the Greeks for punishment of the most heinous crimes), enabling our hero and his surviving crew members to escape from the cave.

Note how the *Odyssey*'s warrior-hero-meets-and-defeats-the-drunken-savage tale is similar in form and tone to the drunken-savage story of the Centauromachy. In both stories, the Homeric heroes prove their arête, their excellence in virtue and valor, by defeating lawless, bestialized, drunken savages. According to the Homeric scheme of moral values reflected in the epics, the warrior-hero earns his immortal fame and honor by justly punishing the savage's violation of a superior civilization's higher law by getting him drunk and then disabling him for life, setting an example for the West in its treatment of indigenous tribal peoples for the next three thousand years.

## HOMER'S INVENTION OF THE CYCLOPS

Like the savage tribes of centaurs referenced by Nestor in the *Iliad*, the *Odyssey*'s depiction of the lawless and inhuman Cyclops monster likely combines elements from several ancient Greek myths and legends. In Greek mythology, the Cyclopes are usually identified as the one-eyed race of giants who forged the weapons used by the gods of Olympus in the overthrow of the Titans. The ancient Greeks believed that the colossal stones comprising the "Cyclopean" walls of Agamemnon's palace at Mycenae had been built by this mythic race of giants.

Some scholars suggest that the Cyclopes were among the group of lesser Greek cult gods adopted by various guilds and associations throughout Classical Antiquity. Blacksmiths in ancient Greece, for instance, were known to wear an eye patch as a preventive measure to save one good eye from blinding flying sparks; thus their profession is often connected to stories, symbols, and myths related to the Cyclopes' single eye.

Other theories associate Polyphemus with some local demon or monster appropriated by Homer into his rendering of the *Odyssey*. The Triamantes of Cretan legend are sometimes cited as an example of a race of man-eating giants with a third eye in the back of the head. Another possible source for Homer's Cyclopean monster may trace to prehistoric dwarf elephant skulls found by ancient Greeks on the islands of Crete and Sicily. Double the size of a human skull with a large nasal cavity in the center for the elephant's trunk, the fossil could have been mistaken for the head of a large, one-eyed, island roaming monster.

We can see how a skillful aiodos like Homer could draw on these myriad myths, legends, and folktales to devise a readily recognizable set of character traits and behaviors that could be used to quickly and efficiently identify the Cyclopes as fierce, threatening savages. They were to be avoided, unless you thought you were some kind of hero. Like the centaurs, their alien remoteness, primitive backwardness, lack of laws, and irrational, violent nature define this race of giants as irreconcilable enemies to civilized humanity. That only great mythic warrior-heroes like Odysseus, Theseus, or Herakles had the arête to take on such monstrous beings could not help but make this dark-sided version of the savage all the more threatening and anxiety-producing for the Greeks as they carried their Homer with them on their colonizing voyages to distant lands inhabited by strange and alien, primitive tribal peoples.

# TWO

# THE LEGEND OF THE GOLDEN AGE AND THE IDEA OF THE SAVAGE

Homer's storytelling device of distant, fierce, savage enemies confronting immortal warrior-heroes in far-off lands was well adapted to the rapidly urbanizing, expansion-minded *polis* (city-state) form of civilization invented by the Greeks during their Renaissance centuries. Homer's epics were embraced by the Greeks as their bible during this critical period of cultural transition and intensified colonizing activities and have often been cited by historians and others as important factors in helping to launch and sustain this era of Greek cultural growth and expansion.

Between the so-called Dark Ages (1100–800 B.C.) following the presumed fall of the Mycenaean Empire and the Greeks' civilization-defining victory in the Persian Wars (490–479 B.C.), hundreds of self-governing, independent, and expansion-minded Greek city-states arose and prospered throughout the Mediterranean world. In this process of unprecedented cultural renascence and development, the Greeks laid the foundations for the Western world's first great imperial civilization centered in Athens during its so-called fifth-century B.C. Golden Age (see chapter 3).

Mainland Greeks had established scores of colonies on the western Aegean coast of Asia Minor (modern-day Anatolia in Turkey) in the first early wave of migrations of the Dark Age centuries. Scholars believe this long period of cultural diaspora may have followed the supposed collapse of the great Mycenaean palace-centered civilization described in Homer's epics. The Greeks themselves believed the ancient stories of fierce, invading Dorian tribes from the north forcing their exodus across the Aegean onto the Anatolian peninsula.

The colonies established during the Greek colonization of Anatolia were made up largely of Ionian speakers (Homer's native language). Well defended with walls and fortifications typically surrounding the urban city-centers of their civilization, the Greeks maintained connections to their ancient Balkan homelands while helping to spread Greek influence and trading relationships throughout the Aegean.

Our knowledge of the period is not as well documented as later centuries; the Greeks seemed to have lost the art of writing during the Dark Ages. But sometime in the late ninth century B.C., Greeks on the mainland begin to experience a gradual but steady population rise, accompanied by improvements in farming and newly acquired shipbuilding techniques, both likely imported from the East.

The pressures on a limited agricultural land base outside the walls of the *polis* and the increased capacity for seaborne trade helped spur the second great wave of Greek colonization activity, commencing around 800 to 750 B.C. Notably, this period is not too far removed from the first conjectured appearance in writing of Homer's epic poems about immortal warrior-heroes invading distant, savage lands.

The Greeks of this second age of colonization were constantly on the prowl for fertile domains far enough away from their overcrowded homelands to sustain independent colonial settlements. Many of the earlier-established Aegean colonies also were heavily involved in this second surge of Greek outmigration. These new Greek colonial settlements reached much farther into the Mediterranean, as far as Cyrene in North Africa, Marseilles in France, and the Costa Brava of Spain.

The Greeks of the Renaissance centuries were in fact developing into what Professor Perry Anderson has called the Western world's first "inherently *colonial*" form of civilization.[1] Focused on acquiring new territories and lands for settlement of excess populations and expanding their trading networks, the Greeks set up scores of new colonies throughout the Mediterranean world.

As occurred with the great city-states of Renaissance Italy in the thirteenth through fifteenth centuries A.D. (see chapter 9), increasing maritime trade and overseas colonial expansion fueled an intense period of cultural renewal and dynamic, civilization-shaping cross-cultural interactions. Greek colonial settlements throughout the Mediterranean, Aegean, and Baltic regions grew into prosperous trading towns and cultural centers. The institution of the polis as an independent city-state begins to assume its unique shape and form in these rapidly urbanizing centers of Greek commercial, political, and cultural life. Burgeoning networks of commerce, trade, information, and military alliances developed, grew, and propagated themselves throughout the Greek Mediterranean world.

Homer's *Iliad* and *Odyssey* celebrated a set of aristocratic norms and values that were highly congenial to the hereditary ruling elites of this new type of expansion-minded form of polis-based civilization. The typical warrior-hero of Homer's poems was a *basileus,* a king or noble warlord like Odysseus, Achilles, or Agamemnon. Usually these rulers were from dynastic families claiming hereditary rights over a traditionally defined territory. The basileus-king provided military protection and a rough form of justice for the city, where his palace sat safely guarded within the city walls, and the impoverished and terrorized peasantry in the countryside.

At the time of the appearance in writing of Homer's poems, the ruling elites who claimed these ancient rights of hereditary succession still largely controlled the petty kingdoms and baronies that dotted the mainland and Peloponnese. These dynastic family groups were typically the primary sponsors and advocates for overseas colonization, seeing it as a convenient device for ridding the kingdom of excess population and troublemakers. Sweetening the pot for this class, new commercial networks and extended trading alliances would be established in the bargain.

Prominent members of leading families, often later-born sons, usually were designated to lead these colonizing voyages, keeping the ventures under firm aristocratic sponsorship and control. Once a foothold was gained in the place chosen for colonial settlement, any resistance by the native population would be quickly suppressed or annihilated by the Greeks' superior technology, tactics, and prior military experience in similar operations.

An easy-to-defend foothold on an island redoubt or some perch of land overlooking a well-protected harbor was ideal (recall Odysseus's detailed reconnaissance of the deserted island located off the coast of the land of the Cyclopes). Once the colony was secured and fortified with sturdy walls and defenses, a temple would be built to honor the gods and sanctify these newly established outposts of Greek civilization.

The most prosperous colonies of this period built some of the largest shrines and temples in the Greek world, advertising the establishment of the divine rule of the Olympian gods in alien, foreign lands. The founders of these successful settlements were typically honored or even mythologized as great heroes after their deaths by their colonies, in classic Homeric fashion.

In this dynamic and highly unstable system of independent, expansion-minded Greek trading settlements, successful colonizing ventures begat the need and desire for new colonizing endeavors. As people were drawn to the most prosperous towns and trading centers, new pressures were imposed on the limited agricultural land base outside the city walls. When the Greeks could no longer feed themselves in their city-states, they went out and founded new ones, in foreign, distant lands.

The Greeks' archaic system of laws regulating rights in landed property added to the dynamic for repeated cycles of social unrest and territorial expansion overseas. Unequal distribution and concentration of ownership and control of what little arable land surrounded the urban core compounded the problems of overpopulation.

The wealthy noble families were able to preserve their country estates outside the city walls by arranged marriages and favorable laws designed for the privileged classes. Such laws carefully regulated inheritance, heiresses, and dowry, and helped maintain the wealth and influence of the family dynasties. But the poorer families with too many sons or undowried daughters were forced to subdivide their plots into smaller and smaller units, inadequate for efficient farming. Eventually, the land-hungry elites would gobble up and reconsolidate these unsustainable family plots through mounting debt, foreclosures, and abandonment.[2] The poor peasants would be evicted from the land, and they would migrate into the city or be told to sail off to some distant overseas colony.

In this sense, the "inherently colonial" character of Greek civilization during this period literally began at home, for the poor farmers in the countryside at least. Once the ruling elites controlled all the land outside the city walls and the settlement had outgrown its limited agricultural carrying capacity, the natural impulse of the propertied classes was to advocate for continual territorial expansion overseas.

The ruling classes perceived such colonies as a relatively painless way to address problems caused by overpopulation and too little land. This noble class of robber barons and marauding warlords picked up plunder, tribute, and slaves along the way as integral parts of the colonizing enterprise.

As many as fifteen hundred Greek settlements were established during this second great age of Greek colonization. Many were very large and prosperous, usually located within a short distance of the coast, as seaborne trade and colonial expansion were vital to their growth. What happened in the hinterlands, where most of the local tribal populations were driven off to eke out an existence, was of little concern to the civilized Greek inhabitants of the polis.

It was a highly successful model for the ruling families and elites who received the great bulk of the economic and social benefits of Greek colonial expansion during the Renaissance. For this group, Homer's tales of aristocratic warrior-heroes advancing civilization's higher law along with the benefits of trade and commerce to distant, savage lands was a lived reality. Or so they liked to imagine.

Other sources from the period, however, tell a different story. The expansion-minded culture of the polis imposed many hardships on the working classes and the poor. Wars, feuds, and evictions appear to have been commonplace, and the turmoil of the times inflicted a heavy price on the poorer classes of Greek society. The small yeoman farmers struggling to survive on the few remaining plots of freehold land in the countryside had little to celebrate. Their complaints become part of a familiar refrain in the West's literary traditions. In fact, their grievances can be said to have invented the tradition of Western protest in word, rhyme, and song.

The first such contrarian ode ever recorded in the history of Western civilization, *Works and Days* by Hesiod, tells the story of a poor dirt farmer being mercilessly oppressed by the evil forces of society.[3] Hesiod, a Boeotian Greek poet, is believed to have been roughly contemporary with Homer. In *Works and Days*, Hesiod retells the famous Greek Legend of the Golden Age at the beginning of time, when humans lived a far more simple and virtuous existence, blessed by the gods, sustained by the bounteous gifts of untamed wild nature, without the benefits and burdens of civilized life in the big polis.

## THE LEGEND OF THE GOLDEN AGE

Given the economic distress, political turmoil, and incessant cries for land reform that characterized Greek life in the polis during the Renaissance, we might expect that the Homeric vision of the aristocratic warrior-hero jaunting off to distant parts of the world and making trouble in other peoples' lands was not a storyline likely to appeal to the poorer working classes. In fact, if *Works and Days* is any indication, some protest-minded Greeks of this era openly questioned whether their highly urbanized form of civilization, with all its luxuries and attendant desires, really was the best way of life a human being could imagine. Perhaps things were better at the beginnings of time, when life was simple and we lived closer to nature, as nature had intended.

Hesiod's subversive ode to the working classes of his time is generally thought to have been first written down close to the time of the appearance of Homer's epics. Along with his *Theogony* (the birth of gods), *Works and Days* was widely cited, read, and copied by the Greeks. It is regarded as one of the primary surviving sources on Greek mythology and the Olympian pantheon of gods from the Renaissance era and has been long considered a canonical text in the literature of the West. *Works and Days* is also the West's first great poetic indictment against the human misery and despair caused by an inherently colonial form of civilization that benefits the aristocratic elites at the expense of the poor, downtrodden, and oppressed in society.

We know little about the life of the first great poet of the oppressed in ancient Greece. We do know that Hesiod was from Boeotia, a large island off the mainland divided up by warring kingdoms that had wreaked havoc on each other over time. He may have been a younger contemporary and even a literary rival of Homer. There is an old story, probably spurious, that he traveled to Euboea and won a tripod in a poetical contest against Homer.

Hesiod's renowned poem and its moralizing celebration of the simpler, more virtuous, and ennobled way of life lived by human beings in the lost Golden Age of humanity predicts the inevitable fall of the corrupt form of civilization that the ruling elites and warlords allowed to fester among the Greeks. The ancient Legend of the Golden Age, he says, shows us "the true way of existence" for humanity.

In *Works and Days,* Hesiod barely mentions the legendary nobles and heroes of the Trojan War. Rather, the reigning aristocrats and robber barons of the present day are cast as the villains and outlaws, oppressing the countryside and devouring the poor peasant farmers' few remaining measly plots of land and humble homes.

*Works and Days* is Hesiod's moral indictment against the rapacious culture of greed and unforgiving avarice he sees all around him. The laws, institutions, and morals of the ruling aristocracy that are celebrated in mythic fashion in Homer's poems are here identified as the scourge of humanity. In Hesiod's time, the gods are dishonored, the poor toil and suffer without protection or justice from their lords, and elders are abused and disrespected.

Hesiod himself feels cursed to live in such a sick and decaying civilization. A society that celebrates the seizure of other peoples' lands as lawful and even virtuous, Hesiod warns, will most surely incur the wrath of Zeus.

There is only one way for his contemporaries to save themselves. Hesiod's moralizing antidote to the misery and decline of the present age is to return to a simpler, more virtuous way of life, one not consumed by the pursuit of worldly riches and not burdened by continual wars at home and conflicts in faraway lands. Hesiod offers us the ennobled, virtuous, and more natural way of life lived by the first human beings of the Golden Age as an example of the true way of existence for humanity.

At the beginnings of human history, Hesiod tells us, the gods created a "golden generation of mortal people." This generation was blessed with a carefree life of primitive simplicity made possible by the bounteous abundance of nature. There were no wars or strife, and humans "lived as if they were gods, their hearts free from all sorrow."

They took their pleasure in festivals, and lived without troubles.
When they died, it was as if they fell asleep. All goods were theirs.
The fruitful grainland yielded its harvest to them of its own accord;
this was great and abundant, while they at their pleasure
quietly looked after their works, in the midst of good things
[prosperous in flocks, on friendly terms, with the blessed immortals].

In contrast to this Golden Age, Hesiod paints a bleak, depressing picture of corruption and decline down through the succeeding ages of human history. He tells us of a Silver Age and then a Bronze Age. There follows the Age of Heroes who fought in the Trojan War. Although each of these ages seems to represent progress for the human condition, in actuality, Hesiod tells us, humanity regresses over time. As each of these epochs pass, we move farther and farther away from the simple, virtuous life enjoyed by primitive humanity in the Golden Age.

Hesiod's own Age of Iron is characterized by a hopelessly fallen generation of men on the earth. He curses his fate that he must live in such a time. Wishing that he had never been a part of this generation "but had died before it came," he laments how the gods "send anxieties to trouble us." Hard work and pain, both day and night, is all that this age knows. Men dishonor their aging parents. Warfare is rampant, and humanity is cursed by the continual attacks of city on city. All virtue is absent in this overacquisitive, greed-driven age. There is no "favor for the man who keeps his oath, for the righteous and the good." Instead, men give praise to perpetrators of violence and evil-doers.

As Hesiod explains, this fallen, debased way of life is far inferior to the free and happy life enjoyed by humanity during the Golden Age. In this utopian vision of the "true way of existence" for humanity, peace reigns over the land, and young boys grow to manhood instead of dying in war. The earth provides sustenance to the people "who are straight and just, they do their work as if work were a holiday." It is literally a land of free acorns and honey from the bees:

on their mountains the oaks bear acorns for them in their crowns,
and bees in their middles.

Their wool-bearing sheep are weighted down with fleecy burdens.
Their women bear them children who resemble their parents.

Keep track of those acorns; they show up throughout the literature of the West from this point on. They can be found as stereotypical food for the primitive savage and rustic peasantry in texts as diverse as *The Metamorphoses* by Ovid, Cervantes' *Don Quixote*, and John Locke's *Second Treatise on Property*.

After laying out the happy blessings enjoyed by humanity in this just and fair land of free acorns, honey from the bees, fleecy sheep, and faithful, fecund wives, Hesiod further sharpens his critique of the Greeks' culture of greed and acquisitiveness. A just society, he warns, prospers "in good things throughout" and does not need to send its citizens off to war to acquire what it needs in other peoples' lands. "They need have no traffic with ships, for their own grain-giving land yields them its harvest."

Hesiod finishes his diatribe against the wickedness of his times by offering a dire prediction: If the Greeks continue down this precipitous path of decadence and decline, the gods will punish them. Zeus will make them die and diminish from famine and plague for their cruel and violent acts. Their women will bear them no children; their houses will dwindle; their armies, navies, and great cities will be destroyed. According to Hesiod, the only way for his fellow Greeks to avoid this inevitable fall is to return to the way of life enjoyed by humanity in the Golden Age.

## THE LEGEND OF THE GOLDEN AGE AND THE INVENTION OF THE NOBLE SAVAGE

Hesiod's retelling of the Legend of the Golden Age represents the founding textual source for one of Western civilization's most familiar and influential adaptations of the idea of the savage. Virtually all of the familiar stereotypes, metaphors, markers, and images associated with the theme of the noble savage in the storytelling traditions of the West can be traced back directly to *Works and Days* and its golden generation of the first humans on earth. Simple and virtuous, relying on wild, abundant nature for subsistence, living a free and unburdened life without wars, disease, or the desire for civilized refinements and luxuries, Hesiod's golden generation embodies the stripped-down version of humanity in its "natural" state that will come to be notoriously represented by the language of ennobled savagery in the literary traditions of the West.[4]

Significantly, in planting the seeds of this ancient mythic theme derived from the Legend of the Golden Age, Hesiod uses the same basic identifying categories as Homer to construct his own contrarian version of the idea of the savage. Like the fierce tribal savages of the *Iliad* and the *Odyssey*, the noble savages of the Hesiodic legend lack laws, sophisticated institutions of government, and the refinements in culture and luxuries that characterize the Greeks' supposedly more advanced form of civilization. They do not trade and lack the technologies, particularly the advanced tools of warfare, utilized by the Greeks of the Renaissance era. Thus, in the technological primitivism of the savage—one of the consistent, unifying, and identifying categories of the Classical idea—they are just like Homer's mythic fierce savages. Further, they are every bit as remote and alien to the Greeks as Homer's savages living on the edges of the earth; it is just that their distance is felt in their temporal separation, rather than in their geographic isolation, from the Greeks.

Hesiod's retelling of the Legend of the Golden Age provides an important thematic counterweight to the Homeric celebration of traditional Greek aristocratic values and norms that prevailed over the day-to-day life of the Renaissance era polis. Hesiod's version of the ancient mythic legend shows that we are happiest when we live the life of the noble savage, free of the cares and worries, wars, and hardships imposed on humanity by an inherently colonial form of civilization.

For a protest poet like Hesiod, the legend's utopian vision of returning to a simpler mode of existence was a highly effective storytelling device that subversively played on the anxieties, fears, and doubts of Greeks regarding life in the polis. By pointing to the incessant wars, corruption, and moral decline of contemporary Greek society, Hesiod was able to show that things really were better in the good old days. From this point forward, this anxiety-producing theme, first inscribed in the protest literature of the West by Hesiod, will be echoed down through history, whenever the noble savage is called on to stand irreconcilably opposed to an inherently colonial form of civilization and the threat it represents to humanity's true happiness and virtue.

## THE LEGEND'S INFLUENCE ON ANCIENT GREEK CIVILIZATION AND CULTURE

The Hesiodic retelling of the legend and its provocative themes of ennobled savagery and simple virtues resonate broadly throughout Greek literature, dramatic poetry, and artistic works. One of the most influential adaptations of the Hesiodic version of the legend was by the fourth-century B.C. Greek Peripatetic philosopher, geographer, and student of Aristotle, Dicaearchus of Messana (ca. 350–ca. 285 B.C.), one of Classical Antiquity's most noted thinkers and historians. His works reflected a general interest in good and bad lifestyles and a deeply pessimistic view of his own contemporary times. For Dicaearchus, the idea of the savage was a perfect vehicle for expressing his profound discontent with modernity.

His oft-cited *Life of Greece,* handed down in fragment form some five centuries later by the Neoplatonist Porphyry (234 A.D.–ca. 305 A.D.), drew on the Legend of the Golden Age to describe a purer and more simple juridical state of nature at the beginning of time. According to Dicaearchus, during this time, humans lived free of the constraining laws of a degraded and overly materialistic form of civilization.[5]

Dicaearchus begins his influential historical narrative with an explicit reference to the Hesiodic version of the Legend of the Golden Age, voicing initial skepticism about its historical accuracy. He nonetheless goes on to draw freely from Hesiod's metallically based scheme of declining ages to tell his story of human history on earth, beginning with "the primeval life of Greece." Using the same rationalist methods and skeptical judgment employed by his famous teacher, Aristotle, he begins to deconstruct the Hesiodic narrative step by step, rebuilding it into a theory of the "natural" growth and development of human society over time. If the Golden Age "is to be taken as having really existed and not as an idle tale," Dicaearchus tells us, "when the too mythical parts of the story are eliminated it may by the use of reason be reduced to a natural sense."

Dicaearchus paints a serene, utopian picture of life for "the men of the earliest age," borrowing heavily from the theme of the more "natural" way of life of the noble savage that emerges out of Hesiod's poem. It was a better time, he explains: "For all things then presumably grew spontaneously, since the men of that time themselves produced nothing, having invented neither agriculture nor any other art. It was for this reason that they lived a life of leisure, without care or toil. . . . And there were no wars or feuds between them; for there existed among them no objects of competition of such value as to give anyone a motive to seek to obtain them by those means."

Having described the envious life of leisure and freedom of care enjoyed by humankind in its most natural, primordial state of existence, Dicaearchus follows the familiar Hesiodic pattern of humanity's precipitous decline through the succeeding ages. There came a period of degeneracy, when humans allowed their desires to multiply beyond the simple mode of life in the Golden Age. Wars and the craving for distinction brought about by luxury and the love of possessions began to characterize this degraded, decadent form of life. "Later came the wandering pastoral life, in which they already sought to obtain superfluous possessions and laid hands on animals." This way of life introduced the institutions and technologies of organized warfare to humanity: "Some men summoned others and gathered them together in groups in order to gain distinction, others did the same for the sake of greater security." Then, as humans "always fixed their minds upon seeming goods, they passed on to a third kind of life, the agricultural."

Dicaearchus drew on the Hesiodic legend to construct his dystopic account of human life on earth as a complex pattern of seeming progress but ultimate decline. The ennobled and supposedly more "natural" idealized way of life enjoyed by humans at the beginnings of time was, according to this pattern, far superior to the way of life characterizing the present-day Greeks' inherently colonial and morally decadent form of civilization.

Dicaearchus's account of human history influenced numerous later Classical writers, including the prolific Roman author Marcus Terentius Varro (116–27 B.C.). Varro wrote more than six hundred books on the Latin language, religion, and historically related topics. Grotius relied on the ancient Greek philosopher as a sound authority in researching his monumental work establishing the foundations of the European Law of Nations and modern international law in the West, *Law of War and Peace,* during the seventeenth-century European Enlightenment (see chapter 11).

The poet Aratus (ca. 315–240 B.C.), another highly influential ancient Greek writer, used the Legend of the Golden Age as a historical beginning point in his oft-cited third-century B.C. poem, the *Phaenomena.*[6] Aratus's poem explained the order of the constellations of stars in the night sky and the simple rules of divine justice that prevailed at the beginnings of time, laid out according to the legend.

Aratus was said to be an acquaintance of Zeno, founder of the Stoic school. Aratus's discussion of the constellations became one of the most influential uses of the legend and its celebration of the superior virtues of a simpler, more primitive mode of human existence by later writers and philosophers.

Aratus's description of the constellation Virgo elaborates a richly evocative integration of Greek mythology and religion, jurisprudential thought, astrology, and social criticism. The poet does all this by using the Legend of the Golden Age as the mythic foundation of his story of humanity's fall from virtue and justice over time.

Aratus tells us that the constellation Virgo is maiden of the gods: "in her hands bears the Ear of Corn gleaming." A tale "current among men," the poet reports, is that "formerly she was on earth, and met men face to face," immortal though she was. "And they called her Justice; and assembling the elders, either in the market place or in the wide streets, she spoke aloud urging judgments more advantageous to the people."

Having elaborated this fundamental notion of justice in ancient Greek legal thought as benefiting a community of people with common civic interests, Aratus describes life in the Golden Age as far superior to the present day. "Not yet did men understand hateful war or vituperative disputes or din of battle, but they lived simply, and the cruel sea was concealed, nor did ships carry men's livelihood from afar; but oxen and the plough and Justice herself . . . furnished all things a thousand fold. This continued as long as the earth nourished the Golden Race."

Aratus proceeds to follow the goddess's course among humanity according to the Hesiodic timeline of a descending series of metallically named ages. Virgo seldom mingled with the humans of the Silver Race, Aratus tells us, longing "for the manners of the ancient peoples." She would come down from her isolated abode in the mountains and curse humans for their wickedness: "What an inferior race the golden fathers have left! But you will breed worse. And wars and monstrous bloodshed will be among men and evil pain will be laid upon them." And, as Virgo had prophesied, a Bronze Race was born, "more deadly than their predecessors." They forged weapons and ate the very oxen that had drawn the plow. Hating this race of men, Virgo "flew to Heaven" to dwell in that country, "where still at night she appears to men."

Aratus's inspired vision of the cosmos, laid out in accord with natural justice and the Hesiodic Legend of Ages, drew numerous reverent commentaries in the literature of later Greek and Roman antiquity. There were several well-known Latin translations of the poem, including Cicero's, contained in his *De natura deorum* (On the Nature of the Gods). Ovid, who would produce his own Hesiodically inspired retelling of the legend in *The Metamorphoses*, relied on Aratus for his *Fasti*, a poem in six books on the origins of the Roman gods.

Though writing about the earliest history of human life on earth, Dicaearchus and Aratus drew on the Hesiodic legend to make an important point about their own times. Such contrarian critics saw the history of the world, with the Greeks at its center, as a complex pattern of seeming progress but ultimate decline. They sought to show that the more natural way of life of primitive humans, living closer to nature without complex laws, institutions of government, sexual hang-ups, private property, or large-scale wars, was far superior to their own fallen, corrupt, and decadent form of civilization in every way. The early protest poets, with their dystopian language of ennobled savagery and plaintive pleas for a simpler way of life, inaugurated one of Western civilization's oldest literary traditions. A source of both resentment and reflection, the theme of the noble savage developed into one of the West's favorite storytelling devices for those who sought to create anxiety and doubt about a civilization whose way of life, they believed, was irreconcilably opposed to human happiness and virtue.

## STORIES OF DISTANT TRIBAL PEOPLES
## LIVING AS NOBLE SAVAGES

The Legend of the Golden Age proved to be the perfect vehicle for subversively playing on the anxieties and fears of the Greeks about the quality and ethics of life in the contemporary polis. The use of the legend and the idea of the savage as ennobled primitive in a stripped-down state of nature sought to show that indeed the Greeks were happy and more virtuous in simpler times, before the rise of their acquisitive, contemporary form of civilization.

A number of different storytelling traditions of the Greeks echoed this basic sense of apprehension about a civilization that seemed deeply flawed by its greed and avarice and in a state of irreversible decline. Some of the most famous and enduring myths and legends of the Greeks imagine distant primitive peoples living an ennobled life of ease and virtue amid the bounties of untamed nature. Such mythic tales reflected the hope that remnants of the Golden Age might still be found to exist on the edges of the earth.

As Professor James S. Romm describes, the Greeks populated the threshold of the earth with a number of different "blameless" locales inhabited by ennobled and blessed humans who enjoyed the benefits of a Golden Age–type existence.[7] Elysium, as one famous example, is described by Homer in the *Odyssey* as being located on the earth's distant boundaries. It is a blessed resting place where heroes such as Menelaus, Agamemnon's cuckolded brother who fought in the Trojan War, are rewarded for their valor and bravery with immortality and a life of tropical ease: "No snow is there, nor heavy storm, nor ever rain, but ever does Ocean send up blasts of the shrill-blowing West Wind that they may give cooling to men."[8]

The Greeks located similar mythic locales, such as the Fortunate Islands and the Blessed Isles, on the brink of the earth, separated from their lands by distant, terrifying Ocean. The recurring tales of remote tribal peoples in Africa, Asia, and northern Europe living in simple harmony with wild, untamed nature, without wars, complex laws, or need for luxuries and extravagance suggests the deep and penetrating influence of the legend in shaping the Greek view of the outer world and its peoples during the Renaissance era.

Homer once again is our earliest written source. He draws on the legend's familiar mythic stereotypes and iconic markers of the ennobled primitivism in his influential descriptions of the "blameless" Ethiopians that appear in both his poems. They are "the furthest of men" living to the south of the Greeks, by the distant "streams of Ocean." They are said to be the happiest humans on earth, to live a blessed lifestyle, and to enjoy the natural abundance of their fair and bounteous land. In the *Iliad*, Zeus, the supreme deity of the ancient Greeks, is said by Thetis, Achilles's divine mother, to travel to feast among them.[9]

Homer reports that other gods go to visit and vacation with the blessed Ethiopians at the far southern edge of the world. In the *Odyssey*, Poseidon, god of the sea, is reported to have been enjoying himself at a festival the Ethiopians had thrown in his honor. There they offered up to the god the traditional "hecatomb," a sacrificial feast involving the slaughter of a hundred sheep and oxen. From Homer onward, the noble Ethiopians are proverbially exoticized in the literature of Greek Classical Antiquity as the happiest and most blessed of humans. Their remoteness is often coupled with their extreme legal and cultural primitivism and their simple, virtuous way of life. Later Greek writers blindly following Homer's poetic lead uniformly refer to them as "blameless," indifferent to power, free from feuds, needing little, and living free of constraining human laws, according to nature. In their far-off lands on the southern edges of the known world, they are special holy peoples of ideal disposition—noble savages in every sense that the Greeks of Classical Antiquity would have imagined them to exist.

Ancient Greek myths and legends also tell of a distant noble people to the far north, the Hyperboreans. They too were holy and just; the founding of the oracle of Apollo at Delphi was attributed to these holy peoples, likely from somewhere in Scandinavia. According to all the ancient hyperbole about the Hyperboreans, their land was covered six months a year in light and six months a year in dark. They were the most just of all people and lived longer than any other humans on earth. Forever joyful, these noble savages of northern Europe enjoyed their festive leisure time without fear of disease, old age, or violent wars, living as humans were meant to live, as if in the Golden Age.

In the *Iliad*, Homer describes another foreign people bordering on the northern frontiers of the Greeks' world. As Zeus turns his weary eyes from the blood-soaked scenes of violence on the plains of Troy to the north, he beholds the land of "the lordly Hippemolgi that drink the milk of mares, and of the Abii, the most righteous of men."[10]

The general region suggested and the Homeric epithets led to the identification of these peoples with the nomadic, horse-breeding Scythian tribes inhabiting the northern Baltic region. The fact that they were milk drinkers associated them in the Homeric mythopoetic imagination with stories of fecundity and the gods and heroes in mythology. Among the many variants on the origin of the Cornucopia, the horn of plenty, in Greek mythology is the story of Zeus, who was committed at birth by his mother, Rhea, to the care of the daughters of Milesseus, a Cretan king, in the hope of saving him from his devouring father, Kronus. As related in Bulfinch's *Mythology*, the daughters fed Zeus "the milk of the goat Amalthea." Zeus, in gratitude, "broke off one of the horns of the goat and gave it to his nurses, and endowed it with the wonderful power of becoming filled with whatever the possessor might wish."[11]

Examples like the "blameless" Ethiopians to the far south, the long-lived Hyperboreans to the far north, and the nomadic horse-breeding, milk-drinking tribes of the Baltic suggest that the ancient Greeks populated the distant frontier boundaries of their known world with a remarkable array of noble savages and virtuous primitives, all blessed by the gods. From this point forward, the inherently subversive, anxiety-producing idea of a more primitive and less technologically sophisticated form of humanity living more naturally, happy, and free in wild, untamed nature, without civilization's constraining laws and confining institutions, is perpetuated as part of an anciently derived storytelling tradition in the West. As represented by the destabilizing counterimage of the noble savage, Western civilization is first taught to see itself as a threat to humanity's desire for happiness and virtue through the ancient Greeks' Legend of the Golden Age.

## CONCLUSION

Western scholars have long commented on the ancient Greeks' fondness for complex dualities and dialectical modes of reasoning in their approach to understanding the world and universe that surrounded them. As I have sought to show in this chapter, the Greeks reveled in applying these dueling paradigms and unresolvable contradictions to the idea of the savage. In stark opposition to the fierce mythic savage of Homer's poems, Greek protest poets and contrarian-minded social critics could always turn to the familiar stereotypes and imagery of ennobled primitives associated with the Legend of the Golden Age for inspiration and examples as to what a life lived free from the complexities, burdens, and woes of contemporary civilization might look like.

Images of the virtuous, happy, and natural way of life of humanity at the beginnings of time, and representations of distant utopian locales and blessed, righteous, and long-lived tribal peoples living on the edges of the earth, sought to prescribe an antidote to civilization's worrisome complexity and precipitous decline. The legend tells us that primitive humanity lived a more virtuous and simple mode of existence, closer to wild nature in all its abundant fecundity. But just like Homer's fierce savages, these ennobled counterexamples lived a way of life irreconcilably opposed to Greek civilization's norms and values.

The idea of the savage as it emerges from the Greek Renaissance centuries already exhibits that anxious, unresolved dual quality that will characterize its use through the ages in the storytelling traditions of the West. Distant, alien, remote, lacking complex laws or institutions, and living a simple mode of existence in a state of untamed nature, the savage from this point forward assumes its familiar identity as an ambiguous, doubting presence, irreconcilably opposed to an urbanized, expansion-minded, and luxury-consuming form of civilization—the same form of civilization that has characterized and defined the Western world since the time of the ancient Greeks.

# THREE

# THE EMERGENCE OF
# THE CLASSICAL IDEA
# OF THE SAVAGE

The idea of the savage underwent a profound transformation in the Classical Age of Greece (fifth and fourth centuries b.c.). The change can be traced in large part to the Greeks' civilization-defining conflict with the Persian Empire in the Persian Wars (490–479 b.c.). The rise of the West's first great imperial civilization during the Athenian Golden Age of the fifth century b.c. was a direct response by the freedom-loving Greeks to the continued threat perceived from the Persian Empire.

No longer confined to the realm of myths, legends, and fabulous tales of subhuman monsters and ennobled primitive tribes in far-off lands, the idea of the savage becomes an increasingly important part of the way the Greeks depict the "barbarian." For Classical Age Greeks, the "barbarian" referred to anyone who did not speak Greek. According to Classical concepts, the most alien, strange, and exotic barbarians were the distant tribal peoples who lived farthest from Greek civilization.

The ancient myths and legends of fierce and ennobled savages handed down from Homer, Hesiod, and other sources from the Renaissance centuries were well known to Greeks of the Classical Age. Schoolboys studied and memorized passages from Homer's two poems. The gods and immortal heroes of ancient Greek myth and legend were celebrated on public monuments, in the religious festivals, on the stage, and throughout the literature, art, and philosophy of the period.

What changes in this unparalleled age of Greek imperial civilization is that the idea of the savage is habitually applied to the "barbarian." The familiar stereotypes and iconic images derived from the ancient myths and legends are no longer just storytelling devices drawn on by traveling bards and contrarian poets. To the Greeks, the lack of sophisticated laws; institutions of government; private property; appropriate religious rituals, dress, and countenance; and meaningful familial or social bonds become key identifying markers of the barbarian's irredeemable primitive nature. The mobilizing, subversive, and anxiety-producing potential of these stereotypes was seized on by writers, dramatists, artists, and philosophers to identify and isolate the most extreme real-life human forms of radical divergence from the Greeks' civilized way of life. For Greeks of the Classical Age, the savage was transformed into the most radical form of the barbarian, the polar opposite of all that was "grand and glorious" about their own highly urbanized, expansion-minded, luxury-consuming form of civilization.[1]

Many influential and well-known literary and artistic works of the Classical Age directly cite or draw on the familiar stereotypes and categorical markers of savagery associated with the ancient myths and legends. Immortal warrior-heroes defeating subhuman monsters and celebrations of the blessed life of primitive humanity in the Golden Age are particularly favored themes. But unlike Homer and Hesiod in their use of the two competing, foundational modes of the idea, the Greeks of the Classical Age drew on these ancient storytelling devices to represent real-life peoples in a myriad of cross-cutting, interrelated, diverse, and complex ways.

Importantly, despite the broad cultural diversity and distant geographical reach of the concept as reinvented during the Classical Age, the essential, unifying notion of savagery in both its dark-sided and ennobled forms as the antithesis of Greek civilization remains unchanged and uncorrupted from the ancient myths and legends. In fact, in the civilization-shaping transition from the Greek Renaissance to the Classical Age, the idea of the savage is now even more strongly unified and made coherent in terms of its basic identifying markers and categorical references. According to the language of savagery invented by the Greeks of this pivotal period in the history of the West's growth and development, those barbarians who are the most distant and remote from Greece will live a way of life radically opposed in all its essentials to the superior form of civilization represented by the polis.

## THE CLASSICAL IDEA OF THE SAVAGE

The idea of the savage was a pervasive presence throughout Greek civilization in the Classical Age. Greeks encountered the ancient myths and legends of fierce and ennobled savages throughout their daily life and rituals, particularly in Athens. Athens had emerged as the center of the West's first great imperial civilization following its navy's decisive victory in 480 B.C. over the fleet of the Persian emperor Xerxes in the Straits of Salamis. The victory ended the Persian Wars, expelled the Persians from Europe, and resulted in the creation of the Delian League. This famed military alliance, led by Athens's indomitable navy, was dedicated to keeping up the fight against the still-dangerous threat of the Persian Empire.

No doubt, the militant obsession with the "barbarian" during this period is but one reflection of the trauma and anxieties the Greeks experienced in repelling the existential threat represented by the Persians. The ancient mythic stories of civilization's irreconcilable conflict with savagery were told and retold with particular intensity during the Classical Age.

As noted in chapter 1, the mythic contest between the Lapiths and centaurs, the Centauromachy, was depicted on the south metopes of the Parthenon on the Acropolis, the ancient fortress mountain that stands in the center of Athens. The famed statesman-orator Pericles (495–429 B.C.) commissioned the sculptor Pheidias to commemorate the Greeks' civilization-defining victory over the Persians by including a sculpted series of legendary triumphs and mythic battle scenes on the monument.

The east front of the temple metopes depicted the Gigantomachy, the mythical battle between the Olympian gods of the Greeks against the giants. The west metopes portrayed the Amazonomachy, the battle between the Amazon tribe of women warriors and the Greeks. The north metopes celebrated the Greeks' triumph over the Trojan Empire in the legendary Trojan War.

Centaurs in general were a favored theme of decorative artists and sculptors during the Classical Age, deployed as a readily recognizable symbol of an extremely deviant form of savagery. Emblematic of the Greeks' underlying ambivalence toward the idea of the savage, an ennobled centaur, Chiron, makes frequent appearances throughout the literature and art of the period. Chiron was the beloved teacher to the mythic warrior-heroes Herakles, Theseus, and Achilles and to the Greek god of medicine and healing, Asclepius. The Roman poet Ovid tells us in his poem on the gods, *Fasti,* that the Greeks honored Chiron by naming the constellation of stars Centaurus after him.

Besides being chiseled in looming bas-relief atop great public monuments or seen in the constellations of the stars at night, the idea of the savage lurks in innumerable nooks and crannies of everyday Greek life. The savage can be found, for instance, leering from the wine vessels used in the symposium, the West's oldest documented male bonding ritual and a central institution for the transmission of traditional Greek aristocratic values and norms.

Plutarch (ca. 46–120 A.D.), the noted Greek historian, once remarked that the well-conducted symposium was "a passing of time over wine which, guided by gracious behavior, ends in friendship."[2] The symposium was where men conversed, often about specific topics, recited poetry, or played music. And, of course, they drank wine. In his famous Socratic dialogue, the *Symposium,* Plato discussed wine drinking as part of the symposium's ritualized activities and how some participants were too hungover from a party the day before to start the process all over again.

Musicians, dancers and high-priced prostitutes (*hetairaira*) might be hired to compliment the evening's games and lively conversation. Wealthy households might have a dedicated room for the symposium, the *andron*—a big improvement over Homer's Cyclopean-appointed man cave.

Inside the special room where the men met, the *symposiarch* (master of ceremonies) would pour carefully measured amounts of water and wine into a large krater. The Greeks took great care in how wine and water were mixed; wine was never served unadulterated; it was always mixed with water according to complex rules and regulations. Drinking pure wine was considered both dangerous and uncivilized, the mark of a savage. Drunkenness, as the Greeks knew all too well from their own myths and stories, could result in madness, violence, or death.

The wine vases and drinking vessels used in the symposium reveal the deep penetration of the stereotypes and iconic images associated with the idea of the savage into interrelated aspects of Greek daily life. Commissioned as fine works of art from skilled artisans and craftsmen, these drinking vessels often depicted exotic tribal primitives or savage mythic monsters.

Drinking vessels from the fifth century B.C., for example, show African Pygmies carrying a dead crane or being eaten by a crocodile. Such pictorial vignettes reminded the holder that the Pygmies of distant Africa lived in a savage, inhospitable world, far removed from the refinements in culture and civilization known to the Greeks.[3] The famous drinking vessel (*rhyton*) by the Brygos Painter, believed to have been produced in Athens in the early decades of the fifth century B.C., is decorated with an African Pygmy, recognizable through a combination of familiar stereotypes and characteristic markers of barbarian savagery in its most extreme forms. He uses a bow, a traditional sign of the primitive tribesman and tribeswoman as well (e.g., the Amazons). Although of African origin, he is efficiently stereotyped as an extreme example of the savage by his leopard-skin Scythian cap. The Scythians were nomadic savages to the north of the Greeks; in painting on the hat, the Brygos Painter was simply embellishing on the clichés associated with the Pygmy's foreign, exotic aspect.[4]

The Pygmy's Scythian-styled cap draws attention to the unique role in the rituals of the symposium of the northern tribes of nomadic hunters who roamed the distant Baltic frontiers of the known Greek world. In the literature and artwork of the period, the Scythians were often stereotyped as both noble tribal warriors and fierce nomadic primitives. But like so many of the savage barbarian peoples of ambiguous nature known to the Greeks, they were routinely caricatured as unable to hold their liquor.

To drink like a Scythian meant to drink wine "neat," unadulterated and undiluted by water. The Greeks coined a term for this practice: to drink *skythizein* style. At the symposium, the symposiarch might even don a Scythian cap to better supervise the mixing and distribution of the wine. Costumed thus, the symposiarch was metaphorically transformed into a symbol of unadulterated wine.[5] Such practices show one of the important ways the Greeks of the Classical era truly enjoyed a higher form of civilization. They got themselves skythizein drunk in their well-appointed man caves.

## "THE INVENTION OF THE BARBARIAN"

Examples like the Parthenon and the wine drinking vessels used in the symposium suggest the subtle but pervasive penetration and widespread diffusion of the idea of the savage in the daily life and ritual activities of the Classical Age in Greece. As we have seen, the concept was an important point of self-reference, cultural identity, and societal cross-comparisons for the Greeks.

The great tragic playwrights of the Athenian stage of the fifth century B.C. seemed to have understood how cultural stereotypes can shape our perceptions of those we see as different from ourselves. Their use of a language of savagery in describing the most extreme examples of the barbarian's divergence from Greek civilization was particularly influential during the Classical Age. In her illuminating book, *Inventing the Barbarian,* Professor Edith Hall describes a "heightening in Hellenic self-consciousness"[6] reflected throughout Greek civilization of the time, but particularly on the Athenian stage following the Persian Wars. According to Hall, this change is felt most palpably in the Greeks' use of the term "barbarian."[7]

Prior to the Persian Wars, there is no overt evidence that the word *bárbaros* (barbarian) held any particularly intense, negative connotations for the Greeks in relation to foreigners. Most scholars believe that up through the early sixth century B.C. at least, bárbaros merely was used to describe those peoples who did not speak Greek or who spoke the language badly, in unintelligible syllables, like "bar-bar." Professor John E. Coleman describes the word as an onomatopoeic term, citing "gibberish people" as a reasonable translation.[8]

But then the Persian Empire appeared as an existential threat to Greek civilization and the independence of the polis. The threat was felt first by the Ionian Greeks in Asia Minor, who were brought under the empire's despotic rule in the late sixth century B.C. and then by the rest of Greece in 492 B.C., when the emperor Darius launched his first invasion of Greece. Darius was followed in 480 B.C. by his son and successor Xerxes I, who marched his massive imperial army across the Hellespont. As Aeschylus's play *Persae,* the only historical drama that survives from the period, indicates, the Greeks regarded this unnatural transgression of the boundary between East and West as a fateful act of hubris against the gods.

The Persians' stated intent of destroying the Greeks' independence and turning them into tributaries and slaves inspired a whole new perspective on the "barbarian" that is palpable throughout the Classical Age. From the Persian Wars onward, the Greeks developed a whole new "vocabulary" of barbarism.[9] Chiefly originating as an Athenian concept, but with echoes and resonances felt throughout the far-flung Hellenic city-states of the Mediterranean, the barbarian comes to represent the polar opposite of everything that was "grand and glorious" about Greek civilization.[10]

Hall has shown how this "polarization of barbarian and Hellene" became a particularly popular theme in Greek theater of the fifth century B.C.[11] Plays were a dominant form of visual spectacle and sacred ritual for the Greeks, helping to shape and define general perceptions and attitudes about the world, the gods, and non-Greeks in particular. Barbarians figure prominently in the tragedies of Sophocles, Aeschylus, and Euripides, so much so that Hall states that "barbarians were a particular preoccupation of the Greek tragedians."[12]

Nearly half of the three hundred tragedies we know something about portray barbarian characters, are staged in barbarian lands, or refer to barbarian customs and exotic rituals or shocking forms of cultural expression and deviance. According to Hall, the intense dramatic focus on the difference represented by the barbarian is part of a vitally important "exercise in self-definition": The Greeks of the Classical Age came to see themselves as a superior form of civilization in opposition to the world of brutish tribal savages and other lesser peoples around them.[13]

The idea of the savage as representing the most extreme example of the irreconcilable differences between the uncivilized barbarian and culturally refined Greek assumed a vitally important role in this process of self-definition that played out on the Athenian stage. In their depictions of barbarian characters, the great tragedies of the period frequently drew on and cited the familiar stereotypes and iconic markers of the most radical, alien forms of savagery associated with the ancient myths and legends.

Euripides's (ca. 480–406 B.C.) plays are particularly noteworthy for their complexity and enduring power in their use of the savage to illustrate the most extreme forms of the barbarian's divergence from the superior cultural norms and political values of the Athenian polis. One of his most frequently staged tragedies, *Medea,* focuses on the mythic warrior-hero Jason, who escaped with the Golden Fleece, aided by Medea, the barbarian Colchian princess and tribal sorceress. The Colchians were a barbarian tribe of savages located on the distant shores of the Black Sea.

In Euripides's version of the famous story, Medea leaves her savage homeland to follow Jason, his Argonauts, and the Golden Fleece back to Greece after the defeat of the man-eating Colchian monster. Once home, Jason decides to choose a Greek wife over Medea and the estranged couple's half-caste children. He chastens the barbarian princess, saying that she actually should be thankful for all he has done for her.

> In so far as you helped me, you did well enough.
> But on this question of saving me, I can prove
> You have certainly got from me more than you gave,
> Firstly, instead of living among barbarians,
> You inhabit a Greek land and understand our ways,
> How to live by law instead of the sweet will of force.[14]

Jason's scolding quite effectively associates Medea with the mythic stereotype of the distant tribal savage in her fiercest feminine form: a lawless, barbarian princess, and a witch to boot. This striking contrast to the more civilized Greek feminine virtues sets the stage for Medea's later murders of her own children, fathered by Jason. Her actions show her true nature as the most extreme type of barbarian savage imaginable. She is the primally driven man-eater, consumed by an unquenchable savage thirst for cruelty and revenge.

Euripides's portrayal of Medea provides his audience with one of the Western world's most enduring and influential character studies of the savage in its most dangerous feminine form. The playwright deploys the Classical idea of the savage as opposite to Greek civilization in a much different way in his play *Iphigenia at Aulis.* The play links the Greek Mycenaean warlord Agamemnon's sacrifice of his daughter, Iphigenia, at the commencement of the Trojan War with the human sacrifices practiced by the Taurians, notorious distant tribal savages in the literature of Greek Classical Antiquity.

Well known as gross violators of the law of xenia, the Taurians of the Crimean region were said to sacrifice Greek sailors captured from wrecked and pirated ships to their virgin goddess. Inside her sanctuary, the Taurians would nail the heads of their victims to poles and then throw their bodies off a cliff. The point of Euripides's dramatic characterization of Agamemnon as acting like a stereotypical Taurian was to show that the freedom-loving, polis-based civilization of Classical Age Athens was far superior to the barbarian institutions of lawless, despotic rule by familial birthright that had once characterized the Greeks.

Euripides's plays represent barbarians in complex fashion; sometimes they are regarded as natural-born slaves and sometimes as full-fledged humans. Nevertheless, they are always identified by their irreconcilable differences from the Greeks. For the playwright's Greek audience, the Classical idea of the savage serves as a familiar point of reference to define those differences in their most extreme and divergent forms.

According to Western scholars, the dramatic plays staged in Athens at the festivals and religious holidays were an important focal point of self-definition for Greek imperial civilization during the Classical Age. As both visual spectacle and sacred ritual, the plays helped to shape, define, and mold widely shared societal perceptions and attitudes about what it meant to be a civilized Greek and a barbarian savage. The tragedies in particular were cathartic, communally shared exercises in consolidating the Greeks' belief that their superiorly regarded, polis-based form of civilization was far different and apart from the rest of the non-Greek world. Much like the blockbuster Hollywood movies we watch today, such as *Apocalypse Now, Dances with Wolves,* or *Avatar,* Euripides's plays became important reference points for the Greeks. Like the centaurs atop the Acropolis on the Parthenon or the Pygmy on a drinking buddy's wine cup, such familiar stereotypes and clichéd images helped to define the essential differences between civilization and the barbarian simply by using the idea of the savage.

## HERODOTUS AND THE CLASSICAL
## IDEA OF THE SAVAGE

The stereotypes, markers, and identifying categories of the language of savagery used by Classical Age Greeks were widely disseminated throughout imperial Athens in the fifth and fourth centuries B.C. The barbarian's lawlessness, despotic political institutions, primitive religious and familial customs, exotic sexual mores, and, most important, remoteness and distance are noted and remarked on in a variety of contexts. Most always the Greeks use this language of savagery to show the barbarian's irremediable lack of civilized refinement and inherent cultural inferiority.

In terms of lasting influence and impact on Western civilization's basic intellectual approach to understanding the barbarian world, Herodotus of Halicarnassus (ca. 484–425 B.C.) stands out as the first Greek writer to comprehensively organize these diverse mythic stereotypes and markers into a systematic account of human savagery in all its divergent and ambiguous forms. Prior to Herodotus's *Histories*, Greek knowledge of the barbarian world was scattered and diffused in stories, folktales, travelers' accounts, myths, and legends. The systematic manner in which he collected and organized all these diverse sources in the *Histories* has had a particularly profound and enduring effect on the way Western civilization has thought about itself and its relation to the non-Western world. Many of the stereotypes and identifying markers used today to describe indigenous tribal peoples trace back to the language of savagery first encountered by the West in Herodotus's influential book.

The *Histories* represents the primary Greek source on the events and major battles of the civilization-shaping Persian Wars. It also represents one of the Classical Age's most influential uses of the savage, a concept Herodotus relied on throughout his historical "inquiries" into the lands and customs of the groups that had come into contact with the Persian Empire—Babylonians, Massagetae, Egyptians, Ethiopians, Indians, Scythians, Libyans, and Thracians. The *Histories* is the foundational source of first reportage for the West on many of these ancient tribal peoples of Europe, Africa, and Asia.

We do not know much about Herodotus, other than what is stated or can be inferred from the *Histories*. He was a native of the Doric Anatolian colony of Halicarnassus in Asia Minor and is believed to have lived in Athens for a time. It may have been his base for traveling throughout the Mediterranean world, including Egypt to the south and as far north perhaps as Scythia.

Parts of the *Histories* appear to have been written to be delivered as oral presentations or readings at religious festivals, wisdom contests, and similar events familiar to Athenians of the Classical Age. Such works would be composed as a series of independent performance pieces, a type of story-telling exercise designed to inform or impress an audience with command of a certain type of useful knowledge.[15] Philosophers and medical treatise writers in fifth-century B.C. Athens, for example, were known to read or de-fend their works in small intellectual gatherings of scholars and aristocrats. Itinerant scholars and intellectuals like Herodotus (we know little of his life or background and how he financed his researches) would display their wares, as it were, through such public recitals.

Not all Greek citizens were literate enough to read Herodotus's *Histories,* but we know from Homer's popularity that the Greeks enjoyed a well-told story. Despite all the criticism through the ages of his methods and usefulness as a historian of the ancient world, Herodotus was an excel-lent storyteller.[16] Central to his method is his free use of a vast archive of Greek and non-Greek myths, legends, stories, folktales, and travelers' ac-counts. Herodotus appears to have gathered most of this flotsam and jetsam of the ancient Mediterranean and Asian world's great storytelling traditions in his own extensive travels. He draws from this rich and varied archive in illustrating one of the central themes of the *Histories,* stated explicitly by Herodotus himself at various points throughout the book: The farther one moved from Greece toward the distant edges of the world, the more strange and different are the lands and life-forms encountered there.

Thus, Greece, Herodotus confidently tells his audience, sits at the stable center of the world, with "far the best and most temperate climate."[17] The most distant lands, he says, will likely have those things the Greeks think the finest and the rarest. He follows this ancient mythic geographic schema of distance determining the degree of cultural and geographical divergence from the comforting Greek norm at the center of the world throughout the *Histories.* The most remote lands also are where the strangest and most primitive tribes of fierce and ennobled savages are found. Nearer at hand are barbaric peoples, the nomadic livestock breeders, like the Scythians to the north, who are less savage but still practice ritual forms of cannibalism typi-cal of highly uncivilized barbarians. Closest to Greece are those barbarians who are more or less civilized like the Greeks, with more or less sophisticated customs and belief systems.

As one example, Herodotus praises many of the cultural achievements of the Egyptians, who are settled cultivators like the Greeks. But their despotic political system of priestly rule and deified kingship distinguishes them from the Greeks—whose largely detribalized, city-state form of civilization was superior to all others known in the world, at least in Herodotus's opinion.

Herodotus's description of the barbarian tribes of the "most easterly" country in the inhabited world, India, closely adheres to this mythic ethno-geographic formula of distance and remoteness determining the degree of strangeness and rarity from the Greeks' experience at the center of the world. According to Herodotus, gold, the finest and rarest of commodities to the Greeks, is found in immense quantities on the far eastern side of India. There, all is desolate because of a great sandy desert. The "most warlike" of the tribes on the periphery of this desert retrieve this gold to pay tribute to the Persians.

Other peoples on this eastern periphery of the known world are equally savage and strange. The Padaei, Herodotus tells us, are the most primitive of all of India's tribes. They are cannibals, the worst type of savages the Greeks can imagine. "Among their customs it is said, that when a man falls sick, his closest companions kill him, because as they put it, their meat would be spoilt if he were allowed to waste away with disease." Even when the person denies that he is sick, says Herodotus, the others will not believe him, but kill and eat him all the same. When a woman is sick, her close female acquaintances treat her the same way. Those who do make it to old age are sacrificed to be feasted on. But not many reach this end, according to Herodotus: "Most of them will have had some disease or other before they get old, and will consequently have been killed by their friends."

Along with these fierce tribal savages, as lawless and wild in their customs and behaviors as the Greeks could imagine, Herodotus describes several tribes of noble savages who live in the most distant parts of India. One remote group enjoys a stereotypical Golden Age-type existence. Confirmed pacifists, they refuse to kill any living creature. They will not plant seeds. Nor do they build houses. When one of their members becomes ill, he goes into the desert to die, "and nobody gives a thought either to his illness or death."

The oscillating patterns of distance defining divergence from the Greeks repeats itself as Herodotus, like Homer before him, describes Ethiopia as the most distant southern land known to the Greeks. This faraway paradise is inhabited by a tribe of ennobled primitives, the "blessed" Ethiopians of Homeric fame and ancient legend: "The furthest inhabited country towards the south-west is Ethiopia; here gold is found in great abundance, and huge elephants, and ebony, and all sorts of trees growing wild; the men, too, are the tallest in the world, the best-looking, and longest-lived."

Consistent with the overall mythic geography informing the *Histories,* Africa has its fierce complement to the noble savages of Ethiopia: the Gyzantes, described by Herodotus as a far-off tribe in the western part of Africa. They live off the honey of the bees, paint themselves red, and eat monkeys. Their way of life is one of the most primitive described by Herodotus in the *Histories.*

Herodotus follows the same basic organizing pattern in describing the northern frontiers of Europe; the lands there "are richest in gold" and reportedly home to fierce savage tribes, such as the one-eyed Arimaspians (who call to mind Homer's legendary Cyclops monster). They are said to steal the gold from griffins, fierce monsters that vigilantly guard the treasure.

Herodotus doubts that there are one-eyed men who "in other respects are like the rest of men," but he does not totally dismiss the possibility of their existence. The reason, of course, is that the Arimaspians are reported to live in the most distant lands, where the strangest and most exotic forms of life are known to be found. "In any case," Herodotus remarks, "it does seem to be true that the countries which lie on the circumference of the inhabited world produce the things which we believe to be most rare and beautiful." According to the organizing schema of distance determining divergence from the Greek norm that pervades the *Histories,* anything is possible on the edges of the world.

The Scythians were one of the nearby tribal groups frequently mentioned or alluded to throughout the literature, art, and even philosophy of the Classical Age as paradigm examples of barbarian savagery. Homer was likely alluding to their simple and hard but virtuous way of life as nomadic herders in the *Iliad* when he called the noble milk-drinking tribes to the north of the Greeks "the most righteous of men."[18] In the Classical Age, as we have seen, they are reduced to clichéd caricatures in the drinking rituals of the symposium.

In the *Histories,* Herodotus depicts the Scythians as a dangerous threat to any imperial power that tries to invade their lands precisely because their "hard," primitive way of life is the source of their most noble virtue as far as he is concerned. As Herodotus describes them, their simple, freedom-loving existence makes them invincible in the rugged wastes of their desolate homeland:

> The Scythians, however, though in other respects I do not admire them, have managed one thing, and that the most important in human affairs, better than anyone else on the face of the earth: I mean their own preservation. For such is their manner of life that no one who invades their country can escape destruction, and if they wish to avoid engaging with an enemy, that enemy cannot by any possibility come to grips with them. A people without fortified towns, living, as the Scythians do, in wagons which they take with them wherever they go, accustomed, one and all, to fight on horseback with bows and arrows, and dependent for their food not upon agriculture but upon their cattle: how can such a people fail to defeat the attempt of an invader not only to subdue them, but even to make contact with them?

Herodotus's subtly detailed account of the nearby Scythians to the north sets the stage for his descriptions of the more distant tribes of savages in that part of the world. He simply repeats the basic formula used throughout the *Histories:* Each tribal group becomes more primitive and savage in its way of life the farther it is removed from the Scythians. The Neuri to the north follow many Scythian customs, but they are reported to be wizards, perhaps even the first werewolves encountered in the history of Western literature. The Scythians, like the Greeks settled near them, swear to Herodotus "that once a year every Neurian turns into a wolf for a few days, and then turns back into a man again."

The Argippaei, another tribe bordering the Scythians, are cast as the perfect counterexample to the Neuri: They are stereotypical noble savages. Herodotus describes them as living a life of extreme primitive simplicity in the "foothills of a lofty mountain chain." Bald from birth, women and men alike, they "live on the fruit of a tree called ponticum—a kind of cherry." Although their land is poor, nature freely provided for this tribe of noble savages: "Every man lives under his ponticum-tree, which he protects in winter with bands of thick white felt, taking them off in the summer." Blessed by the gods, the Argippaei are not burdened by the evils that plague life in the polis. "[P]rotected through a mysterious sort of sanctity[,] they carry no arms and nobody offers them violence; they settle disputes amongst their neighbours, and anybody who seeks asylum amongst them is left in peace."

Although Herodotus has long been criticized for his serial faults as a historian of the ancient world, he was remarkably consistent in his descriptions of the barbarian kingdoms and tribes of savages surrounding the Greeks. Throughout the *Histories,* he organizes his exotic stories and descriptions of distant peoples according to a geographical set of coordinates that turns to the idea of the savage as the most extreme form of the difference from the Greeks. The farther he moves from Greece at the center toward the outer edges of the world, the stranger and more different are the lands and peoples described.

Naturally, the fiercest and most ennobled tribes of savages are randomly scattered at the distant edges of the earth, where chaos and confusion reign. Nearer at hand are barbaric peoples, like the Scythians, who practice ritual forms of cannibalism typical of the most uncivilized savages. At the same time, they also exhibit certain noble qualities in their preference for a simple, "hard," nomadic way of life.

The language of savagery used by Herodotus throughout the *Histories* is nuanced and complex. He draws freely on both fierce and ennobled elements of the idea of the savage in developing his hard and soft accounts of primitive life. But the basic categorical markers of savagery derived from the ancient myths and legends—distance and remoteness, living without laws or property, sexually deviant and culturally unrefined in manners, customs, and religion—remain the same. Herodotus manages to give coherence and order to the barbarian world by organizing its orienting coordinates according to the Classical idea of the savage. From this time on, the *Histories* will become an important point of self-reference and self-identification for the Greeks as well as for the West. In using the stereotypes and categorical markers associated with the Classical idea of the savage to describe far-off barbarian peoples, Herodotus confirmed the ancient mythic belief that the most extreme forms of human difference from the norms and values of civilization are to be found on the remote edges of the world.

## CANNIBALISM AND THE CLASSICAL IDEA OF THE SAVAGE IN THE *HISTORIES*

Herodotus's use of cannibalism to organize his descriptions of the barbarian world provides one of the more interesting illustrations of the Classical idea of the savage at work in the *Histories'* account of distant tribal peoples. Going back to Homer's famous scary monster stories about the man-eating Cyclops monster and Lestrygonian giants, cannibalism was a universally recognizable and feared marker of irredeemable human savagery to the Greeks. Herodotus begins by noting that, although the Scythians do not eat human flesh, they do practice a type of cannibalism: drinking the blood of their vanquished enemies, whose skulls are gilded and used as cups. They also make garments of their enemies' skins and defile the gods by rejoicing in human sacrifice.

Thus, the Scythians are savages, according to the *Histories'* criterion of cannibalism as a definitive marker of the most extreme forms of barbarism. But, as the *Histories* shows, the degree of cannibalism, and thus of savagery, increases the farther one travels beyond the Scythians' barren land. The Issedones, Herodotus tells us, piously eat the flesh of their dead relations and gild their skulls. Then there is a dangerous tribe of cannibals called the Androphagi to the north. According to Herodotus, they are the "most savage of men, and have no notion of either law or justice." They are nomads and dress like the Scythians, but they speak a language of their own.

To the west of the Caucasus are the Massagetae. Herodotus describes their country as "an immense tract of flat country over which the eye wanders till it is lost in the distance." They are much like the Scythians in terms of their uncivilized, "hard" way of life, but more so. They eat wild food and raw fish. But their copulation is impersonal or even open, like that of cattle. Their country is easily entered but unconquerable; they have no silver or iron, but they live a primitive existence in an age of gold and bronze. They are sexually deviant. Among the Massagetae, "every man has a wife, but all wives are used promiscuously." They are primitive in their religious customs, worshipping only the sun. They have no agriculture, living on meat and fish, of which "there is an abundant supply" in their native lands. Like other barbarian savages, the Massagetae practice a ritualized form of cannibalism, determining the appropriate time for their elders to die and then sacrificing them along with some cattle. They then boil and eat both at the same time. Herodotus says it is their way of favoring those who went before them.

For Herodotus, the degree of cannibalism is an effective and readily recognized categorical marker for identifying the most extreme forms of the barbarian's degeneracy from the civilized norms and values of the Greeks. According to the Classical idea of the savage as elaborated by the *Histories,* cannibalism was just one of the many divergent cultural practices the Greeks could expect to encounter the farther they moved toward the most distant, savage parts of the barbarian world.

## CONCLUSION

The metopes atop the Parthenon in Athens, the drinking vessels used in the rituals of the symposium, the tragedies on the Athenian stage, and Herodotus's reports on the degrees of cannibalism encountered in the barbarian world all help us better understand the pervasiveness of the idea of the savage throughout Greek imperial civilization in the Classical Age. Such examples, for all their diversity in form and content, reveal a familiar shared set of essential features that define what the savage is as far as the Greeks were concerned: the most extreme form of the barbarian imaginable. Distant and remote, lacking laws and sophisticated political institutions, culturally backward, sexually deviant, linguistically confused, technologically unsophisticated, and dependent on the hunt and what nature might provide for subsistence, the savage emerges out of the Greeks' ancient myths and legends to assume a new, radicalized identity in the Classical Age. The polar opposite of everything a superior civilization stands for, the savage escapes from the realm of myth and legend to become the real-world embodiment of the irreconcilable differences represented by the stereotypes, iconic images, and categorical markers used by the Greeks to invent the barbarian.

# FOUR

# THE CLASSICAL IDEA OF THE SAVAGE AND THE INVENTION OF WESTERN PHILOSOPHY

The earliest beginnings of philosophy in the West reflect the ancient Greeks' obsession with the idea of the savage as the most extreme form of the barbarian and the polar opposite of everything that was supposedly grand and glorious about their own civilization. The founders of the Western philosophy—Socrates (469–399 B.C.), in his debates with the Sophists; Plato (ca. 429–347 B.C.), in his own highly influential philosophical system; and Aristotle (384–322 B.C.), in his theory on natural slavery—all used a language of savagery to create a stripped-down version of humanity in a state of nature.

Without laws, assemblies, religion, private property, technology, sexual shame, or familial and civic bonds, the savage became the perfect philosophical vehicle for defining what was most essential for human happiness and flourishing. In this process of reinvention into a philosophical construct, the idea of the savage becomes an important part of the Greeks' ethical and moral reflections on the meaning of the good life. From this point forward in Western philosophy, the stereotypes, iconic images, and categorical markers that had been used to identify the barbarian as the most extreme form of human savagery are now transformed into a philosophical model of our essential human selves, without the benefits and burdens of a highly urban-ized, expansion-minded, luxury-consuming form of civilization. Without the idea of the savage, as I show in this chapter, Western philosophy would never have been able to construct the anxiety-producing image of what our lives would be like if Western civilization had never been invented. As the Greek philosophers would probably tell us, we would all be living like savages.

## THE SOPHISTS, PROTAGORAS, AND THE IDEA OF THE SAVAGE

The idea of the savage can be identified as a key conceptual device of Greek speculative thought beginning with the early Sophists of the fifth century B.C., at the birth of the West's major philosophical traditions. Socrates's in-fluential dialogues with the Sophists, as related by his dutiful student Plato, initiate the debate that will consume Greek philosophy from this point for-ward: Can a highly urbanized, expansion-minded, luxury-consuming form of civilization promote human flourishing and happiness, or are we better off living the simple and unadorned life of the primitive savage?

Today, the word "sophist" carries a highly negative connotation. A sophist is someone regarded as too clever by half, a specious obfuscator. But at least prior to the humiliating defeat of Athens and its allies by the Spartan League in the Peloponnesian War (431–404 B.C.), the term "soph-ist" (*sophiste*) was generally applied by the Greeks to anyone who taught or possessed some sort of special "wisdom" (*sophia*). The word was applied at times to rhapsodes, professional performers of epic poetry who could give precise, by-the-word recitations of Homer's poems. Revered poets like Hesiod, gifted healers, and even Orpheus, "the father of songs," according to Pindar, are all respectfully referred to as "sophists" in the literature of Classical Greek Antiquity. At least in the early part of the Classical Age in Greece, no insult was intended if someone called you a sophist. It was meant as a compliment—it was a way of saying you were sophisticated and wise.

But in the period of widespread social disruption, chaos, plague, and imperial disintegration that accompanied the setbacks and defeats of Athens in its prolonged civil war with the Spartans, the sophists' reputation began to change. The well-paid group of itinerant teachers and scholars who drilled their students in the art of rhetoric and public speaking—vitally important survival skills in the increasingly litigious imperial civilization of Athens in the Classical Age—became Sophists with a capital "S." They were caricatured, reviled, and even lampooned on the Athenian stage as amoral parasites, living off the handsome fees paid for their services in teaching the careful choice of words and rhetorical tricks that could be used to move and cajole the assemblies and law courts of the polis.

The Sophists earned this less-than-stellar reputation largely by teaching their students how to make the weaker argument appear stronger and the stronger appear weaker, regardless of the overriding merits of either appeal. Their methods of teaching the art of persuasion reflected an underlying philosophical belief that knowledge and truth are illusory, since people cannot agree on what they are. And the Sophists were there to make sure of that, by demonstrating the hopeless relativity of all systems of knowledge. They taught their students to be deeply skeptical about the possibility of mere mortals ever discovering some absolute truth or pure form of justice in the world. People would be better advised to concentrate instead on making really clever arguments designed to appeal to the prejudices of your audience. Some Sophists were even said to argue in nihilist fashion that, in the end, might makes right and the stronger always wins, regardless of the merits of a particular argument. But you might as well try because sometimes a good speech can really make a difference.

Aspects of this skeptical philosophical perspective are reflected in what we know of the views of one of the most famous Sophists, Protagoras (ca. 490–420 B.C.). His most notorious teaching that everything is relative is best captured by his oft-quoted aphorism: "Man is the measure of all things; of what is, that it is; of what is not, that it is not."[1] Conclusions about the world, in other words, all depend on the person making those conclusions. Protagoras's deep intellectual and moral skepticism is expressed in his lost (perhaps publicly burned) book, *On the Gods,* of which only a few fragments survive: "About the gods, I am not able to know whether they exist or do not exist, nor what they are like in form; for the factors preventing knowledge are many: the obscurity of the subject, and the shortness of human life."[2] He is sometimes referred to as the first humanist of the Western philosophical tradition for his intensely secular, demythologized approach to the quest for human knowledge.

Like many of the Sophists, Protagoras did not worry much about the gods or the afterlife. He believed that life in the polis as he idealized it was the highest stage of perfection for humanity. The art of government, laws, and the higher virtues that make for the good life are possible of being achieved and perfected only by living in cities.

In the famous dialogue by Plato that bears his name, Protagoras uses the idea of the savage as handed down from the ancient Greek myths and legends to show how humanity acquired "justice and reverence."[3] According to Protagoras, these prime political virtues were given to the Greeks as a gift from the gods. Rejecting the Hesiodic Legend of the Golden Age, which tells of humanity's decline over time, Protagoras explains how the first humans lived miserable lives in the absence of these higher virtues. They gained their precarious "sustenance from the earth," living dispersed and in fear of the brutalities of a savage, untamed world. "[T]here were no cities. But the consequence was that they were destroyed by the wild beasts, for they were utterly weak in comparison of them, and their art was only sufficient to provide them with the means of life, and did not enable them to carry on war against the animals: food they had, but not as yet the art of government, of which the art of war is a part."

Protagoras goes on to explain that "the desire of self-preservation gathered them into cities; but when they were gathered together, having no art of government, they evil intreated one another." Zeus, seeing that humanity was about to cause its own self-destruction, sent Hermes, the messenger of the gods, to earth, "bearing reverence and justice to be the ordering principles of cities and the bonds of friendship and conciliation." Zeus further instructed Hermes to make sure that all humans shared in these divine gifts: "for cities cannot exist, if a few only share in the virtues, as in the arts. And further, make a law by my order, that he who has no part in reverence and justice shall be put to death, for he is a plague of the state."

For Protagoras, this act of divine intervention in delivering the political virtues to urbanized humanity is what differentiates civilization from savagery. To better illustrate the degraded, regressive nature of humanity in the savage state of nature, Protagoras points to the comedic play (now lost) *Savages*. Written by Pherecrates, a popular Athenian comedic playwright of the Classical Age, the basic idea behind the play, as much as we can tell from surviving fragments, is to highlight the advantages of the superior form of civilization enjoyed by the Athenians by contrasting it with the brutish life of the primitive savage. As Protagoras explains to Socrates:

> In like manner I would have you consider that he who appears to you to be the worst of those who have been brought up in laws and humanities, would appear to be a just man and a master of justice if he were to be compared with men who had no education, or courts of justice, or laws, or any restraints upon them which compelled them to practise virtue— with the savages, for example, whom the poet Pherecrates exhibited on the stage at the last year's Lenaean festival. If you were living among men such as the man-haters in his Chorus, you would be only too glad to meet with Eurybates and Phrynondas, and you would sorrowfully long to revisit the rascality of this part of the world.

According to Plato's dialogue, the great Sophist Protagoras taught his students that the laws and political institutions of the Greeks were literally gifts from the gods. Protagoras's use of the idea of the savage to underscore the superiority of life in the polis represents a vigorous philosophical defense of Greek civilization and its capacity for achieving human happiness and flourishing. At the same time, his influential philosophical digression on teaching the political virtues reinforced the ancient mythic stereotypes and categorical markers of lawlessness and cultural backwardness that the Greeks had long associated with the idea of the savage. In fact, Protagoras's teachings underscore the fundamental irreconcilability of savagery and civilization by assigning divine origins to the establishment of the imperial polis. According to the language of savagery used by this influential Sophist, to be civilized is to be blessed by the gods, an idea that will resonate down through the history of Western civilization's relations with the non-Western world.

## SOCRATES AND THE IDEA OF THE SAVAGE

Protagoras's celebration of Greek civilization's demonstrable virtues in securing a happy life for humankind in comparison to the life of the primitive savage was designed to appeal to the prejudices of sophisticated Athenians who might distrust the Sophists and their teachings. It did not sit too well, however, with Socrates. Regarded as the first real philosopher in the history of the Western world (that is why philosophers before him are called pre-Socratic), Socrates, at least in the dialogues in which his words and teachings are reconstructed or invented by Plato, did not care much for the Sophists' clever arguments. He particularly disfavored using the idea of the savage as a philosophical construct to celebrate the superiority of life in imperial Athens.

Ironically, Socrates himself was once notoriously lampooned as being a Sophist of the worst type by Aristophanes (ca. 446–ca. 386 b.c.) in his play, *Clouds* (423 b.c.). The play has been called the first great comedy of ideas in the literature of the West.[4] The center of the action is a place called the "Thinkery," where Socrates is depicted as teaching his students just enough knowledge and wisdom to be able to avoid paying any of their debts. *Clouds* gained particular notoriety in the literature of Classical Antiquity thanks to Plato's infamous charge in the *Apology* that it was a factor that contributed to the trial and execution of his beloved teacher.

Despite Aristophanes's caricature, Socrates would never have regarded himself as a Sophist of the type represented by Protagoras. In fact, according to Plato's dialogues, Socrates strenuously opposed much of what the Sophists stood for, particularly their methods of teaching rhetoric and oratory as central to the art of persuasion. In Plato's *Protagoras,* Socrates says he fears that if the youths of Athens listen too much to the clever and beguiling Sophist, they will be seduced and corrupted.

A lifelong citizen of Athens and veteran of the Peloponnesian War, Socrates became disenchanted with his fellow Athenians' conduct during the closing phases of the conflict. Although he opposed the Thirty Tyrants— the antidemocratic group of rulers installed after the Athenian defeat by Sparta—some in the capital identified Socrates as an enemy of democracy and a Spartan (or "Laconian") sympathizer. Sparta was located in Laconia, a region on the Peloponnese. Socrates, the self-described gadfly of Athenian society, was known for at times expressing a preference for things "Laconian." This tendency made him extremely unpopular among those Athenians who resented the undemocratic terms dictated by the Spartans to end the war.

In the *Protagoras,* Socrates does indeed praise the Spartans for their "Laconic brevity." He says such simplicity in expression was the earliest characteristic of philosophy in ancient times. *Birds* (414 B.C.), another comedy by Aristophanes, viciously lampooned Socrates's youthful followers for dressing and grooming themselves in the "Laconian" (Spartan) fashion.[5] As Aristophanes declares, "All men had gone Laconian-mad." Everywhere, gangs were going around "[l]ong-haired, half-starved, unwashed, Socratified." By this charge, Aristophanes's play underscored the belief that Socrates himself had apparently gone "Laconian mad." (The philosopher was notorious for going about Athens barefoot and unkempt while wearing a simple cloak to protect him against the elements.)

Socrates's primitive manner of dress can be seen as one of the ancient Greeks' most innovative and influential uses of the idea of the savage as a philosophical construct. He employed the notion of primitive humanity's simple and seemingly more deprived way of life to represent the extreme opposite of Greek civilization's ethical norms and values. Improvising on the familiar stereotypical images of humanity in its stripped-down, "hard" savage state, Socrates developed his own philosophical portrait of what the good life looked like for his fellow Greek citizens. His Laconian-inspired manner of living and dressing sought to show that a more "natural" mode of life in conformity to nature was more according to reason for humankind than was indulging in the luxuries and refinements that characterized the degraded, materialistically oriented life of the imperial polis.

Socrates's subversive, ironic manipulation of the idea of the savage to undermine the assumptions of his fellow Greek citizens about the superiority of their way of life accepts the basic claims of a Sophist like Protagoras; Socrates's Laconian-inspired version of the good life is no clichéd Golden Age–type existence for humanity. In the *Memorabilia,*[6] Xenophon's collection of Socratic dialogues, Socrates acknowledges as much in his exchange with another Sophist philosopher, Antiphon. Antiphon states that the simple, austere life advocated by Socrates is simply too hard for most Greeks to endure:

Socrates, I supposed that philosophy must add to one's store of happiness. But the fruits you have reaped from philosophy are apparently very different. For example, you are living a life that would drive even a slave to desert his master. Your meat and drink are of the poorest: the cloak you wear is not only a poor thing, but is never changed summer or winter; and you never wear shoes or tunic. Besides you refuse to take money, the mere getting of which is a joy, while its possession makes one more independent and happier. Now the professors of other subjects try to make their pupils copy their teachers: if you too intend to make your companions do that, you must consider yourself a professor of unhappiness.

Socrates's reply is telling about his views on the necessary components of the good life for humanity. Humanity was happiest living in primitive simplicity and virtue.

Do you not know that the greater the enjoyment of eating the less the need of sauce; the greater the enjoyment of drinking, the less the desire for drinks that are not available? As for cloaks, they are changed, as you know, on account of cold or heat. And shoes are worn as a protection to the feet against pain and inconvenience in walking. Now did you ever know me to stay indoors more than others on account of the cold, or to fight with any man for the shade because of the heat, or to be prevented from walking anywhere by sore feet? . . . You seem, Antiphon, to imagine that happiness consists in luxury and extravagance. But my belief is that to have no wants is divine; to have as few as possible comes next to the divine.

Socrates believed that reason dictated that a simpler way of life without complex laws, institutions of government, or the other luxuries and refinements proffered by Greek civilization would make us most happy and content in the end. He makes this point clear in Plato's *Republic* in speaking to his friend Glaucon, Plato's eldest brother and a major figure in this central dialogue in Western philosophical and political literature. Glaucon is the questioner during Socrates's famous telling of the Allegory of the Cave.[7]

Glaucon admits to Socrates that he has reservations about living in too minimal a civilization. Socrates, somewhat cynically, notes that one advantage of creating "a luxurious State" is that "in such a State we will be more likely to see how justice and injustice originate." But in his opinion, the true and healthy constitution of the state is the one that satisfies the basic needs of all members of society. Always the realist, Socrates admits that many "will not be satisfied" with the simpler way of life. They will want sofas, tables, and other fancy furnishings, luxuries like perfumes and incense, call girls, and cakes of all varieties. A never-ending cycle of desires, a theme familiar to any Greek who had ever heard of the Legend of the Golden Age, has now been initiated, assuring a never-ending cycle of frustration and imperial aggression to satisfy those desires and frustrations: "[W]e must go beyond the necessities of which I was at first speaking, such as houses, and clothes, and shoes: the arts of the painter and the embroiderer will have to be set in motion, and gold and ivory and all sorts of materials must be procured. . . . Then we must enlarge our borders; for the original healthy State is no longer sufficient."

According to the language of savagery used by Socrates, the luxurious, resource-consuming state must constantly expand in order to meet its citizens' insatiable demands for increased consumption of other peoples' resources and lands. Human beings can never be ultimately happy and content in such a society because the desire for more material goods and wealth can never be satisfied.

This is just the type of irreverent challenge to contemporary norms and values that earned Socrates the enmity of those who believed his teachings corrupted the minds of the youth of Athens. For such offenses, he was made to drink hemlock in 399 B.C. From this point forward in the history of the West, this "Socratified" language of savagery was available to any philosopher who wanted to show that a more "civilized" way of life is fundamentally at odds with humanity's hopes of achieving true happiness. By employing the familiar stereotypes of a more primitive, Laconian-inspired manner of dress on his own body, Socrates was able to suggest in ironic fashion that civilization itself is the source of all our discontents, a notion that further reinforced the idea of the savage's fundamental irreconcilability with a highly urbanized, expansion-minded, luxury-consuming way of life.

## THE SOCRATIFIED SAVAGE

The Socratified, minimalist image of the savage represented a vision of humanity stripped bare of the laws, institutions, customs, and manners of

Greek imperial civilization in the polis. Socrates's innovative use of the idea of the savage to illustrate his minimalist vision of the good life for humanity influenced, either directly or indirectly, many of the major schools of Greek philosophy that emerge out of the Classical Age centuries. This Socratified construct also reinforced the familiar ancient stereotypes of savagery's fundamental irreconcilability with civilization by focusing on the ethical implications of a way of life tied to consumption and the acquisition of material wealth that typified the polis.

The Cynic school, for example, shows how the Socratified idea of the savage could be deployed in a most annoying fashion as a subversive tool of social critique and ethical condemnation. The Cynics dutifully followed Socrates's teachings by using the idea of the savage on their own bodies, but in a much cruder and more confrontational manner than Socrates would likely have approved. Called "the mendicant friars of antiquity,"[8] Cynic adherents literally assumed the persona of a primitively dressed savage, living without property, laws, or even good manners among the citizenry of the polis. The Cynics sought to flesh out what a life of human savagery, stripped of all but its essential needs, would look like for the benefit of their fellow citizens. They would go about the city in a coarse and vulgar manner, deprecating all "knowledge, refinement, and the common decencies" of civilized life.[9] Some Cynics were reported to defecate, urinate, and masturbate in public.

The practical morals of the Cynics drew from the Socratic teachings received by Antisthenes (445–ca. 365 B.C.), one of the school's founders. Like Socrates, the Cynics believed that humans will be unhappy and irrational in proportion to the multiplicity of their desires. Thus, in order to be truly happy, our desires should be kept simple, "in accordance with nature." This fundamental teaching was reinforced by a principle that was also popular with the Sophists: Things are best as "nature" made them.[10]

According to Lovejoy and Boas, the Cynics' basic challenge to Greek civilization's urbanized, consumption-oriented vision of human happiness was "the first and most vigorous philosophic revolt of the civilized against civilization in nearly all its essentials."[11] Like Socrates, the Cynics used the idea of the savage on their own bodies and in their lives in an effort to persuade their fellow citizens to return to a better, simpler, more natural way of life. To the Cynics, that meant a life unburdened by contemporary civilization's worrisome laws, attachments, and constraints.

The Cynics adopted perhaps the most extreme interpretation of the idea of the savage as handed down from Socrates. The Stoic school developed a more subtle approach in their use of a stripped-down version of humanity in a state of nature. The founder of the school, Zeno of Citium (333–262 B.C.), was a student of the Cynics and was also heavily influenced by Socrates. The influence is demonstrated by Zeno's famous maxim: Live according to nature (*Zen kata physin*).

The Stoics basically took the Socratified concept of the savage and internalized its stripped-down model of humanity, turning it into a self-regulating ethical ideal of how life should be lived and grounded. For the Stoics, life should be lived naturally, according to reason. Like the Cynics, the Stoics' ethical premises favored an essentially backward-looking scheme of values found in the way of life lived by primitive humanity. Human beings, as nature made us, must have been perfect, and therefore humanity must have fallen from the primeval and natural excellence achieved during the first age of humanity on earth.

The Stoics did not uniformly deny that humanity could use the refinements and conveniences of modern society profitably. But the Stoic adherent had to be emotionally indifferent to the external goods produced by contemporary civilization. The Stoic should be able to let go of such material goods and the pleasures they bring without losing that sense of inner imperturbability. Get over it, or at least get along without it, might be the modern-day translation of the Stoics' philosophy. But like the Cynics, the Stoics sought to raise the anxiety level of their fellow Greeks in the polis by demonstrating that we are most happy and free when we live our lives more simply according to nature, like primitive humans at the beginnings of time.

The subversive and destabilizing appropriations of the idea of the savage by the Cynics and Stoics show us two examples of how early Greek philosophers sought to understand and illustrate the ethical implications of living in a materialistically driven, consumption-oriented society. Their stripped-down version of humanity sought to show that we can be perfectly content and happy without the material benefits and baubles of big-city life in the polis. Drawing on the same basic language of clichéd stereotypes and familiar cultural markers that identified the barbarian as the polar opposite of everything the polis stood for, these early contributors to the foundations of the Western philosophical tradition sought to show us that savagery and civilization were not just two different ways of living in the world. These two competing constructs represented radically different philosophical approaches to a question with ethical implications that have haunted the West since Socrates's debates with the Sophists: Would we all be happier if Western civilization, as handed down from the Greeks, had never been invented?

## ARISTOTLE'S THEORY OF NATURAL SLAVERY AND THE IDEA OF THE SAVAGE

Aristotle is without question one of the most important and central figures in the history of Western philosophy. His influential answer to the question of whether we would be happier if Western civilization had never been invented by the Greeks was a definitive no. Aristotle used the idea of the savage to show us how human beings can reach the highest stage of perfection in an imperially minded civilization; they simply make slaves of the most primitive and uncivilized barbarians they can find to serve the needs and desires of a higher form of civilization's privileged leisure class of ruling aristocrats.

Aristotle is reported to have written more than a hundred philosophical treatises, although only about thirty survive in the form of lecture notes taken by his students. His major contributions to the Western canon of knowledge include agriculture, biology, botany, ethics, logic, medicine, metaphysics, mathematics, physics, and politics. He is credited as a founder of the natural law tradition in the West and of the related concepts of the law of nature and natural right. He also developed one of the most influential theories based on the idea of the savage in the history of Western philosophy. Aristotle reportedly thought that some barbarians were so inferior and irrational that they were incapable of understanding reason and therefore could be regarded as natural slaves, fit only for menial service to the Greeks.

To understand Aristotle's idea of the savage as a natural slave, it helps to begin with Plato, his teacher. Both Aristotle and Plato took up the rationalist strains in Socrates's thought but rejected the Socratified interpretation of a stripped-down version of human happiness based on the idea of the savage. Both Plato and Aristotle were closer to the Sophist Protagoras's views (and, remember, Plato is the primary conduit through which we have those views) in the way they used the idea of the savage to illustrate Greek civilization's potential for securing human happiness and virtuous flourishing.

Plato's most influential use of a language of savagery to illustrate his philosophical defense of the polis as representing the highest state of perfection for humankind occurs in his account of the origins of government in Book III of the *Laws*. It is a later dialogue, and Socrates does not figure as a character in the text, so it is generally assumed that the work reflects Plato's own more mature and far more rationalist cast of thought.

The *Laws* describes a small, primitive band of mountain shepherds who subsist by herding and hunting wild beasts. Their simple way of life lacks the defining laws and institutions of the Greek polis. Plato then goes on to tell of humanity's progressive development and advance over time, commencing with the decisive "turn to agriculture." From this critical first step, Plato describes the beginnings of legislation, the institution of private property, and the undeniable benefits for humanity as we advance from this savage, primitive state to the civilized urbanity and laws of the contemporary polis.[12]

Aristotle's famous theory of natural slavery builds on the same basic stereotypes and categorical markers of primitive humanity's inferior mode of existence used by Plato. In his *Politics,* Aristotle closely follows Plato in characterizing the lives lived by the herdsman, the husbandman, and the hunter as being inherently inferior to the more civilized way of life lived by those who procure their food by barter and trade.

> Men's modes of life differ widely. The laziest are the nomadic shepherds, for they live an idle life getting their subsistence without labor from tame animals; as their flocks have to wander from one pasturage to another, they are obliged to follow them, cultivating, as it were, a living farm. Others live by various kinds of hunting, such as brigands, some—those who dwell beside lakes or marshes or rivers or a sea,—by fishing, still

others live on birds and wild beasts. But the greater number of men obtain a living from the cultivated fruits of the soil.[13]

To Aristotle, the more primitive modes of life are inherently inferior because they are incapable of helping us to realize our full potential as human beings and achieve the good life. Such modes of being are focused on fulfilling only our most basic human needs. Because we are "by nature a political animal," Aristotle holds that the only way we can achieve "a good way of living" is in the city-state governed by the perfect constitution. This is the stage of civilization that ensures to individuals "leisure" and the time needed for "liberal" pursuits. However, this way of life, the "virtue" it secures, and the property and "abundant means" needed to sustain it, of necessity, can be enjoyed only by a very limited class: the enlightened rulers. As Aristotle explains, his perfect state needs people to work the soil, and these "will necessarily be either slaves or immigrant aliens." It will also need artisans and merchants. None of these workers, however, can be allowed to enjoy the benefits of citizenship, for their way of life "is ignoble and unfavorable to virtue, since leisure is needful for the production of virtue and for participation in politics."[14]

What seems clear from Aristotle's views on the conditions for human happiness is that without the idea of the barbarian savage as a natural slave, his perfect state could not exist. In the *Nicomachean Ethics*, Aristotle famously brands those humans who "are irrational by nature and live only by their senses" as foolish beings. Such peoples "are like the beasts, as are some of the races of the distant barbarians."[15] They are at the bottom of the food chain, so to speak; brute savages. These are the barbarians who are fit only for subjugation by a superior civilization, such as the Greeks who need leisure time in order to be happy and fulfilled. According to Aristotle: "Where then there is such a difference as that between soul and body, or between men and animals (as in the case of those whose business is to use their body, and who can do nothing better), the lower sort are by nature slaves, and it is better for them as for all inferiors that they should be under the rule of a master. For he who can be, and therefore is, another's, and he who participates in rational principle enough to apprehend, but not to have, such a principle, is a slave by nature."[16]

Human progress for Aristotle is thus measured by the development of cities ruled by a leisure class that controls all the property in society, dutifully served by slaves culled from the dregs of the barbarian world. Freed from manual labor and mercantile pursuits, this privileged class can enjoy the good life of intellectual stimulation, cultural refinement, and disinterested self-government under an ideal constitution made available only by a life lived in the polis.[17]

At the time Aristotle was writing (the fourth century B.C.), the Greeks' way of life (particularly in Athens) was largely dependent on the use of foreign-born "barbarians" as slaves. A ubiquitous presence, they served as laborers in the Greeks' mines, fields, vineyards, and households. Many Greek households had slaves, even some of the poorest. Some skilled slaves served their masters as revenue-producing artisans. By Aristotle's time, slavery had become the most common means by which Greeks came into contact with foreigners. Aristotle discusses the status of slaves in detail in the *Politics*, and slaves play an important role as agricultural workers in Xenophon's ideal estate, as set forth in *Oeconomicus*.

Slavery, in fact, has been recognized as one of the most important factors in Greek attitudes toward foreigners. Due to the pervasiveness of slavery, Greeks of all ages, regardless of their own social rank, had numerous exchanges and contacts with foreign-born slaves. The degraded, servile status of these peoples served to confirm the Greeks' worst prejudices and stereotypes about the barbarian foreigners' inherent savage nature and the attractiveness of Aristotle's theory that such wretched beings were so uncivilized and irrational that they were made only to serve the Greeks as slaves.[18] In the language of savagery that infuses Aristotle's influential philosophical system, the barbarian's way of life is so primitive and irrational that the best thing that the Greeks could do for their well-being was to enslave them.

## CONCLUSION

The Classical idea of the savage as handed down from Greek antiquity to Western civilization first emerges out of Homer's epic tales of fierce, monstrous enemies to mythic warrior-heroes and the ancient Legend of the Golden Age and the more "natural" way of life enjoyed by human beings at the beginnings of time. According to the Classical language of savagery, these two types of uncivilized beings are identified by certain essential shared qualities that differentiate them from the civilized Greeks. They live without laws, sophisticated institutions of government, or cultural refinement and are irreconcilably opposed to the norms and values of civilized existence in the polis. Both mythic versions of the idea agree that the savage represents the extreme opposite of everything Greek civilization epitomizes: civic order, cultural refinement, and material wealth—or, as some contrarian-minded Greeks thought, political corruption, social decay, and spiritual poverty. This ambivalence about what the savage represents to a supposedly more sophisticated form of civilization is one of the concept's most distinctive, anxiety-producing features in the storytelling traditions of the West. From the time of the ancient Greeks, the savage has been used in this anxious, ambiguous fashion to stereotype and categorize non-Westernized peoples as fierce, irrational enemies to civilization and as ennobled exemplars of a happier way of life opposed in all its essentials to the West's ethical norms and values.

The habitual resort to the idea of the savage to define the virtues and vices of an expansion-minded form of civilization is one of the oldest and most frequently told stories in the history of the Western world. As we shall see, a language of savagery comprised of the clichés, stereotypes, markers, and images first used by the ancient Greeks to tell that story will shape and inform the way Western civilization seeks to define itself in relation to the non-Western world from this point forward in its history.

# FIVE

# THE IDEA OF THE SAVAGE AND THE RISE OF ROMAN IMPERIAL CIVILIZATION

"*Gallia est omnis divisa in partes tres.*"[1] One of the most famous opening lines in all of Western literature, even if it is written in Latin, a dead language, translates as "All Gaul is divided into three parts." But what comes next in Julius Caesar's (100–44 B.C.) *Commentaries on the Gallic Wars* indicates that the famous Roman military general knew a bit of Greek in addition to his famously precise Latin. He goes on to describe the three groups of barbarian tribes that inhabit Gaul: the Belgae, the Aquitani, and the Celts, each differing from the other in "language, customs and laws." Then Caesar uses a language of savagery clearly borrowed from the Greeks to describe these three tribal peoples.

> Of all these, the Belgae are the bravest, because they are farthest from the civilisation and refinement of [our] Province, and merchants least frequently resort to them and import those things which tend to effeminate the mind; and they are the nearest to the Germans, who dwell beyond the Rhine, with whom they are continually waging war; for which reason the Helvetii also surpass the rest of the Gauls in valour, as they contend with the Germans in almost daily battles, when they

either repel them from their own territories, or themselves wage war on their frontiers.

Rome had absorbed Greece and Hellenistic East Asia into its empire a century prior to Caesar's military invasions of Gaul. Romans, particularly those from elite, aristocratic families with long-established records of service in the Senate, quickly began to colonize Greek learning, literature, art, architecture, mechanical and engineering science, and many other aspects of Hellenic civilization as well.

Well-educated slaves who could teach the Greeks' language, literature, and skills in rhetoric and oratory to sons of the nobility were regarded as prized captives in Rome's foreign wars of empire. In his youth, Caesar had been tutored by Marcus Antonius Gnipho, believed to be a former slave from either Gaul or the Hellenistic East who taught in Rome. We know little of Gnipho; he is reported to have been educated in Alexandria, the Harvard on the Mediterranean of the Roman world. His students included Cicero, six years older than Caesar.

Caesar's precisely declaimed account of the military situation on Rome's northern barbarian frontier indicates that he had been immersed in a language of savagery derived from Greek Classical sources. His opening paragraph in the *Gallic Wars* efficiently utilizes the same basic organizing categories, familiar stereotypes, and identifying markers invented by Greek writers like Herodotus in describing Rome's barbarian enemies as distant and fierce, war-loving savages.

Caesar's *Gallic Wars* represents one of the most influential and enduring examples of the Romans' appropriation of the Greeks' idea of the savage. The genius of the Romans is reflected in the many ways they reinvented the concept to serve the purposes of their own highly urbanized, expansion-minded, luxury-consuming form of imperial civilization.

## THE TOURISTS' VIEW OF THE SAVAGE IN MODERN-DAY ROME

We can get a pretty good sense of what the idea of the savage looked like to Romans in the glory days of their empire by walking around the Eternal City

with a decent guidebook in hand. The savage, particularly in its dehumanized, barbarian form, was an all-pervasive presence in the Roman imperial
era. Depictions of the barbarian enemies conquered by Rome can be seen
with their dejected faces, uncouth dress, and hairy heads and beards (the
Romans had adopted Greek preferences for shorter hairstyles and clean-
shaven faces) on public monuments, buildings, and works of art throughout
the city today. Invariably, if we dig into the history of many of these iconic
works, a strong Greek influence can be found.

The Romans were particularly fond of using the idea of the savage
to commemorate their military triumphs over the barbarian tribes on the
northern European frontiers of the empire by constructing towering monuments in the city. The repeated stereotypes and identifying markers on these
structures suggest a fairly stabilized mental image of the barbarian in imperial Rome. Trajan's Column is located on the site of Emperor Trajan's Forum
near the Quirinal Hill, north of the Roman Forum. Completed in A.D. 113,
it is believed to be the first monument of its type constructed in Rome. Built
to commemorate Trajan's victory in the wars against the Dacian tribes (A.D.
101–102 and 105–106), its construction has been credited to the famous
Greek architect Apollodorus of Damascus (second century A.D.), who is believed also to have designed the Pantheon in Rome.

The Dacians were well known as extreme examples of barbarian savagery in the literature and ancient folklore of the Greeks. They were called
the Getae by Herodotus, and ancient reports associated them with werewolves in what is now Romania. The upwardly spiraling bas-reliefs on the
column depict Roman soldiers defeating the barbarously dressed and primitively armed Dacian warriors. The laborious construction of forts, roads,
bridges, and the familiar infrastructure of Roman imperial civilization is also
depicted on the column. Dacian men are always shown as unkempt, hairy,
and unshaven. Dacian women are depicted torturing Roman soldiers. Heads
of several Dacian warriors are hoisted upon pikes—such is the fate of those
who resist the empire. As Trajan's Column illustrated for the citizens of
Rome, the empire treated them like the barbarian savages they were.

Following Trajan's successful campaigns, the Dacians' territory was colonized and integrated into the empire. So was the practice of commemorating Rome's victories over the barbarian tribes of Europe on colossal public

*Trajan's Column, Rome (photograph by R. Williams)*

*Trajan's Column, Rome (detail) (photograph by R. Williams)*

monuments in the Eternal City. The Column of Marcus Aurelius, modeled after Trajan's Column, was constructed toward the end of the second century A.D. Commemorating the emperor's victory over the Danubian tribes in the Marcomannic Wars from A.D. 166 to 180, the column looms over the Piazza Colonna. The defeated barbarians, easily identified by their rough dress and bearded, unkempt, hairy heads, are depicted in various stages of disarray, despair, and defeat. Their villages are torched and their women and children are marched off into slavery as the sculpture winds its way up the column's façade. All the while, Emperor Marcus Aurelius (author of the influential Stoic philosophical text the *Meditations*) is shown watching over the conquest, in total command of the decimation of a people regarded by the Roman Empire as barbarian savages.

One of the most interesting adaptations of the idea of the savage on a Roman triumphal monument is found on the Arch of Constantine, located between the Coliseum and the Palatine Hill in Rome. The great arch was dedicated in A.D. 315 to commemorate Constantine I's victory over the

*Arch of Constantine, Rome (photograph by R. Williams)*

Roman emperor Maxentius at the Battle of Milvian Bridge. The towering structure incorporates sculptures of defeated barbarian savages taken from older Roman monuments in an effort to rehabilitate Constantine's image after his victory in what was essentially a civil war. The arch is a jumbled pastiche of scenes and pieces carved out from other monuments commemorating military victories won by Rome's "good emperors" (a phrase coined by Machiavelli) over various barbarian tribes. The attic of the arch shows the effort to associate what we today would call Constantine's brand with the valiant deeds of those notable barbarian killers. It is decorated with battle scenes and surrenders of barbarian prisoners taken from earlier monuments commemorating the deeds of Marcus Aurelius's victory over the German tribes and Trajan's conquest over the Dacians.

These hyperrealistic depictions of vanquished barbarian savages on public monuments and buildings were complemented by innumerable

*Arch of Constantine, Rome (detail) (photograph by R. Williams)*

Greek-inspired (or sometimes simply copied) works of art that can be seen in many of Rome's most famous museums. For example, featured in the center of a gallery in the Capitoline Museum, a Roman copy of a lost Greek statue, the famous "Dying Gaul," mournfully evokes the theme of the noble savage in its depiction of a wounded Gallic warrior. The original statue is thought to have been commissioned sometime in the early decades of the third century B.C. by Attalus I of Pergamon, an Ionian city-state in Asia Minor. Attalus, a loyal ally of Rome's empire, had defeated a group of Celts that had invaded Asia Minor from Thrace, spreading terror across the land.

The "Dying Gaul" draws on familiar Greek stereotypes and clichéd markers of the barbarian savage, particularly in its nakedness. Diodorus Siculus, a Greek historian of the first century B.C., describes Gallic warriors who fought naked. Polybius (ca. 200–118 B.C.), another Greek historian, de- scribes the battle dress of one particular tribe of Gauls in his account of the Battle of Telamon of 225 in this way: "[T]he Gaesatae, in their love of glory and defiant spirit, had thrown off their garments and taken up their position in front of the whole army naked and wearing nothing but their arms. . . . The appearance of these naked warriors was a terrifying spectacle, for they were all men of splendid physique and in the prime of life."[2]

Dionysius of Halicarnassus (ca. 60 B.C.–after 7 B.C.), a Greek historian who went to Rome to teach rhetoric during the reign of Augustus Caesar,

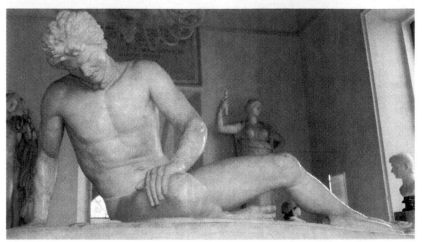

*"Dying Gaul," Capitoline Museum, Rome (photograph by R. Williams)*

lists the stereotypical attributes of the Gallic warrior in dismissing their effectiveness on the battlefield: "Our enemies fight naked. What injury could their long hair, their fierce looks, their clashing arms do us? These are mere symbols of barbarian boastfulness."[3]

The large hands and feet, mustache, and especially the collar, or torc, around the neck of the "Dying Gaul" all project popular Greek stereotypes of the way a barbarian should look and dress—or not dress. The torc, the telltale mark of the barbarian to the Romans, was worn by the Scythians, Thracians, Celts, and other tribal groups considered fierce, savage warriors by the Greeks.

The statue has been greatly admired throughout the course of Western history. Napoleon liked it so much that he took it with him to Paris in 1797 after invading Italy. Lord Byron celebrated its pathos and emotive power in his famous poem *Childe Harold's Pilgrimage* in the early nineteenth century:

> He leans upon his hand—his manly brow
> Consents to death, but conquers agony,
> And his drooped head sinks gradually low—
> And through his side the last drops, ebbing slow
> From the red gash, fall heavy, one by one.[4]

The noted art historian F. B. Tarbell, quoting Byron, described the "savage heroism" of the "Dying Gaul" in this way: He " 'consents to death,' and conquers agony. Here, then, a powerful realism is united to a tragic idea, and amid all vicissitudes of taste this work has never ceased to command a profound admiration."[5]

Roman appropriations of more fanciful versions of the Greeks' idea of the savage are represented by the frescoes and sculpted figures of centaurs, fauns, and satyrs favored by the aristocratic elites of the imperial era. The famous wall paintings of Pompeii featuring Pan and other Roman gods borrowed many of their themes and ideas from the Greeks. Intricate mosaics of Theseus defeating the Minotaur and famous mythic battle scenes between immortal Greek warrior-heroes and monstrous savages graced the vacation homes and villas of Rome's wealthiest and most powerful families.

The Romans even carried the idea of the savage with them to their graves, literally speaking. Roman sarcophagi decorated with bas-relief carvings of famous Greek myths and legends such as the Amazonomachy or intricate renderings of famous Roman battles and triumphs over barbarian tribes can be found on display in the museums of modern-day Rome.

With these sarcophagi as well, the influence of the Greeks lies submerged, just beneath the surface. Prior to the first century B.C., the Romans probably did not use sarcophagi for burials. The practice was adopted from the Greeks. One of the most famous Roman battle sarcophagi, the Grande Ludovisi from the third century A.D., is on display at the Palazzo Altemps in Rome. Discovered in 1621, the front of the sarcophagus depicts clean-shaven Roman soldiers and abject Germans defeated in battle, stereotyped by their distinctive clothing, beards, and unkempt heads. Roman soldiers tower over the defeated barbarians, checking their teeth to determine their suitability as slaves. The noble-looking Roman on the horse in the center top of the sarcophagus has been identified as Hostilian, son of the emperor Decius, who died in 252.

A tour of modern-day Rome will show that the Romans did not lack for their own indigenous myths and legends of the savage. The famous statue of the "Capitoline Wolf" in the Museo Nuovo in the Palazzo dei Conservatori shows Romulus and Remus, Rome's legendary founders, being suckled by a wolf. But even this foundation myth was most famously told by a Greek, the historian Plutarch (ca. A.D. 46–120), who related the legend in the first

*"Grande Ludovisi," Palazzo Altemps, Rome (photograph by R. Williams)*

chapter of his best-known book, *Parallel Lives,* a compilation of detailed biographies pairing famous Greeks and Romans to show their common virtues and vices.

Even from this brief tour of Roman imperial-era art and architecture, we can begin to sense how the idea of the savage was a pervasive presence in everyday Roman life, habitually turned to in celebrating the achievements of an empire that sought to bring civilization to the barbarian world. Told as part of their foundation myth, taken to their graves, chiseled in bas-relief on the great public monuments of their empire, and painted on the walls of their baths and vacation retreats, the idea of the savage as found reflected throughout the great public monuments and enduring works of art reveals the true genius of the Romans. Even the casual tourist who walks through the Eternal City today can appreciate how the Romans invented the Western world's greatest imperial civilization by conquering the barbarian tribes of Europe and then using the Greeks' language of savagery to memorialize their triumphant deeds.

## THE GENIUS OF THE ROMANS IN USING THE IDEA OF THE SAVAGE

As our brief tour of the sights of modern-day Rome suggests, the genius of the Romans is found in their ability to take the ideas and knowledge from the peoples they conquered and put them to good use in service to their own imperial ambitions. The process of Rome's absorption of the Greeks began relatively early in the history of the Republic (509–31 B.C.) and the city's rise as the preeminent imperial power in the Mediterranean world. The Hellenizing process was initiated first through contacts with the long-established Greek colonies of Magna Graecia (or "Great Greece") on the southern Italian peninsula. The independent Hellenic city-states that had been established as colonies in the early Greek Renaissance period were all eventually annexed as part of Rome's unification of the Italian peninsula into its expanding empire in the mid-third century B.C.

The Macedonian Wars of 205 to 148 B.C. increased Roman contacts with the Greek mainland city-states and the eastern Greek world in Asia Minor. With the decisive victory over the Achaean League in the Battle of

Corinth in 146 B.C., Rome completed its imperial absorption of virtually all the Greeks.

This remarkable and unprecedented series of imperial conquests, annexations, and encounters resulted in the extensive penetration of Greek-inspired ideas and systems of knowledge into virtually all aspects of Roman life. As we have seen with Caesar's early education, Roman elites preferred Greek-educated tutors or slaves to instruct their sons in the skills regarded as indispensable for a career and advancement in public life.

Typically, the young Roman student would read and memorize the best-known and respected works of Greek literature: Homer's *Iliad* and *Odyssey*, of course; Hesiod's *Theogony* and *Works and Days;* and the plays of Sophocles, Aeschylus, and Euripides. The major Greek philosophers and their schools—Plato, Aristotle, Epicurus, and Zeno of Elea (founder of the Stoic school)—would also be studied. Well-known historical works by Herodotus and Thucydides would likely be assigned. In order to serve capably in the Senate, the best and brightest young sons of the Roman nobility were trained in oratory and rhetoric, typically by Greeks or Latin scholars adapting Greek methods or teaching from Greek texts.

The effect of this Hellenizing influence was a source of controversy in the Republic from the outset of Rome's contacts with the Greeks. Cato the Elder (234–149 B.C.), Roman consul and censor during the Republican period, warned his fellow citizens to beware of the influence of the degraded Hellenistic world. Seeking to reclaim Rome from its descent into debilitating luxury and vice, Cato himself, however, was apparently unable to avoid echoing the familiar refrains of the Greek protest poets. Sounding much like Hesiod, he preached to the Romans about the need to return to the simpler virtues of an agrarian way of life, leaving others alone in their homelands to do the same. Identifying colonial wars, homosexuality, and the "mixture of elements" that they inevitably brought into the imperial capital as a source of moral decline, Cato sternly warned his fellow Roman citizens to beware: The reception of Greek culture would mean ruin for the Roman state.[6]

In violating his own censorious prescriptions against Greek influences while railing against them at the same time, Cato, like many of Rome's ruling class, was simply drawing on the lessons of his youth. As Plutarch notes, Cato's books and writings were full of citations to Greek authorities; at times he translates them word for word into Latin. As a young man, Cato had developed a close relationship with the Greek Pythagorean philosopher Nearchus, taking great pleasure in hearing him talk of philosophy.

The censor Cato apparently could not control himself when it came to relying on the Greeks in expressing his grave concerns over the deterioration of the Republic—caused, in his opinion, by too much exposure to the Greeks. Nor could his fellow Romans ignore the temptation. From the very beginning of their contacts, the Romans borrowed, stole, and plundered from the Greeks anything of value or insight they could take from that failed imperial civilization, in hopes of perfecting their own.

## THE GERMANS AND THE IDEA OF THE SAVAGE IN CAESAR AND TACITUS

As Cato's failed attempts at censorship demonstrate, Greek ideas and modes of seeing and reflecting on the world were a pervasive presence in Roman imperial civilization and its rise to ascendancy over the ancient Mediterranean world. As mentioned, one of the most important ways that the Romans used the Greeks' language of savagery is reflected in their basic understanding of the European barbarian world and the peoples in it. Recall Caesar's statement about the Belgians: "The Belgae are the bravest, because they are farthest from the civilisation and refinement of [our] Province, and merchants least frequently resort to them, and import those things which tend to effeminate the mind." Caesar's use of distance from Roman civilization to explain the degree of the barbarian savage's divergence from civilized norms and values was one of Herodotus's organizing principles in the *Histories* and a popular convention of imperial-era Roman writers.

Similarly, Caesar's conclusion that a luxury-consuming civilization was fundamentally at odds with the nobler virtues of the barbarian's "hard" way of life was also a familiar cliché among Roman writers, inherited from the Greeks and the literature of social protest associated with the Hesiodic Legend of the Golden Age. Caesar reveals the full scope and extent of his Greek-inspired geopolitical strategic vision of the world when he explains exactly why the Belgians are so brave and fierce: They have to defend themselves from the German tribes to the north, who, being even farther removed from civilization, are naturally more savage in their manners and customs.

Caesar's *Commentaries* were designed and written as propaganda pieces to promote his political career back in Rome. As tallied by Plutarch, Caesar's armies killed one million barbarian enemies of Rome, enslaved another million or so along the way, subjugated some three hundred–odd tribes of savages, and destroyed eight hundred of their towns and cities during his seven-year-long campaign. His victories over the barbarian tribes situated on Rome's vulnerable northern frontier, as documented in his year-by-year chronicle, made him extremely popular among the urban mob that controlled the Roman Assembly. Like Caesar, they opposed the aristocratic rule of the Senate.

Caesar's contemporaries greatly admired the *Commentaries* for their simplicity and precision in phrasing and grammar. Cicero, for example, remarked that Caesar's *Commentaries* merit the highest approbation: "for they are plain, correct, and graceful, and divested of all the ornaments of language." There is nothing more pleasing, Cicero wrote, "than a correct and elegant brevity of expression," and Caesar had mastered the skill in the exact and lucid phrasings of his prose.[7]

Caesar's terse, unexaggerated prose writing style reflected the influences of his Greek-styled education. As mentioned, he had initially been instructed by the former slave and grammarian, Marcus Antonius Gnipho. As a young man with political aspirations, Caesar then sought out the famous Greek orator Apollonius Molon of Rhodes, who also instructed Cicero. From what we know of his teaching methods, Appollonius emphasized the famous "three Ds" of the Greek statesman, orator, and one-time professional speech writer Demosthenes (384–322 B.C.): "Delivery, delivery, delivery."[8]

What Caesar delivers throughout his *Commentaries* is a concise recapitulation of the familiar stereotypes and categorical markers of barbarian primitivity handed down from the Greeks to describe the major tribal groups of Europe who opposed Rome's imperial authority. The Germans, as he describes them in his opening paragraph, being the furthest tribe from the Romans, are naturally the most warlike and uncivilized in their manners. Caesar runs down in checklist fashion all of the familiar markers and indicia of barbarian backwardness used by the Greeks. Living the "hard" life of the primitive savage described by Greek writers and philosophers, the Germans, Caesar reports, have no priests and do not sacrifice to the gods. They subsist on a simple diet determined by their nomadic, cattle-herding way of life. They eat mostly milk, cheese, and meat. They have no single king or ruler in times of war, "but the chiefs of provinces and cantons administer justice and determine controversies among their own people." Dishonest to the core, robbing any foreigner they might come across, their entire life, Caesar informs us, "is occupied in hunting and in the pursuits of the military art; from childhood they devote themselves to fatigue and hardships."

Like other Roman writers during the era of imperial conquests and acquisitions, Caesar notes that the Germans do have a few noble qualities that are worthy of emulation. Unlike the Romans who, Caesar seems to suggest, indulge themselves too much in bodily pleasures and sensuous luxuries, the Germans avoid all sexual relations until their twentieth birthday. The most honored among them are those who remain chaste for the longest period, believing that "by this the physical powers are increased and the sinews are strengthened. And to have had knowledge of a woman before the twentieth year they reckon among the most disgraceful acts." They freely open their houses to their welcomed guests, treating them with the utmost respect and gladly sharing their food. They refuse to recognize private property in land, holding it communally for several reasons. As Caesar explains, the Germans fear being ensnared by the steady habits of the farmers' life that might make them change their "ardor in the waging of war for agriculture." Believing that the accumulation of wealth incites jealousy and feuds among them, they maintain "a contented state of mind" by having each see his own possessions "placed on an equality with [those of] the most powerful." They live in simple huts, fearing that the construction of elaborate houses would make them less able to deal with the cold and heat.

Roman writers following Caesar continue to draw on the familiar categories and identifying markers of the Classical language of savagery handed down from the Greeks to describe the fierce and ennobled qualities of the "hard" life of the Germans and other barbarian tribes of northern and central Europe. A good deal of what we know about the German tribes during Rome's imperial era comes from Tacitus (ca. A.D. 56–120), a renowned historian and the son of a Roman knight. Tacitus served Rome as a senator, consul, and governor of Asia. He was a staunch Republican throwback at heart, who had witnessed in his time both the madness of Nero and the noble deeds of "good emperors" like Vespasian. What is clear from his works is that Tacitus longed for the stability and peace of the good old days of the Republic that prevailed prior to Caesar's overthrow of the Senate in 49 B.C. Interestingly, he uses the same basic language of familiar clichés and stereotypes as Caesar in describing the barbarian tribes of Germany to make his preferences for the virtues and glories of Republican Rome felt.

Well educated in rhetoric and law by the famous rhetorician Quintilian, Tacitus describes the Germans as fierce but noble warriors whose hard way of life could teach his fellow Romans a thing or two about virtue. As depicted by Tacitus, the Germans are a hodge-podge collection of primitive stereotypes and rude behaviors. They place little value on gold, reject the luxuries of civilized life, and know nothing of the security of private property. They are prone to drunkenness and blood feuds, dress like bums, and govern themselves according to primitive laws and exotic customs. As for their attitudes toward farming, they are, as Tacitus concedes, your basic barbarian, war-loving savages: "A German is not so easily prevailed upon to plough the land and wait patiently for harvest as to challenge a foe and earn wounds for his reward. He thinks it tame and spiritless to accumulate slowly by the sweat of his brow what can be got quickly by the loss of a little blood."[9]

But, according to Tacitus, the Germans do have their good points. Like Caesar and other Roman writers who attempt realistic accounts of the barbarian tribes of Europe, Tacitus calls on the familiar themes of ennobled savagery associated with the Legend of the Golden Age in favorably remarking on the righteousness of the remote Chauci tribe:

> They are the noblest people of Germany, and one that prefers to maintain its greatness by righteous dealing. Untouched by greed or lawless ambition, they dwell in quiet seclusion, never provoking a war, never robbing or plundering their neighbours. It is conspicuous proof of their valour and strength that their superiority does not rest on aggression. Yet every man of them has arms ready to his hand, and if occasion demands

it they have vast reserves of men and horses. So their reputation stands as high in peace as in war.

Tacitus also follows Caesar in adopting the Greeks' organizing principle of the barbarian savage's distance from Rome as determining the degree of cultural divergence from civilized norms and values. The most distant tribes, he writes, live on the shores or in the vicinity of the Suebian Sea (Baltic Sea). This body of water, he tells us, is "believed to be the boundary that girdles the earth." The tribes of this distant and remote region are among the most savage encountered anywhere in the world, according to Tacitus.

In the *Germania,* Tacitus describes the Fenni, for example, as being among the northernmost tribes of this region. Scholars surmise that he may have been writing about the ancient ancestors of the Sami or proto-Finns, or perhaps a group of indigenous Scandinavians.[10] According to Tacitus, the Fenni live a very "hard" life, perhaps the hardest of all the barbarian tribes of Europe, since they are at the ends of the earth. They are "astonishingly savage and disgustingly poor," with no horses or household goods. They lack iron and therefore sophisticated armaments. Their arrows are made out of bone. "They eat wild herbs, dress in skins, and sleep on the ground," surviving by the hunt. These miserable savages take refuge "from wild beasts or bad weather" by hiding "under a makeshift covering of interlaced branches."

Yet the Fenni too, as savage as they are, can teach the Romans something about what it means to be truly happy and virtuous. They refuse "to groan over field labour, sweat over house-building or hazard their own and other men's fortunes in the hope of profit and the fear of loss." They have no gods or religion, but that is fine as far as Tacitus is concerned; the Fenni "have reached a state that few human beings can attain: for these men are so well content that they do not even need to pray for anything."

Tacitus concedes that he had little knowledge, direct or indirect, of the tribes beyond the Fenni. Referring to the ancient legends and myths, he writes: "What comes after them is the stuff of fables," animals with the "faces and features of men, the bodies and limbs of animals. On such unverifiable stories I shall express no opinion." He really does not have to; he has written down everything he thinks the Romans need to know about the Germans. As defined by the familiar stereotypes and cultural markers appropriated from the Greeks' language of savagery, they are fierce but noble barbarian warriors irreconcilably opposed to the imperial civilization of Rome.

## THE IDEA OF THE SAVAGE IN
## STRABO AND PLINY THE ELDER

Tacitus's last sentence in the *Germania* about his complete lack of knowledge of what lies beyond the "boundary that girds the earth" underscores an important point about the Romans' geographical understanding of the world. Beyond the barbarian tribes of Europe and the great trading civilizations of Asia and Africa brought into Rome's imperial orbit, Roman knowledge of the outer world was heavily dependent on Greek sources.

The two most influential geographers of the Roman imperial era, Strabo (64–63 B.C.–ca. A.D. 24) and Pliny the Elder (A.D. 23–79), maintained complete fidelity to their Greek sources and legends, placing the location of the Fortunate and Blessed Islands, for example, to the far west and associating these distant lands with the Homeric myth of Elysium. Their works tend simply to repeat the familiar stereotypes and fanciful accounts of distant tribal peoples encountered throughout the ancient Greek myths, legends, and travelers' tales. In reading their Greek-inspired geographical works, we are still on the lookout for noble Ethiopians, milk-drinking Scythians, and just Hyperboreans.

Strabo himself was Greek, from a prominent family in Amaseia in Asia Minor, which had been incorporated into the Roman Empire. He traveled around the Mediterranean world, seeing Egypt and Kush, coastal Tuscany, and good parts of Asia Minor. This type of scholarly travel was popular during the era of relative peace that characterized the reign of the emperor Augustus (27 B.C.–A.D. 14), Caesar's great-nephew and heir who succeeded him after his assassination. Strabo settled in Rome in 44 B.C. to study and write, finishing his most famous surviving work, the *Geography*, before he died.

Strabo's influential treatise on world geography, dutifully cited and faithfully relied on down through the European Renaissance era, sometimes just repeats or embellishes on Homer's well-worn accounts and clichéd stereotypes of distant tribal peoples, strange lands, and exotic customs. Strabo, in fact, regards Homer as the founder of geography. He habitually draws on the Greeks' language of savagery to theorize about the differences in the modes of subsistence displayed by different barbarian tribes in comparison to the Greeks and Romans. The Albanians, a Scythian tribe, "are more pastoral and more like the nomadic tribes except that they are not savage. And therefore they are only moderately warlike."[11] Fusing the literary traditions of the Hesiodic Legend of the Golden Age with Homer's famous description of the land of Cyclopes in the *Odyssey*, Strabo explains why "a people of this kind has no need of the sea. Nor do they use the land to the full extent of its value, the land which bears every kind of fruit, even the cultivated, and every kind of plant. For it bears ever-blooming plants. Nor does it require the slightest attention, 'but all things grow there untilled and unsoiled,' as the soldiers say, living a Cyclopean life."[12]

Pliny the Elder is another influential geographical writer who freely and copiously relied on Greek sources to describe things he knew absolutely nothing about, such as the far edges of the world. In his well-regarded encyclopedic text, *Natural History* (which served as the model for all similar works in the West), he cites a long list of Greek authorities that includes Herodotus, Aristotle, Ctesias, Eudoxus, Artemidorus, Hippocrates, Asclepius, Hesiod, Ephorus, Xenophon, Democritus, and Thucydides, along with Strabo. His account of the most distant parts of India is a typical example of his thorough grounding in the Greeks' language of savagery and total lack of incredulity about anything his Greek sources might say to him:

> There are satyrs in the easternmost mountains of India (in the region said to belong to the Catarcludi); this is a very fast-moving creature, going at times on all fours and at other times upright, in human fashion; because of their speed only the older and sick members of the tribe can be caught. Tauron says that the Choromandi tribe are forest-dwellers, have no power of speech yet shriek horribly, have shaggy bodies, grey eyes, and dog-like teeth. Eudoxus says that in southern India there are men with feet as long as a cubit, and women with feet so small that they are called Sparrowfeet. Megasthenes says that among the Nomad Indians is a tribe called the Sciritae, who have only holes instead of nostrils, like snakes; they are also club-footed.[13]

Like the great monuments and works of art that celebrated the triumphs of Rome's Empire over the barbarian tribes of Europe, the works by this small sample of Roman writers—Caesar, Tacitus, Strabo, and Pliny—can only begin to suggest the broad, pervasive influence of the Greeks and their idea of the savage on Roman imperial civilization. The language of savagery that the Romans inherited from the Greeks provided form, content, meaning, and coherence to the way distant tribal peoples were described and perceived as barbarian enemies to a higher form of civilization. In their acts of cultural appropriation, the Romans perpetuated a vital, civilization-defining legacy for the West: a language of anciently derived stereotypes, categories, and cultural markers that identified those barbarian peoples whose way of life was regarded as irreconcilably opposed to an expansion-minded form of civilization and its fated rise to empire.

# SIX

# PARALLEL LIVES

## The Idea of the Savage and the Decline of the Roman Empire

Julius Caesar himself had proclaimed that the borrowings from foreign peoples that characterized the culture of the expanding Roman Empire was a source of strength, not weakness. "Our ancestors," he once remarked, "were never deficient in conduct or courage; nor did pride prevent them from imitating the customs of other nations, if they appeared deserving of regard."[1] As Professor Charles Norris Cochrane writes, "The record of the city was, indeed, one of persistent borrowings, the tradition of which goes back to her earliest contacts with her neighbors in prehistoric Italy."[2]

The genius of the Romans in appropriating Greek ideas for their own uses is particularly evident in the way Roman writers sought to understand their own historical development from a tiny agrarian republic to a great imperial civilization. The Greeks themselves confirmed what seemed an inevitable historical pattern of decline for all imperial civilizations. In their efforts to understand that pattern, the Romans turned to the Greeks' idea of the savage for guidance and insight.

The Roman view of history in general was heavily indebted to the Greeks. Even Rome's foundation story, as told in the *Aeneid* by Virgil, borrowed from Greek storytelling traditions. The Greeks and their language of savagery provided an agreed-on starting point for Roman philosophers, poets, and even comic entertainers who sought to understand and illuminate the causes of decline that seemed to plague all great empires.

## THE IDEA OF THE SAVAGE AS THE STARTING POINT OF HUMAN HISTORY IN LUCRETIUS AND CICERO

Greek philosophy and ethics exercised a particularly profound influence on the way the Romans approached a broad range of issues and concerns relevant to the problems of sustaining their empire. Amid the diversity of all these approaches, the Romans remained characteristically utilitarian, borrowing extensively from the Platonists of the Academy, the Epicureans, the Stoics, and teachings from other major Hellenistic schools of philosophy.

From Greek philosophy and ethics generally, the Romans absorbed a number of important, foundational principles and maxims about the nature of the human condition: There existed a fundamental, natural state of being for man; our unhappiness is caused by our inability to satisfy our desires for things that in reality are quite superfluous; and in the end, happiness can be obtained only by returning to those things that are essential and that make us truly ourselves.

Given their incorporation of these Greek-inspired elements, Roman philosophers tended to use the idea of the savage in much the same way as the Greeks did. It was a convenient starting point for trying to identify those things that were most essential to human beings' true natural selves. The Romans, though, in typical fashion, went one step further. They used the Greeks' stripped-down philosophical model to identify the things that were most essential to understanding not only themselves but also Rome's fortune (*fortuna*) and fate as an empire.

*De Rerum Natura* (On the Nature of Things or On the Nature of the Universe), by the Roman Epicurean poet, Lucretius (99 B.C.–ca. 56 B.C.), represents one of the most important works of philosophy in the history of Western civilization.[3] Lucretius also produced one of the West's most influential accounts of human history from the beginning of time by using the Greeks' language of savagery to begin his Epicurean-inspired account of the hard life of primitive humanity.

Lucretius was more of a protest poet, in the tradition of Hesiod, than a philosopher. But he was a true believer in the school of philosophy founded by Epicurus (341–270 B.c.) in Athens in 306 B.c. He lived during the tumultuous period of the late Republic and Rome's descent into civil wars and chaos leading up to Julius Caesar's overthrow of the Senate. A troubling and sometimes disturbing reflection on the nature of the universe, the human condition, and the cravings and desires for power that were tearing the Republic apart in his own time, *De Rerum Natura* was rediscovered during the late Renaissance after centuries of suppression by the Catholic Church (see chapter 9). The poem has been celebrated ever since as the most precise distillation of Epicurean philosophy handed down from the Classical era and one of Western civilization's greatest works of literature.

Epicurus, the Greek philosopher and founder of the school that Lucretius reverently follows in *De Rerum Natura*, was born on the island of Samos in Ionia. As a youth, Epicurus studied the philosophical works of Plato, Aristotle, and Democritus, and he went on to found his own school, the Garden, in 306 B.c. The school was notable, among other things, for its radical egalitarianism in accepting both women and slaves.

Epicurus's philosophy is sometimes misunderstood as being focused obsessively on pleasure, represented by the Epicureans' supposed motto that can be loosely translated as "Eat, drink and be merry, for tomorrow we may die." We have no evidence, however, that Epicurus himself ever advocated such a frivolous approach to life. He knew that, at times, happiness can only be gained through pain and suffering, and that sometimes, the unbridled pursuit of pleasure can lead to great suffering. Regardless, the ultimate happiness for Epicurus was in achieving *ataraxia,* the sense of peace and tranquility attained by profound contemplation on the art of making life happy. This can be done by following Epicurus's true motto, as reported by Plutarch: *"Lathe biosas"*—live unknown or unobtrusively (i.e., avoid fame and the hatred, envy, and contempt it brings).

Ataraxia, the pure state of intellectual pleasure or serenity sought by the true Epicurean, is the only good worthy of being sought after by humankind. Epicurus himself was largely indifferent toward religion. He was, however, greatly concerned that people abandon their superstitious fear of the gods. While conceding the gods existed, he described them as busy with their own affairs and not caring about humans. Epicurus stands as one of the great founding figures of the Humanist tradition in Classical Greek philosophy, advocating a wholly secular, demythologized approach to the solution of the intensely human problem of trying to make ourselves happy in the world.

Lucretius seeks to carry on that tradition of using philosophy to promote human flourishing and happiness in *De Rerum Natura*. His use of familiar Greek stereotypes and cultural markers of hard savagery to describe the human condition at the beginnings of time draws on a tradition that traces back through the works of Protagoras, Herodotus, and Aristotle and their influential accounts of humanity in a primeval state of wild and untamed nature.

In Book V of his poem, Lucretius describes "the childhood of the world" and humanity's inevitable decline over time. He begins his dystopian account of human history with the ancient Greek cosmographical myths of a great primordial chaos at the beginnings of time. Nature was in its period of greatest vigor and fecundity. All sorts of monsters were propagated. Some survived, and some did not.

From this undifferentiated, primordial chaos, the first human beings emerged. Invoking one of the Greeks' most favored categorical markers of human savagery, Lucretius describes these first humans as giants, "built on a framework of bigger and more solid bones, fastened through their flesh to stout sinews." Their indifference to heat and cold builds on the familiar Greek stereotype of the "hard" life of the savage in a primal, hostile state of nature. They preferred simple foods and were free from "bodily ailments in general." They may as well have been Germans.

These primitive giants do not bother much with agricultural pursuits. Why waste their strength "in guiding the curved plough," Lucretius writes, or pruning fruit trees and vines, when they can enjoy the simple fare of nature? "Their hearts were well content to accept as a free gift what the sun and showers had given and the earth had produced unsolicited." They ate acorns and berries to stave off hunger. The "lusty childhood of the earth," Lucretius writes, "yielded a great variety of tough foods, ample for afflicted mortals."

In typical Roman fashion, Lucretius borrows widely from a diverse catalog of Greek-inspired clichés and images in constructing his account of primitive humanity's way of life. He is careful to note that this early time for humanity on earth was no Hesiodic Golden Age. The first humans lived like "wild beasts roaming at large," not knowing "how to enlist the aid of fire, or to make use of skins, or to clothe their bodies with trophies of the chase." Their homes were the forests, caves, and mountains. They sought shelter for "their rugged limbs among bushes when driven to seek shelter from the lash of wind and rain." They lacked sophisticated laws or effective institutions of self-government. They were ignorant of marital vows: "Venus coupled the bodies of lovers in the greenwood. Mutual desire brought them together, or the male's mastering might and overriding lust, or a payment of acorns or arbutus berries or choice pears."

Like Caesar and Tacitus, Lucretius focuses his reader's attention on the simpler virtues associated with living this type of hard and "rugged" way of life. In fact, he tells us that this mode of existence was far superior to what followed as human history progressed, or actually regressed, through time. In Lucretius's highly pessimistic adaptation of the Hesiodic time frame, humanity regressed from a state of relative misery to more misery.

He notes, for example, that mortality among primitive humans "was not appreciably higher then than now." In those early times, it was true that "it more often happened that an individual victim would furnish living food for a beast of prey." But, as Lucretius explains, there were no wars either, so "it never happened then that many thousands of men following the standards were led to death on a single day." There were no ships to carry the huge armies that invaded other peoples' lands, as "the mariner's presumptuous art lay still unguessed."

What seems like progress over time for humanity, the poet explains, is really a step in the wrong direction toward a steep and steady decline in our fortunes. The Roman Republican ideal, as Cato had lectured his fellow citizens, was to live the noble life of the simple yeoman farmer on the land. Lucretius argued that humanity was better off before farming was even invented; lack of food may have been a prime cause of mortality in primitive times, he tells us, but now "it is superfluity that proves too much for them. The men of old, in their ignorance, often served poison to themselves. Now, with greater skill, they administer it to others."

This quintessentially Greek philosophic theme, distilled through the teachings of Epicurus, of living the simple life as the best course for securing

our happiness is reiterated throughout the book-length poem. Lucretius repeats the theme at several points. He wants to make sure his fellow Romans
understand that their desire for fame and power, "so that their fortune might
rest on a firm foundation and they might live out a peaceful life in the enjoyment of plenty," is an "idle dream." Such a desire, he says, can lead only
to decline and ruination. "In struggling to gain the pinnacle of power, they
beset their own road with perils. And then from the very peak, as though
by a thunderbolt, they are cast down by envy into a foul abyss of ignominy."

Relentlessly advancing his depressing theme of human regress through
the ages, Lucretius moves forward in time, depicting the inevitability of decline as a fundamental law of human history on earth. Civilization's most revered institutions are actually a curse on humanity. Even though "some men
showed how to form a constitution, based on fixed rights and recognized
laws," Lucretius says, this form of progress was purchased at a price. For now
man submitted his "own free will to the bondage of laws and institutions."
According to Lucretius, "[e]ver since then, the enjoyment of life's prizes has
been tempered by the fear of punishment."

Ultimately, for Lucretius, human progress always contained the inevitable seeds of human decline and misery: "The discovery of something new
and better blunts and vitiates our enjoyment of the old." His point is that
an imperially minded, consumption-oriented civilization like that desired
by his fellow Romans will never be able to make a person truly happy, and,
of course, he uses acorns to make the point: "So it is that we have lost our
taste for acorns. So we have abandoned those couches littered with herbage
and heaped with leaves. So the wearing of wild beasts' skins has gone out of
fashion." "Skins yesterday," sighs Lucretius, "purple and gold today—such
are the baubles that embitter human life with resentment and waste it with
war." Such plaintive pleas for simplicity, a staple of Epicurean philosophy,
appear throughout the poem. Lucretius makes those pleas by inventing his
own uniquely inflected, Epicurean-inspired language of savagery, adapting
the Greeks' convention that human desires for material goods and luxuries
are the root cause of all human misery. He deploys this language to reveal
the doomed fate of Rome's imperially minded civilization. For Lucretius,
virtually every story of human progress is really a story of human decline,
caused by our insatiable desires for worldly wealth and power. As we move

away from the conditions of savagery in the state of nature, toward the refinements and luxuries so desired by civilized Romans in their pursuit of creating the world's greatest empire, we create the seeds of our own destruction. "So mankind is perpetually the victim of a pointless and futile martyrdom, fretting life away in fruitless worries through failure to realize what limit is set to acquisition and to the growth of genuine pleasure. It is this discontent that has driven life steadily onward, out to the high seas, and has stirred up from the depths the surging tumultuous tides of war."

This theme of humanity's inevitable decline, of course, was the essential lesson that had been taught by the Hesiodic Legend of the Golden Age. Lucretius absorbs most of that lesson into his poem, while rendering one of Western civilization's most profoundly depressing meditations on the fate of all empires. According to Lucretius, the citizens of an empire never really enjoy a Golden Age period of virtue and happiness. All empires inevitably go into an irreversible cycle of decline and then fall. Ultimately, he tells us, "everything is gradually decaying and nearing its end, worn out by old age."

Writing against the backdrop of the Romans' intense fears and anxieties in a time of fierce and bloody civil war, recriminations, and chaos, Lucretius seeks to show his contemporaries that things will only get worse for humanity, so perhaps they should enjoy life while they can. This bit of Epicurean advice characteristically reflects the genius of the Romans in appropriating Greek ideas in contemplating the fate of their own empire. In Lucretius's case, he thought about that fate by using the Greeks' idea of the savage, filtered through the philosophy of Epicurus. By such acts of cultural appropriation, Lucretius came to understand that the good times for Republican Rome were about to come to an end.

It is interesting to compare Lucretius's use of the stereotypes and identifying markers of savagery in *De Rerum Natura* with the use of that same basic vocabulary and set of themes by the Roman orator and political philosopher Cicero (106–43 B.C.) in several of his major philosophical works. Cicero helped to invent one of Western philosophy's most influential accounts of human history and the development of the rule of law. A towering intellectual and political figure in the chaotic period that witnessed Julius Caesar's overthrow of the power of the Republican Senate (50–48 B.C.) and Caesar's assassination (Ides of March, 44 B.C.), Cicero used the idea of the savage to show his contemporaries that without the rule of law, Rome would descend into the disorder and chaos of the rule of the stronger.

Famous throughout the history of Western civilization as a statesman and an unparalleled orator, Cicero was also a primary interpreter of a considerable part of Greek philosophy to his Roman countrymen, particularly the Greeks' teachings on natural law. Roman contemporaries immediately recognized the significance of his ideas. Seneca thought it superfluous to "enlarge upon his accomplishments."[4] Plutarch tells us that Emperor Augustus Caesar (r. 27 B.C.–A.D. 14) himself praised Cicero as a great scholar and patriot, and Quintilian, the great polymath of Latin antiquity, "equates his name with eloquence itself" and considers him the rival of Plato in philosophy.[5]

Cicero had been instructed in rhetoric by Apollonius, the same Greek tutor Caesar had sought out as a young Roman with political ambitions. Cicero also had studied in schools that claimed descent from Plato's Academy. What Cicero took away from his Greek-inspired education was a basic commitment to skepticism, rationalism, a life of virtue, the rule of law, and the broad scheme of Classical Humanist values that the Greeks had taught him were vital to the restoration of the Republic and its virtue. The corrupt and venal politicians of his time, he believed, suffered from a loss of virtue that had characterized the great leaders of Republican Rome. The rule of law had given place to the rule of the stronger and the worldly desire for fame, fortune, and power.

The concept of the "rule of law" is central to Cicero's understanding of the differences between a savage state of nature, where brute force reigned, and civilization, where men lived "naturally" in a free community as social beings. Following Plato and Aristotle, Cicero believed that civilized society was man's most "natural" state. The way of life of the savage represented the very opposite of this perfected form of human existence, and civilization's job was to triumph over it. Cicero explained the reason for Rome's picking fights with far-off barbarian tribes: They were men known to the Romans as "wild, savage and warlike, tribes which *no one who has ever lived* would not wish to see crushed and subdued."[6]

In one of his most famous speeches, *Pro Sestio* (56 B.C.), Cicero explains the desperate state of primitive humanity, without the benefits of the rule of law, in terms drawn directly from Plato and Aristotle: "For who does not know the condition of nature to have been once such that men, in the days before either natural or civil law had been drawn up, wandered dispersed and scattered about the fields, and that each possessed no more than he could seize or keep by his own strength, through killing or wounding others?"[7]

Cicero goes on to narrate his own interpretation of human history as a cycle of the ages. His elaboration of human progress over time clearly contradicts Lucretius, instead echoing Plato's *Protagoras* in identifying the improvements in the human condition achieved through the great lawgivers of antiquity: "But those who first arose endowed with superior virtue and prudence, having recognized a kind of intelligence and teachableness in man, gathered these scattered individuals together in one place and converted them from wildness to justice and gentleness."[8] Cities were built, says Cicero, "and they fortified all these with law, human and divine, as with walls."[9]

Cicero's vision of human happiness was strongly biased toward a highly urbanized way of life, governed by the rule of law, which he equated with natural reason. Cities formed because of the natural sociability of men. He writes in *De Officis* (On Duties), completed in the last year of his life in 44 B.C., that because of cities, "laws and customs were established, and then the equitable determination of rights, and a settled discipline of life." These were the natural conditions in which "a more humane spirit" and greater developed sense of morality emerged among men, "so that life was more secure, and that, by giving and receiving, by mutual exchange of goods and services, we were able to satisfy all our needs."[10]

According to Cicero's view of history, humans of the present day enjoyed a much better quality of life due to the civilizing influence of the city and its rule of law, which was the refined expression of the natural law bonds of our shared humanity. Without the association of men, he writes in *De Officis,* there would be no cities, and therefore no laws would exist to make life secure. Only the city could sustain the conditions in which a more humane spirit and greater developed sense of morality emerged among men.

Unfortunately for Cicero, he himself would come to feel that wretched difference between the rule of law and the rule of the stronger that prevailed in a savage, uncivilized state of nature. He ended up opposing Caesar's close ally, cousin, and co-consul, Mark Antony (83–30 B.C.), in the chaos following Caesar's assassination. His angry tirades against Antony in the Senate are preserved in his *Philippics*. They are modeled on the speeches of Greek orator Demosthenes against Philip II of Macedon. Cicero's preference for this particular form of Greek oratory, however, put him on the wrong side of Roman history and Anthony's brief reign of shared power in Rome following Caesar's death. According to Plutarch's *Lives*, the great Roman statesman's head was cut off on Antony's orders as an enemy of the state. It was then put on display in the Forum of Rome, along with his severed hands, a punishment thought appropriate for his writings against Antony. Much later, Cassius Dio (ca. A.D. 150–235), the Roman consul and historian who wrote an eighty-volume history of Rome in Greek, reported that Antony's wife, Fulvia (83–40 B.C.), got into the act as well. She reportedly grabbed Cicero's severed head, pulled out his tongue, and jabbed it repeatedly with her hairpin, exercising her spousal privileges of revenge under the rule of the stronger that prevailed in Rome at the final fall of the Republic. Such acts of political savagery, however, could not silence Cicero's unparalleled legacy for Western civilization and its political and philosophical traditions. The genius of his words and speeches, left for posterity in his writings, many of which are still studied and cited throughout the West today, had already secured his fame. Whenever the idea of the savage is used to show the irreconcilable differences between the rule of law and the rule of the stronger in the invention of Western civilization, Cicero's influence is felt.

Like Lucretius, for Cicero, the idea of the savage was the perfect vehicle for expressing his own anxieties about the fate of Rome's empire. Both of these influential Romans helped perpetuate in their own profound, enduring, and quite different ways the Western world's use of a language of savagery handed down from the ancient Greeks to understand the vices and virtues of their own contemporary form of imperial civilization.

## VIRGIL AND OVID AND THE LEGEND OF THE GOLDEN AGE IN IMPERIAL ROME

Virgil and Ovid, the two greatest Roman poets of the reign of the emperor Augustus Caesar (r. 27 B.C.–A.D. 14), both used the idea of the savage associated with the Hesiodic Legend of the Golden Age to develop two very different views on the history and fate of Rome's empire. The legend in fact becomes a dominant motif of the Augustan Age. Following the civil wars and social chaos after the assassination of Julius Caesar in 44 B.C., Rome completed its transformation into an empire during the reign of Augustus, Caesar's great-nephew and heir. Seizing power in 27 B.C., Augustus ruled as emperor until his death in A.D. 14. His reign inaugurated an era of relative calm and consolidation of Rome's imperial borders known as the *Pax Romana,* the Roman peace. The peace was emblematic of the Augustan pledge to restore the republic to its former grandeur and place it on a secure foundation. Augustus's grand vision was to make real the Eternity of Rome (*Aeternitas Populi Romani*) in the form of an eternal empire: "May I be privileged to build firm and lasting foundations for the Government of the State. May I also achieve the reward to which I aspire: that of being known as the author of the best possible Constitution, and of carrying with me, when I die, the hope that these foundations which I have established for the State will abide secure."[11]

We have seen how even prior to Augustus, Roman writers such as Lucretius had adopted the Greeks' historiographical idea that there was a generalizable declining "pattern of empire" whereby "nations succes-sively achieved dominion only to have the scepter turn from their grasp."[12] Industry gave way to laziness; moderation and justice lost out to greed, avarice, and desire.

Livy (59 B.C.–A.D. 17), who lived through the tumultuous period of the civil wars, viewed Rome's transition from a republic into an empire as result-ing in what seemed an inevitable decline in moral standards. In his monu-mental *History of Rome,* Livy appealed for a return to a Golden Age when humanity lived a much simpler and more virtuous way of life as the prescrip-tion for a restoration to Rome's former Republican virtues. Prior to empire, Livy writes, Rome was a community in which poverty and thrift were held in "high esteem." "The fewer our resources, the less there was of cupidity. It is but recently that an accumulation of wealth has stimulated avarice; the superabundance of material goods an itch on the part of men to indulge a passion which is ruinous to everything including themselves."[13]

The Romans sought to develop an antidote to this disease, which they believed corrupted all empires, by striving to create an imperial order unique in its ideals, existing for purposes beyond mere acquisition of wealth and power. Augustus's vision of Rome's empire sought to create an eternal order, "in sharp contrast to the ephemeral character of other systems."[14]

Given the Augustan pledge to restore the Republic and place it on a secure temporal foundation, the myth of a Golden Age and the cyclic theory of history attached to it proved to be an irresistible combination for poets, playwrights, satirists, and dystopian critics of Roman imperial civilization. The Greeks' language of ennobled savagery was the perfect vehicle for assessing the job the Romans were doing in living up to Augustus's exalted vision of Rome as an eternal empire.

The use of the legend by the two greatest Roman poets of the Augustan age, Virgil (70–19 B.C.) and Ovid (43 B.C.–A.D. 18), once again reveals the Roman genius for cultural appropriation. Augustus had been a patron of both poets, and his support of their art was part of his grand imperial vision to make real the Eternity of Rome.

Both Virgil and Ovid freely appropriated Hesiod's notion of the Golden Age into their poetry in ways that are at times complementary but at other times diametrically opposed. Virgil's *Aeneid*, his epic poem influenced by Homer's *Odyssey*, imagines the potentiality of a renewed Golden Age during the reign of Augustus Caesar: "son of a god, whom shall again set up the Golden Age in Latium amid the fields where Saturn once reigned, and shall spread his empire past Garamant and Indian."[15]

Virgil's alignment of the Golden Age concept with Augustus's reign reflects the optimism engendered by the emperor's pledge to restore the Republic and the Roman people to their state of former virtue. That is why, for Virgil, the first Golden Age was not at the beginning of time. That came later. Following Cicero and Lucretius, Virgil says the first age of humans on earth was characterized by "a race of men born of tree trunks and hard oak, who had neither a rule of life nor civilization, nor did they know how to yoke bulls or store up their wealth or husband their gains, but fed themselves from trees and the rough fare of the huntsman."[16]

To Virgil, the elements of the Roman spirit that were essential to its greatness and virtue were to be found in the simple, virtuous life lived by human beings following this first "hard" age. This was when the mythic figure of ancient Roman mythology, the hero-redeemer Saturn (the Greeks'

Cronus), brought together "that ignorant race scattered on the mountain-tops and gave them laws." These are the ancient ancestors of the Latins, the people who came to occupy the place called Latium by Saturn. "Golden is called the age," Virgil tells us, in which Saturn reigned as king.[17]

In Virgil's reinvention of the Greeks' Legend of the Golden Age for the purposes of telling the Romans' foundation story, the divine introduction of more civilized modes of life, particularly by the enactment of a code of laws, is what differentiates civilization from savagery. Saturn "ruled the people in calm peace." But "little by little the age grew worse, its brilliance dimmed, and the madness of war and love of possession took its place."[18]

What happened to bring this age down was the institution of private property. Without privatized property, humans have no need of sophisticated laws. All that was required to sustain a life of peaceful simplicity in the Golden Age were the simple rules of just conduct given to humanity by Saturn, the lawgiver. But the "love of possession," writes Virgil, gave birth to the institution of private property. And private property gave birth to war, for war is waged among humans in order to seize the goods of other peoples in distant lands.

Virgil's adaptation of the ancient Greeks' legend enables him to critique the moral flaws of his fellow Romans in failing to live up to the Augustan vision of their Eternal Empire while also promoting a more primitive scheme of values. The revival of Roman virtue promised by the Augustan settlement can occur, Virgil tells his fellow Romans, only with a rejection of the vices of empire. If the Romans are going to reinvent themselves according to Augustus's exalted vision, they need to embrace the more primitive virtues of the Golden Age and give up their "love of possession."

That type of patriotic appeal was one way poets on the emperor's dole used the idea of the savage to curry favor in Augustan Rome. Telling Romans to refrain from asking what their empire can do for them in terms of satisfying their desire for more possessions likely pleased the emperor's ear. Virgil's slightly older contemporary Ovid took a much different approach. He used a Greek-inspired language of savagery to tell his fellow Roman citizens that their empire was doomed from the start and that there was nothing the emperor could do about it, given human nature. The emperor was not pleased with Ovid.

Ovid's great poetic masterpiece, the *Metamorphoses,* paints a lively and raucous hexameter-verse picture of a utopian Golden Age populated by primitive human beings living a life of ease amid the abundance of wild nature. In this long-ago lost era, "[e]arth herself, unburdened and untouched by the hoe and unwounded by the ploughshare, gave all things freely." Humans were content with simple foods produced "without constraint," gathering fruits of the tree, berries, and acorns (there's those acorns again), fallen to the ground. Untilled, "the earth bore its fruits and the unploughed field grew hoary with heavy ears of wheat." It was literally a time of milk and honey: "Rivers of milk and rivers of nectar flowed, and yellow honey dripped from the green oaks."[19]

Ovid draws on a favorite theme of the Greeks in pronouncing at length on the advantages of this life lived free of the rules and laws of civilized society. Expanding significantly on this Hesiodic theme, he writes that in the first age, all human beings were virtuous by nature and had no need of lawyers, judges, or courts. "The first age was golden. In it faith and righteousness were cherished by men of their own free will without judges or laws. Penalties and fears there were none, nor were threatening words inscribed on unchanging bronze; nor did the suppliant crowd fear the words of its judge, but they were safe without protectors."[20]

Ovid's idealized rendering of the Golden Age sets up his searing indictment of the vices of contemporary Roman civilization. His poem seeks to show that human beings actually become more "savage" as they progress from their primitive, simple way of life to life in modern-day Rome. Human decline, he shows, is brought about by what conventionally would be thought of as the technological advances of modern civilization.

Borrowing Hesiod's basic time frame, the third race of human beings, Ovid says, lived in an age of bronze, "more savage than its predecessors." This was because humans were "prompter to [take up] bristling arms." This age was superseded by an even worse age of "hard iron," a time when "[s]ails were spread to the winds." Trees, which in prior ages "grew up ignorant of the waves," were now cut down to make sailing ships. These advances in technology made it possible to reach distant lands. The earth, "hitherto a common possession like the light of the sun and the breezes, the careful surveyor now marked out with long-drawn boundary line." And all of these advances led to increased population on the land. Corn and other foods had to be planted in the richest soil. Competition for land led to a recognition of legally defined property rights. And so humans even began to bore "into the bowels of the earth, and the wealth she had hidden and covered with Stygian darkness was dug up, an incentive to evil." In this "age of baser metal" (his own era), writes Ovid, "all manner of evil, and shame fled, and truth and faith. In place of these came deceits and trickery and treachery and force and the accursed love of possession."[21]

The troubling question raised by Ovid's retelling of the Legend of the Golden Age is of course the same basic query posed by Virgil: Do humans truly benefit from living in an expansion-minded, imperial form of civilization, consumed by the "love of possession"? Ovid's poem provides a somewhat depressing answer to that question, much in the vein of Lucretius: The transformative, technological achievements of civilization are really evidence of humanity's inexorable decline from prior ages. Our life was happiest when we lived according to nature, removed from the economic, technological, and institutional dislocations of an imperial civilization. Better to live like the noble savages of the Golden Age.

Ironically, Ovid got his wish, sort of. Having given offense to Augustus for what he called in his *Tristia* (Sorrows) *carmen et error,* "a poem and a blunder,"[22] Ovid was banished to live and die in exile among the legendary noble savages of the Black Sea region, the barbarian Scythian tribes. The parallel lives of Virgil and Ovid suggest the virtues and vices of their different poetic strategies in using the Greeks' language of ennobled savagery to critique the possession-minded form of civilization that had developed during Rome's transition from a tiny agrarian republic to the Western world's most celebrated empire.

## JUVENAL AND LUCIAN AND THE SATIRICAL SAVAGE IN THE POST-AUGUSTAN AGE

As the works of Virgil and Ovid suggest, Roman writers reveled in the use of the Legend of the Golden Age to warn their contemporaries to change their ways or suffer the inevitable consequences of imperial decline. The great satirists of Rome's post-Augustan imperial era were particularly attuned to the irony and comedic potential of the Golden Age legend in making the point that Romans had failed miserably in achieving Augustus's grand vision. Their response to what they caricatured as a hopelessly irredeemable age of corruption and degeneracy, marked by insane emperors and widespread decadence, took full advantage of the comedic potential of the idea of the savage as handed down from the Greeks.

Two of the greatest satirical poets of post-Augustan Rome, Juvenal (c. A.D. 55–127) and Lucian (c. A.D. 125–180), drew on the legend to depict a simpler and more natural mode of life without the luxuries of contemporary civilization that no Roman in his right mind would find at all appealing. Their depictions of human existence in the "natural state" of noble savagery turn the mirror on contemporary society. The legend proves the perfect launching point for their biting satire and often hilarious insights into Roman civilization's complete depravity and decline.

Juvenal, the great satirical poet of the first century A.D., alluded to the legend and its familiar stereotypes and iconic images to construct one of his most scathing attacks on contemporary Roman society, contained in his famous *Thirteenth Satire*.[23] The poet viciously caricatures a detestable age of luxury and vice as "worse than that of iron, for whose crimes no name has been found." Chastising a "childish old man" as being out of touch with the times, his poem asks: "Do you not know how your simplicity moves the crowd to laughter?" The "aborigines" once lived by this rule of the simple life. But men no longer bother to follow this rule, says Juvenal. "Dishonesty was a thing for wonder" in those long-ago times. Back then, "it was deemed a great crime and punishable by death for a youth not to rise before an old man and for a boy not to do likewise before a person with a beard, although he might have at home more fruits and greater heaps of"—you guessed it—"acorns."[24]

Juvenal's broadly drawn satire is pointed directly at the luxuries and excesses of his contemporary Roman society, where material possessions are the debased measure of all values. His Greek-inspired language of savagery constructs an image of primitive humans living virtuously and happily in as stark and unattractive terms as possible. In his *Sixth Satire*, for example, he writes that only "an icy cavern provided a man's little home." His "mountain wife" was "often more savage than her acorn-belching mate." Juvenal is clear, however, in drawing out the moral of his tale: These acorn-eating primitives are as "savage," as wild and uncivilized as human beings can be, yet they are morally superior to the civilized Romans of his own debased age. Back then, "no one feared the theft of his cabbages and apples, and men lived in an open garden." But subsequent ages, writes Juvenal, have produced every crime known to man.[25]

Juvenal's clever deployment of the familiar stereotypes associated with the idea of the savage functioned as a highly destabilizing satirical device for biting social commentary and devastating critique. His skilled comic re-telling of the Legend of the Golden Age reveals an emptiness at the heart of modernity that is likely irremediable. Like all great satire, his use of the legend is meant to show us that, in the end, the joke is on us if we think we can be anything other than what nature made us.

An even more biting, cynical, and ultimately disquieting use of the legend and its ironically intended themes of ennobled savagery can be found in the *Saturnian Letters* of the Greek verse writer Lucian. Composed in the second century A.D., Lucian's famous satire deployed the legend to condemn the excesses of a ruling class of Roman elites wallowing in a decaying imperial culture's exorbitant luxury and decadence, oblivious to the misery of the masses. In Lucian's satire, the joke is not on all of us, just the poor saps at the bottom of the social ladder.

Invoking the memorable Ovidian image, Lucian writes of the "old days" spoken of by poets, when Cronus was still king and earth brought forth her goods for men, "unsown and unplowed; there were meals more than sufficient made ready for each man; rivers ran wine and milk and honey." He then launches his attack on the festering class divisions in Rome: "Most important of all, they say that the men of that time themselves were of gold, and poverty never approached them. But we would hardly seem to be of lead, but rather of something cheaper than this. Most of us earn our food by toil, live in poverty, want and helplessness, with cries of 'Ah me!' 'Whence comes this?' and 'Oh that such a fate should be!'—such is the lot of us poor men."[26]

Our suffering would be less, remarks Lucian, were it not for the wealthy enjoying such a happy lot in life, with their "stores of gold and silver" and "wardrobes, slaves and carriages and houses and fields." Though they own such abundance, "they share none of it with us, but deem the many unworthy of even a glance."[27]

Lucian uses the Legend of the Golden Age to condemn his contemporaries for their vices and decadence. But he also recognizes that the life of the noble savage without laws, private property, and other confining social institutions was a dream and fantasy; it never existed, and it would never return even if it had. Rome's corrupt rulers and elites were acting according to human nature in pursuing their "love of possession" and doing all they could to keep those below them on the social ladder permanently down at the bottom rungs.

In his satirical poem *True History,* Lucian gives us a wildly humorous first-person account of a band of vagabond adventurers who land on the Island of the Blest, with its city of gold surrounded by an emerald wall. The inhabitants of this enchanted island have no bodies "but are intangible and incorporeal, and they exhibit form and idea alone, and though bodiless yet they stand and move and think and give voice, and their naked souls seem to walk about wearing the likeness of a body." Nor do the inhabitants grow old; they remain at the age at which they came to the island. The island itself knows "but one season of the year."[28] "For it is always spring there. And one wind blows among them, Zephyr. The country abounds in every flower and in every cultivated shade tree. And the vines bear twelve times a year, and each month they gather in the fruit."[29]

Lucian uses a Greek-inspired language of savagery to tell his fellow Romans that the Golden Age was a dream impossible of existence. Wake up to the reality of a Rome that had been corrupted to its core by the love of possession. Juvenal used that same basic language of familiar stereotypes and cultural markers to tell his contemporaries that even if the Golden Age did exist at one time, Romans would never be able to re-create it, having acquired an insatiable desire for material wealth. The genius of both Lucian and Juvenal was to combine their satirical insights with the Greeks' idea of the savage to show their fellow Romans that the joke ultimately is on them; they had invented a form of civilization that they could never hope to escape, even if they wanted to.

# SEVEN

# THE MEDIEVAL CHRISTIAN CHURCH'S WAR ON THE CLASSICAL IDEA OF THE SAVAGE

The idea of the savage as a civilization-defining force in the history of the West experienced a dramatic transformation as a result of the fall of the Western Roman Empire in A.D. 476. The rise of the Christian Church in Europe during the Middle Ages (fifth through fifteenth centuries) was accompanied by an all-out assault on Greek and Roman forms of pagan religion and knowledge. The Church's close supervision and control of the literature of pagan antiquity cleared the ground for a radical reformulation of the Classical idea of the savage. Church dogmatists and theologians ignored, allegorized, and suppressed any pagan notions that challenged Christian teachings. Those elements disfavored by the Church simply disappeared from medieval Christian literature. What survived was twisted and subverted to complement and reinforce the medieval Church's version of human savagery, unredeemed by the Christian God, represented in the form of the biblical Wild Man (whose history and characteristics are described in chapter 8).

As I describe in this chapter, those aspects of the Classical idea represented by the Legend of the Golden Age and the theme of the noble savage directly contradicted the biblical story of the Fall of Adam and Eve and

Christ's redemption on the cross for all humankind. They therefore were not allowed to flourish in the dank intellectual soil of the Christian medieval era. Those aspects of the Classical idea that were not stamped out as heretical survived, along with the well-known stereotypes and iconic images drawn from pagan fables and myths of distant monstrous races on the edges of the world and demonic spirits and witches intent on seducing and corrupting good pious Christian souls.

## THE WAR AGAINST PAGAN LITERATURE

The early Church Fathers saw Christianity as being in a state of perpetual war with the entire system of Greek and Roman pagan religious belief and knowledge. The ancient legends and myths of the gods were anathema to the Church. Pagan philosophy, with its skepticism and incessant inquiries into the potentiality of a virtuous and happy life lived free of knowledge of the Christian God, was regarded as an existential threat to the Church's worldview. Converting the masses of the Roman Empire to the true Christian faith required the obliteration of all pagan forms of worship and belief. Church doctrine taught that redemption was possible only through God's saving grace and membership within his universally conceived Christian commonwealth.

The Church's assault on the pagan system of belief was swift, decisive, and uncompromising. Under Emperor Theodosius I (A.D. 347–395; r. A.D. 379–395), the Catholic Church was raised to the position of the state religion, thus making adherence to paganism a political offense punishable by death as treason to the state. The "refuge of old Roman tradition," the Altar of Victory that held the famous gold statue of the goddess *Victoria*, was banished from the Roman Senate while zealous monks and vagabond armies of angry Christians roamed the land, destroying sanctuaries to pagan gods and toppling blasphemous works.[1] Villages suspected of continuing the impious worship of the pagan gods were plundered and sacked. Bans were imposed on pagan sacrifice. The reading of entrails was prohibited on pain of death. Visiting pagan temples and celebrating pagan holidays, even within one's own home, were proscribed. The last known staging of the ancient Olympic Games was in A.D. 393, during Theodosius's reign as emperor. It is assumed that he banned those ancient festivities held in honor of the supreme pagan deity Zeus as well.

The campaign on the ground against paganism was effectively won during the early centuries of Christianity's elevation to the official religion of the Roman Empire. Then the Church Fathers sought control over the literary corpus of Greek and Roman Classical civilization. Early Christian writers recognized that many of the ideas perpetuated by pagan literature were a direct threat to the integrity and stability of Christian doctrine, belief, and moral code. Pagan works were therefore carefully scrutinized and monitored. St. Jerome (ca. A.D. 347–420) was one of the most influential of the early Church Fathers. He translated the Bible into Latin (the Vulgate) and is the patron saint of translators, librarians, and encyclopedists. He was also well versed in Classical rhetoric and philosophy, having been trained by the noted Roman grammarian Aelius Donatus. Jerome made it quite clear that pagan literature must first be purified from all errors. "Then it is worthy to serve God."[2]

Church dogmatists throughout the Middle Ages habitually cited the biblical passage from Deuteronomy on the "beautiful woman" made captive slave as a scripturally approved approach for relying on pagan authors in their writings: "When thou goest forth to war against thine enemies, and the Lord thy God hath delivered them into thine hands, and thou hast taken them captive, And seest among the captives a beautiful woman, and hast a desire unto her, that thou wouldst have her to thy wife; Then thou shalt bring her home to thine house; and she shall shave her head, and pare her nails; And she shall put the raiment of her captivity from off her, and shall remain in thine house."[3]

As Professor Peter Gay notes, St. Augustine (A.D. 354–430), a devotee of the Greek neo-Platonist philosopher Plotinus, adopted this "beautiful woman" approach in his highly influential early Christian writings. The author of *The City of God*, the most important theological text from the Patristic period of the early Church Fathers, found no problem in taking from pagan literature whatever might be of use to the Church.

This basic censorious approach to the literature of Greek and Roman pagan antiquity is seen at work throughout the Middle Ages. In his twelfth-century work, *Dialogus super Auctores* (Dialogue on Authors), the

Benedictine monk Conrad of Hirsau wrote that pagan learning should be used liked spices and herbs, thrown out once the food has been flavored and cooked.[4] In the same century, the Abbot of Hildesheim vigorously promoted the study of the ancient classics with the following tactical advice: "You go over to the camp of the enemy not as a deserter, but as a spy."[5]

In the Christian system of thought that dominated the Middle Ages, pagan learning could be treated as a beautiful captive slave girl, stolen treasure, sauce for the goose, or military intelligence to bolster and advance the cause of the Church. All these tortured metaphors imply that a selective and judiciously cultivated knowledge of pagan literature was regarded as an essential tool in upholding the authority of Christian doctrine and the supremacy of the Church over all questions of faith. But as Gay explains, pagan literature reflected a system of alien knowledge and ideas that could never be treated as wholly "respectable." Works by Classical authors had to be closely "shaved, pared, and kept in the house of Christianity to serve a Christian master."[6]

## THE AFRICAN MADMAN, TERTULLIAN

A good deal of Classical learning and knowledge did survive Church censorship and suppression in the Middle Ages. Christian dogmatists, many of whom were highly conversant with a broad range of pagan literature and writers, played a central role in this process of selective transmission of Classical works. But they were highly discriminating in their use and selection of pagan texts and writers; those that could not be twisted or contorted to support Christian doctrine were censored, ignored, or hidden away in the carefully guarded monastic libraries controlled by the priestly hierarchy.

The Church's efforts at total control were aided considerably by the fact that most, if not virtually all, of those who were learned and literate, particularly in the far western provinces of the old Roman Empire, were priests and clerics. Under the firm control of the Church's machinery for enforcing dogma, such pious Churchmen were not inclined to perpetuate pagan works or ideas that challenged fundamental Christian beliefs. Pagan writers were carefully screened and monitored to ensure that their works did not contradict the biblical account of the creation and Adam and Eve, salvation through God's grace alone, the divinity of Jesus Christ, humanity's redemption through his death on the cross, the existence of the Holy Trinity, the divine authority conferred on the pope through Peter the Apostle, and virtually any other important or even trivial aspect of Church teaching.

The Church's Founding Fathers were particularly fond of echoing St. Paul's warning in the epistle to the Corinthians that God will "confound the insight of the wise" by the " 'sheer folly' of the Christian message."[7] Tertullian (ca. A.D. 160–220), a highly influential Church Father from Carthage in Roman Africa, illustrates the maddening degrees to which early Christian dogmatists could take the Pauline message to heart. His notorious *credo quia absurdum*—I believe because it is absurd—unashamedly embraced St. Paul's warning to the faithful to avoid the ratiocinations of pagan philosophy by affirming the utter ridiculousness of the resurrection of Jesus: "The Son of God was crucified: I am not ashamed—because it is shameful. The Son of God died: it is immediately credible—because it is silly. He was buried, he rose again: it is certain—because it is impossible."[8]

Voltaire, writing during the European Enlightenment, would insult this highly influential Church Father by calling him the "African Madman."[9] But Tertullian was not crazy. His rejection of all forms of pagan knowledge that could not be harmonized with Church doctrine was based on the true Christian believer's faith in the authority of Holy Scripture. With the advent of Jesus Christ and the Gospel, Tertullian simply felt there was no longer any need for curiosity about pagan ideas. When St. Paul traveled to Athens, as Tertullian tells the story, the apostle was totally unimpressed "with that loquacious city."[10] Tongue-in-cheek, Tertullian blames the fact that the "divine doctrine" gets no respect from the "huckstering wiseacres and talkers" there on Jesus, who sent "forth fishermen to preach, rather than the sophist."[11]

"What has Athens to do with Jerusalem?"[12] Tertullian once defiantly asked, opposing the falsehoods of those "patriarchs of heretics,"[13] the Greek philosophers, to the revealed truth of the Christian Bible. He even went out of his way to chastise the condemned Socrates for ordering a rooster to be sacrificed to Asclepius before he committed suicide.

Yet despite all his expressed hostility and fulminations, like most of the early Church Fathers, Tertullian would cite pagan writers in his theological writings with no hesitancy if they were helpful to the cause. He wrote at least three books, now lost, in Greek. He knew some Roman law, and, although he was a Christian apologist, he would not hesitate to call on the rhetorical teachings of Cicero and the Stoics to bolster a zealously made argument in defense of the faith.

As Tertullian had absorbed so much of Classical learning and the pagan worldview, we should not be surprised to learn that he was also familiar with the language of savagery invented by the Greeks and perpetuated by Roman Classical writers. He certainly was familiar with the Greek and Roman stereotypes of distant tribal peoples and their primitive manners and customs, as evidenced by his attack on Marcion, the founder of a heretical Christian sect. Marcion was from Sinope in Pontus, in the northeastern Black Sea region of Turkey. The Scythian tribes of that area, Tertullian writes, were notoriously fierce savages. One should not assume their homeland "to be friendly," he says, "so far removed is it from our more humane seas, as if it were ashamed of its barbarity."[14]

> The most savage tribes dwell in it, if, indeed, one can be said to dwell in a wagon. Their domicile is unsettled, their life is rude, their lust is promiscuous and for the most part open. . . . They do not blush even at their weapons. They devour the bodies of their parents slaughtered with their cattle at their feasts. Those who have not died to be eaten meet an accursed death. Nor are the women softened by their sex as modesty dictates: they cut off their breasts, their distaff is the axe; they would rather wage war than wed.

Even the climate of the region inhabited by these far-off peoples is "hard" according to Tertullian. The days are dark, the sun does not shine, it is winter all year round, he reports. "All is torpid," he rages, "all is stiff. Nothing there is hot except savagery."[15]

The clichéd stereotypes and cultural markers used by Tertullian to describe the Scythians are all too familiar; they are drawn directly from the extensive literature of Greek and Roman Classical Antiquity devoted to these notorious nomadic savage tribes. They wander over a barren wasteland, live in the harsh elements without a roof over their heads, are sexually promiscuous, and they cannibalize the remains of their own parents. Their feral females adopt the self-mutilating habits and primitive weaponry of Amazon warrior-women.

Tertullian's ravings against the Scythians suggest the degree to which the early Church Fathers had absorbed the worst stereotypical elements from the Classical language of savagery into their own biased views on the barbarian tribes of Europe. Tertullian even tells us the Classical sources where the irredeemable savage nature of the Scythians is on full display: the great tragic plays of the Greeks, which were a major influence on Roman drama. The savagery of these barbarians, Tertullian observes, "has furnished plots for the theatre: the sacrifices of the Tauri, the loves of the Colchi and the tortures of the Caucasus."[16]

Tertullian's classically inspired screed against the pagan Scythians with its litany of Greek-inspired stereotypes and caricatures is characteristic of those early Church Fathers who were conversant with pagan literature. Having absorbed all those negative images and descriptions of distant tribal peoples from their favorite Classical Greek and Roman sources, Christian dogmatists used the worst stereotypes they could dig up to describe the non-Christianized barbarian tribes on the frontiers of the Roman Empire as irredeemable savages.

## TAMING THE SOURCES

As the African Madman Tertullian shows us, the early Church Fathers, despite their fulminations and protests, had no hesitancy in drawing on pagan literature and Classical references when it suited their purposes. For the Church, the problem was in maintaining control over the more unruly sources of Greek and Roman knowledge. Particularly with respect to the Classical idea of the savage, pagan authors who celebrated the happiness and unbridled virtue of a way of life free of knowledge of the Christian Church had to be carefully controlled. Those pagan works that echoed the Hesiodic Legend of the Golden Age or the contrarian themes of the language of ennobled savagery, for example, were recognized as throwing into question the biblical account of Eden and the utter impossibility of redemption and grace outside the universal Church. Such pagan works therefore were suppressed; some were even outright banned.

Those pagan works, or parts thereof, that did manage to survive in this dank climate of intellectual rigidity and religious intolerance were reinterpreted, reinvented, and domesticated for Church purposes. The taming process was always tortuously complicated, often perverse, and at times even ridiculous.

A good deal of Platonic philosophy, for instance, was brought within the close orbit of the Church's system of control by St. Augustine, who used Plato and the neo-Platonists to help structure his early systemization of Christian dogma.

Cicero is another example of a pagan author found suitable for use by the Church for select purposes. Christian didacticians praised his contributions to rhetoric and educational theory. Those more humanistically inclined of Cicero's works that focused on natural law and philosophy, however, were recognized as contrary to the Christian system of thought. Whenever they were glossed or digested, any of Cicero's thoughts that challenged Church teachings were twisted and contorted to uphold the Christian system of knowledge and truth.

Aristotle's treatment at the hands of the Church is indicative of the culture of close surveillance and control maintained by Christian dogmatists over the literature of Classical Antiquity. Christian theologians had long been familiar with the great philosopher's works through the efforts of the Churchman Boethius (ca. A.D. 475–525), consul and minister to the Ostrogoth king, Theodoric the Great. Boethius had translated several of Aristotle's logical treatises in the sixth century.[17] Isidore of Seville (ca. A.D. 560–636), the Spanish encyclopedist, bishop, and saint, used Aristotle's concept of *argumentum* in developing his influential theory of rhetoric.

In the twelfth century, however, the Church had to deal with the "new" Aristotle, transmitted through the growing number of Latin translations and compendiums of the works of the Spanish Arabic philosopher Averroës (A.D. 1126–1198). Averroës's presentation of Aristotle's views on natural history, metaphysics, ethics, politics, and natural law were quickly recognized as a significant threat to the integrity of Christianity's most basic teachings. Beginning in the early decades of the thirteenth century, Church authorities issued a succession of bans and restrictions on Aristotle's more dangerous works. But the theologians apparently could not help themselves, particularly at the Church's leading institutions of higher learning, such as the University of Paris. The prohibitions were repeatedly infringed, requiring repeated renewals.

In 1231, for instance, Pope Gregory IX (r. A.D. 1227–1241) prohibited the use of any of Aristotle's books on nature in Church educational institutions. Although the pope acknowledged that the pagan philosopher's works contained "both useful and useless matter," he told the Dominicans at the University of Paris that, in examining Aristotle's books and teachings, "you entirely exclude anything which you may find there to be erroneous or likely to give scandal or offense."[18]

The Dominicans, of course, were the mendicant priestly order that had also been entrusted with carrying out the papal inquisitions against heretics and witches initiated around this same time. Whatever might have given "scandal and offense" to the Church during this reign of priestly terror fell under their jurisdiction.

The scholarly friars took up their assigned tasks of reconciling Aristotle's teachings with Church dogma with the same fervor and commitment they demonstrated in prosecuting the Inquisition. The Dominican scholar and teacher Albert the Great was one of the earliest Christian Humanists. He set out to paraphrase each of the pagan philosopher's works. He was succeeded in his efforts at synthesis and reconciliation by his star pupil, the great Christian Humanist theologian Thomas Aquinas (A.D. 1225–1274). Aquinas's *Summa Theologica* purified Aristotle's teachings to make them suitable for Christian study.

Virgil provides another example of the tortuous methods used by Church dogmatists to domesticate the works of pagan authors. Virgil's reputation as the greatest poet of Roman pagan antiquity, and particularly his celebration of the highest ideals of the Roman Empire, presented a number of problems for Christian theologians.

In the *Aenied*, for example, the pagan poet had recycled Hesiod's Legend of the Golden Age to celebrate the Augustan vision of an Eternal City on earth—an idea that was intolerable to Church teachings. Christian apologists who bemoaned his bad luck for being born before Christ's appearance on earth basically excused him for such lapses. He was quasi-deified and turned into a Christian oxymoron, a pagan saint, complete with his own cult.

In the fourth century, the emperor Constantine, who was willing to let go of all his pagan beliefs upon converting to Christianity, would not abandon Virgil. He somehow managed to claim the poet for Christianity as a prophet of Christ's coming to earth. John of Salisbury, an influential twelfth-century Christian writer, told of Virgil's performing a great miracle that relieved the city of Naples from a swarm of insects.

The legend of Virgil was reverently celebrated in the Middle Ages, but his works were consistently interpreted in ways that the poet himself would likely have found odd, to say the least. Christian writers, for example, converted the *Aeneid* into an edifying allegory of humanity's pilgrimage on earth.

Ovid, whose *Metamorphoses* unashamedly celebrated primitive human-ity's virtuous and happy way of life in the Golden Age, provides another well-known example of an ancient writer who could be transmitted to pious Christian readers only by tortured allegories of his more notorious works. For centuries, Ovid had served as an example of pagan licentiousness and immorality. This was, after all, the poet who had declared in one of his scan-dalous works, *Amores* (The Loves), that the subject of his verse was usually "a lad or else a long-tressed maid."[19] Ovid first had to be cleared of the charge of personal debauchery by a rehabilitation of his historical personality, be-coming transformed into another pagan saint, in line with Virgil.

All the while, his poems were being carefully screened for their suit-ability for Christian society. His double meanings and sensuous metaphors were closely monitored and supervised. In the twelfth-century university curriculum lists, for example, Ovid's *Fasti* and *Ex Ponto* are "tolerated," but his erotic poems, most notably the *Metamorphoses*, are rejected. One such list, for example, recommends his lesser work, the *Remedia amoris* (Love's Remedy), as an antidote to the unlisted *Metamorphoses*.[20]

During the late Middle Ages, Ovid's lecherous litany of sexual assaults by pagan gods on mortal maidens and lads, his tales of satyrs and nymphs cavorting in forests and glens, and his vision of ennobled primitives living happy and free without knowledge of the Christian God had to be tamed and brought into line with Church teachings. Pious Churchmen allegorized and reinvented the *Metamorphoses* to make it more acceptable for Christian readers. The gods and goddesses of the pagan pantheon were transformed into clerics and nuns, while their sensuous couplings were turned into chaste meetings—"a metamorphosis perhaps more astounding than any that Ovid himself had recorded," in the words of Professor Gay.[21]

As the close supervision of Ovid's poetry on the gods' scandalous exploits and the happy life of primitive humanity in the Golden Age suggests, pagan literature was considered a dangerous and subversive threat to the medieval Christian worldview. Even the most innocuous works were treated as a temptation to sin and worldliness. Indulging in the sensuous allure of pagan literature could bring on fear, sexual anxiety, and self-loathing for even the most pious priest or cleric. Otloh of St. Emmeram, an eleventh-century German Benedictine monk, related that reading the Roman poet Lucan gave him rashes and nightmares. After recovering, he vowed to reform: "What then were Socrates to me? Or Plato, Aristotle, or even Tullius [Cicero] the Orator?" We can assume he was off the stuff for good.[22]

Nicolas, chancellor of the University of Paris in 1285, recognized the pagan threat but apparently could not do anything about it: "We are in danger, we who read the writings of the pagan poets."[23] "How shall I be rid of these things?" says the tormented priestly novice in Cassian's *Dialogues*. "At mass, in the very act of contrition the old stories flaunt before my mind, the shameless loves, the sight of the old heroes going into battle."[24]

Ermenrich of Ellwangen had to stop himself in the middle of writing a grammatical treatise in the ninth century after quoting Virgil so many times that he knew he was going to have nightmares about it: "Not that I have any wish to see him, whom I believe to be in a Very Bad Place, and besides the sight of him terrifies me. Often indeed when I have been reading him, and after reading put him under my head, in that first sleep which should be sweetest after toil, comes to me a dark monster carrying a codex with a pen behind its ear as one about to write, and mocks at me."

Awaking from his bad dream, Ermenrich makes the sign of the cross and hurls his Virgil across the room. Once again able to sleep, he vows to his abbot to give up reading the pagan poet for good, although it seems that his heart is not in it: "[L]iar that he is, sunk with Apollo and the Muses in the foulest swamp of the Styx. There let him hug Proserpine and listen to Orpheus fiddling for his Eurydice from the infernal gods." God, the erudite grammarian writes, sets his curse on such falsehoods. "Why then do I harp upon them?" He answers his own anxious question with the typical dodge of the Church dogmatist: "Since even as dung spread upon the field enriches it to good harvest, so the filthy writings of the pagan poets are a mighty aid to divine eloquence."[25]

The "filthy" sensuousness of pagan art and sculpture was always a temptation to otherwise good Christian souls. In the mid-twelfth century, an English cleric, Master Gregory (Magister Gregorius), wrote up the equivalent of the medieval tourist's guide to Rome, *De mirabilibus urbis Romae* (The Marvels of Rome). In it, Gregory describes one of his favorite works of art in the city, a statue of Venus, standing up naked and covering her private parts, showing herself to Paris. He notes that it is "fashioned of Parian marble with so marvelous and inexplicable art that rather did she seem a living creature than a statute." He confesses that "her amazing beauty," combined with "I know not what magical persuasion," led him to visit her three separate times, "though she was distant two miles from my lodging."[26]

Of course, it was not all just about sex. Christian anxieties about the tempting allure of pagan literature, art, and ideas generally extended well beyond the realm of the senses. Pagan views on the potentiality of human life lived free of the constraints and confining institutions of Christian society raised the troubling possibility that God's grace in the Church was superfluous and even detrimental to the question of human happiness and the attainment of virtue on earth.

Infected by pagan attachments to worldliness, sensual pleasures, and intellectual skepticism, Classical ideas and influences could be highly dangerous to the stability of the Christian worldview if left unsupervised and uncensored. Pagan literature therefore had to be closely controlled and monitored; if necessary for the defense of the faith and protection of the faithful, it had to be suppressed or banned. Whatever pagan works that could be purified through allegory or cleansed of heretical or infectious impulses were permitted to survive. Where Classical literature and knowledge had nothing to say of interest, use, or concern to devout Christian minds or, worse, spoke of heresies and scandalous and worldly things, the Church simply ordered those works destroyed, ignored, or locked away, guarded closely only by the pious, learned, and wise.

## THE SUPPRESSION OF THE LEGEND OF THE
## GOLDEN AGE BY THE MEDIEVAL CHURCH

It is not difficult to see why certain aspects of the Classical idea of the savage found little room to flourish in the Christian Middle Ages. In particular, the Legend of the Golden Age, its themes of noble savagery, and its historical assertions of a declining cycle of the ages were highly problematic. From the Church's perspective, such pagan notions were presumed to be heretical. Christian theologians and writers had no need for a carefully calibrated instrument of pagan self-reflection and contrarian social critique that began with the assumption that humankind was better off before there even was a Christian Church, a Jesus Christ, or the Bible.

The benignly imagined, humanizing elements of the language of ennobled savagery perpetuated by the Legend of the Golden Age reflected a whole range of pagan values and an approach to life that was antithetical to the Christian message of redemption solely through the Church and grace of God. Thus, it is not surprising that Christian writers seldom discussed or commented on the legend. When it or any of its associated clichés and imagery are mentioned, Church dogmatists typically dismissed such things as just more instances of pagan foolishness and heretical falsehoods, artifacts of a worldview that the Church looked at with horror.

In his *Etymologiae* (Etymologies), for example, Isidore of Seville refers to the "Fortunatae insulae," the legendary Fortunate Isle, located to the west on the distant uncharted Ocean. As the highly respected Renaissance scholar and one-time Major League Baseball Commissioner A. Bartlett Giamatti explains in his splendid book on the idea of the earthly paradise in European thought, Classical Greek and Roman authors had often referred to the island as being "marked by fruit, precious trees, slopes covered with vines, crops, and garden vegetables," terms that evoked the Legend of the Golden Age. Isidore believed that because of the reputed fertility and lushness of the place, both gentile and pagan poets had confused these islands with the Garden of Eden. The problem was that these writers, according to Isidore, had failed to preserve the appropriate distinction between the pagan legends of the Fortunate Islands as a Golden Age–type locale and the Bible's description of the Garden of Eden as the earthly paradise. As Giamatti notes,

Isidore's insistence on maintaining this distinction was typical of Christian writers who were zealously on guard against any intrusion of false pagan ideas on the Bible's historically unchallengeable account of creation.[27]

One response by Church dogmatists to this type of loathed infiltration of the pagan myth into Christian consciousness was simply to subsume the Golden Age legend into the concept of the earthly paradise of the Garden of Eden. The ancient myth of Elysium, for example, represented another well-known pagan variation on the Legend of the Golden Age. The Classical poets, beginning with Homer, described Elysium as the resting place of the great warrior-heroes of ancient battles and triumphs. These heroes had been transported to this fair, bountiful, and blessed utopian land at the edges of the earth by the gods as a reward for their immortal deeds in war. Tertullian, the African Madman, tried to show how pagans, although they were unaware of it, were actually worshipping Christianity, as evidenced by the fact that the pagan poets' descriptions of the Elysium were derived from the Bible.

Early Christian writers' accounts of the earthly paradise were influenced by a number of Classical elements derived from the Golden Age legend.[28] The Spanish Christian poet Prudentius (A.D. 340–c. 405), for example, described the earthly paradise in terms that are traceable to Virgil's description of Elysium. Such "Virgilian echoes"[29] are heard throughout medieval Christian writers' descriptions of Eden and the earthly paradise. In time, these echoes so dominate Christian descriptions of place that they become a rigidified convention and even somewhat of a cliché, reverberating down into the Renaissance Age of Discovery. Columbus, for example, tells us in his journals that he was searching for an earthly paradise on the distant edges of the earth when he set out to discover what turned out to be a whole New World (see chapter 10).

## THE WANDERING GOLIARDS

It would not be entirely accurate to say that all the unruly aspects of the pagan Legend of the Golden Age completely vanished during the Middle Ages. But the story of the Wandering Goliards reveals the risks and rewards for those Christians who sought to celebrate the works and ideas of pagan poets deemed heretical and dangerous by the Church. The relentless efforts during the later Middle Ages to suppress this ragtag group of wayward scholarly monks and wisecracking schoolboy clerics demonstrates the degree to which the Church hierarchy sought to maintain tight control over any and all harmful pagan influences on Christian society.

As Helen Waddell explains in her leading study of the wandering scholars of the late Middle Ages, the Goliards' vagabond lifestyle and licentious hymns impiously embraced Ovid as their patron saint and his scandalous verse as their holy creed. For their offenses in seeking to keep the full scope of the Classical idea of the savage alive, they became the subjects of censure and scorn within the institutional Church. The *clericus* who turned *vagus* (vagabond), worshipping the pantheon of pagan gods of the *Metamorphoses*, was regarded as a rebel against the authority of the Church. In their wild and wandering ways, the Goliards represented everything that the pious Churchman was not or should never be.

Their origins are shrouded in mystery, like most secret societies that might never have really existed. These errant souls had succumbed to temptation by indulging in the vices spawned by absorbing too much pagan literature. Gerald of Wales (c. A.D. 1146–c. 1223), writing in the thirteenth century, tells us of a "certain parasite, Golias by name, notorious alike for his intemperance and wantonness." A "tolerable scholar, but witnout morals or discipline," he would "vomit forth against the Pope and the Roman Curia a succession of famous pieces, as adroit as they were preposterous, as imprudent as they were impudent." He even dared to scandalize eternity by celebrating his vices and vile misdeeds by writing his own epitaph. But not to worry, Gerald assures us; Golias would get his comeuppance in the end: "[A]lthough he may escape the vengeance of men, hardly might he shirk the divine fury, which suffers not that sin shall go unpunished, unless it be redeemed by penitence."[30]

Learned clerics who had been defrocked or forced to leave their monasteries or who simply liked the road typically were marked down as members of the Order of Golias. The medieval Church always frowned on this class of wandering clerics. Stability (*stabilitas*), staying in one place, was central to the disciplinary regime imposed within the monastery. It was one of the three obligations of the Benedictine vow. "Sit in thy cell," warned St. Anthony, the

Egyptian hermit who resisted the temptations of the devil in the desert, "and thy cell shall teach thee all things. The monk out of his cell is a fish out of water." The Abbot of Clonfert in Ireland advised the wandering scholar to "[d]ig and sow" so that "you may have wherewith to eat and to drink and be clothed, for where sufficiency is, there is stability, and where stability is, there is religion." This absolute rule of stability for the brother was only slightly relaxed for the *clericus saecularis*, secular clerks (ordained clergy who were not monks): "No clerk may leave the diocese without permission and letter of licence from the bishop; no bishop may receive him without such letter."[31]

The stereotypical Goliard, by virtue of his wild and wandering nature, could never abide by such rigid rules and silly vows. These vagabonds of the road were defined by their inability to stay in one place for too long and their love of the pagan poets. St. Benedict used the Latin epithet *gyrovagus* (wandering around in circles) to castigate "those monks whose whole life is spent, three days here, four days there, in the hospitality of different monasteries, ever wandering and never in one stay, and minding only their own pleasures and their wretched gullets."[32]

Your typical gyrovagus of the late Middle Ages would claim the Ovid of the *Metamorphoses*, uncensored and unexpurgated, as his patron saint. Singing sweetly in "Goliardic lyric" and Latin rhymes, he would earn his keep for the night by using satire, mockery, and invective to celebrate the sexual appetites, revelry, and human longings for love in this cloistered, pent-up age.

Christian writers used the term "vagus" to capture not only the physical condition of the life of the wandering scholars but the moral depravity that went along with it. Ekkehard tells the tragic story of a young monk of St. Gall, "of a mind incorrigibly *vagus* [wandering], with whom discipline could do nothing." Forbidden to leave the monastery, he still climbed the bell tower, "to look abroad, and missing his foot, crashed to the ground," bringing his sad life to an end."[33] One gets the sense that Ekkehard felt that the young man got precisely what he deserved.

For all these reasons and more, Church councils throughout the Middle Ages sought to closely monitor the giving of the habit and tonsure (the shaving of the crown of the monk's head by the bishop). They were not to be used as a "cloak for wandering."[34]

In the early tenth century, a Church council specifically calls out the Goliards by name, condemning those bawdy clerks "who are vulgarly called the family of Golias." They eat and drink "more at one sitting than the Blessed [St.] Martin did in his whole life."[35] Eleventh-century letters of license and introduction from high Church officials describe the vagus as a fraud while giving assurances that "[t]he present bearer is not such."[36] Even the Holy Roman Emperor is implored to rid his court of absentee clerks and hang-abouts.

At the Council of Rouen in 1231, which was around the time that the papal Inquisition was just gearing up, the Church imposed its second most severe sanction, degradation, on the wandering Goliards. Degradation meant loss of the benefit of clergy. The punishment was not intended to be as serious as excommunication, but for the degraded clerk, it meant losing all privileges previously conferred by the rite of tonsure. This mark of the Church was more than a new haircut; it secured relief from the taxes and impositions of the secular authorities. Clerics were exempt from military service. They did not have to face trial in a secular court of law for their crimes and offenses against the king's peace. The "neck verse"—a passage of the Bible that, when read by an offender, entitled him to benefit of clergy— could save a pious man of the Church from a hanging for his crimes. In this sense, the benefit of clergy was truly a life-saving privilege. As Waddell explains, the cleric found to be vagus lost all those privileges: "*clericus* no longer: he is to be shaven, so that no trace may be left of that order to which he is a disgrace: henceforth he will go out from the bishop's or monastery prison, an Ishmaelite indeed."[37] Abbots were warned not to give shelter to such fugitive monks.

To the Church, the Goliards amply demonstrated all the dangers of indulging in forbidden pagan knowledge. Their worship of Ovid and other scandalous Classical poets required the harshest forms of suppression. To the Church, Adam's Creation and the Fall were not mere stories or allegories of how the earth and human beings were created; they were undisputed historical facts, as stated in the Bible. They explained the unredeemed state of humankind in the world at the beginning of time as told in Genesis, and they had to be maintained in their orthodoxy. Persecuting a group of wandering monks who challenged the medieval Church and its teachings by celebrating the Classical idea of the savage in all its unruly aspects was only one minor front in Christianity's thousand-year-long holy war against the pagan worldview.

## CONCLUSION

We can now begin to get a better sense of the role of the Classical idea of the savage in the medieval Christian era. If a myth, legend, or stereotype could be used to support Christian doctrine, it was allowed to survive. As we have seen, some Classically derived stereotypes and cultural markers, such as those applied by the African Madman Tertullian to the nomadic barbarian tribes on the far frontiers of European Christendom, flourished and perpetuated themselves throughout the Middle Ages. But pagan notions like the Legend of the Golden Age and myths of noble savages directly contradicted the biblical story of the Fall of Adam and Eve and Christ's redemption on the cross for all humankind. They simply could not be allowed to flourish or propagate. The dank intellectual soil of the Christian medieval era killed off their growth and development, except where they survived in the form of bawdy roadhouse lyrics sung by drunken Goliard monks or in subtle and sublime Virgilian echoes buried deep within the verses of the Bible.

As it did with other aspects of the Classical system of ideas that ran counter to or challenged in the slightest Christian teachings and doctrine, the Church declared holy war on those aspects of the idea of the savage that it did not like. Pagan nonsense like the Legend of the Golden Age and a golden race of godless savages living it up at the beginnings of time in a place that looked just like the Garden of Eden simply could not be tolerated. Christianity's dogmatic view on what it meant to be a happy and virtuous human being required obliterating the full scope of the Classical idea of the savage. It was replaced with something much different and far less nuanced. Church theologians wanted to show what a human being untouched by the grace of God and cast out in the wilderness from Christian civilization really looked like. And so they invented the biblical Wild Man.

# EIGHT

# THE WILD MAN
# AND THE MEDIEVAL
# CHRISTIAN IDEA
# OF THE SAVAGE

## THE INVENTION OF THE WILD MAN

The Church's all-out assault on those works and ideas of pagan Classical Antiquity that could not be reconciled with Christian dogma cleared the ground for a much different, less nuanced, and unambiguous interpretation of the idea of the savage during the Middle Ages. The biblical Wild Man, emerging out of the Hebraic Old Testament, is the savage in the most dark-sided sense of the term: alone in the desert or wilderness, a castoff from humanity, a hunter, a giant, a subhuman beast; without knowledge or the saving grace of the Christian God. The Wild Men of the Bible—Cain, Ham, Nimrod, and Ishmael—are accursed figures, without hope of redemption.

Church dogmatists and theologians had no problem with absorbing and assimilating the most negative elements of the Classical idea of the savage into their writings on the biblical Wild Man. The more humanizing aspects of the idea associated with the Legend of the Golden Age and its language of ennobled savagery in particular were suppressed and replaced by the biblically derived image of the Wild Man as an unredeemable, irrational, and forsaken enemy to the Christian message of salvation and hope in the Church.

In the Bible's Old Testament, the Wild Man represented the human being "from whom no blessing flows because God has withdrawn the blessing from him."[1] He is accursed, with no hope of salvation. Wildness appears early on in the Book of Genesis as a sign of depravity, insanity, a kind of ill or evil demon force that reflects man's falling away from God. It is "a state of degeneracy below that of 'nature' itself, a peculiarly horrible state in which the possibility of redemption is all but completely precluded."[2]

The degraded, bestialized, irrational nature of the Wild Man makes him a highly detestable character in the Bible. In Christian thought, the archetypal Wild Men of the Old Testament are radically opposed to the paradisiacal image of Adam, the first man, in the Garden. Cast out into the wilderness, the Wild Man embodies the biblical counterimage of human potentiality represented by the Christian theme of Adamic man.

The offspring of these Wild Men in the Bible are the children of Babel and Sodom and Gomorrah. They are "men who have fallen below the condition of animality itself." They are the result of "*species corruption*."[3] In the Old Testament, such stories of species corruption tell of bestialized forms of humanity, particularly gigantism. As with the Greeks and Romans, gigantism is an almost universally credited attribute of savagery and wildness in the Bible. For Christian writers of the Middle Ages, the image of the Wild Man represented humanity in its most forsaken, accursed form, an unredeemed state of existence, an aberrant creature in God's mysterious order of creation.

Given the static nature of the stereotype, salvation was not imagined as possible for the Wild Man. By nature, the Wild Man was irreconcilably opposed to the order and stability of Christian civilization. He could redeem his status only by accepting salvation in the Church by the grace of God. At that point, he was no longer a Wild Man. But until that time, the Wild Man was regarded as a perpetual enemy to the Christian faith. Through this dehumanizing process, the Wild Man, in all his monotonous one-dimensionality as the personification of evil and accursedness, came to embody the medieval Church's idea of the savage.

## THE CLASSICAL IDEA OF THE
## SAVAGE AND THE WILD MAN

The Founding Fathers of the Church quickly seized on the worst elements and stereotypes taken from the Classical language of dark-sided savagery to give life and dimension to the Wild Man in their commentaries on the Old Testament. In *The City of God*, St. Augustine identifies Nimrod, the son of Cush, the Giant slain by David, as founder of the biblical city of Babel (Babylon), "whose people had tried to raise a tower against the heavens and brought down upon mankind the confusion of tongues which has afflicted it ever since." According to Augustine, "[a]s the tongue is the instrument of domination, in it pride was punished."[4]

Even aside from his biblical reference to the onomatopoeic term "Babylon," Augustine's focus on linguistic confusion as a characteristic sign of wildness shows the striking convergence of pagan and Christian ideas on the identifying markers of savagery in the medieval Christian era. Augustine throws down another of those parallel markers in his reading of the biblical passage identifying Nimrod as "a mighty hunter *against* the lord." "And what is meant by the term 'hunter,'" Augustine asks, "but deceiver, oppressor, and destroyer of animals of the earth?"[5]

Even at this early point in the institutional history of the Church, we can begin to sense how Christian writers were able to subsume and assimilate the negative oppositional elements and stereotypes of the Classical idea of the dark-sided savage into the biblically grounded iconography of the Wild Man. Pagan literature provided innumerable examples of species mixture, gigantism, and irreconcilable forms of human and subhuman savagery, sexual lewdness, and cultural deviancy. Church dogmatists were able to use their familiarity and acquaintance with the most negative and antihumanistic elements of the Classical idea to maximum effect in affirming and amplifying the unredeemable, irreconcilable nature of the Wild Man.

Ancient pagan histories, geographical works, and familiar travelers' accounts circulated widely throughout Christian Europe in the Middle Ages, and Christian writers drew freely on these sources in seeking to prove the existence of Wild Men in the world. Such accursed creatures served as the embodiment of true demonic evil and a warning to pious Christian souls to beware. Here again, Augustine leads the way in raising the anxiety level of every good Christian pilgrim by describing in vivid detail the wild races of men reported by ancient travelers. As Hayden White notes in his leading essay on the iconography of the Wild Man in the Middle Ages, Augustine catalogs "races of men with one eye in the middle of the forehead, feet turned backward, a double sex, men without mouths, pygmies, headless men with eyes in their shoulders, and doglike men who bark rather than speak."[6]

Showing off his characteristic penchant for learned synthesis of pagan and biblical references, Augustine speculates that the bestial creatures described by the pagan writers of Greece and Rome were really descended from Ham and Japeth. These Wild Men were Noah's accursed sons, "archetypal" heretics and sinners, devoted to "monstrous gods"[7]: the perfect fusion of the Classical and Christian idea of an irredeemable savage.

The fabled conquests of Alexander the Great in India and the East provided a particularly rich corpus for medieval Christian writers to pick over for examples of Wild Men accursed to God located on the far edges of the world. Many of the stories of Alexander's discoveries in India were collected in the widely popular compilation known as the *Alexander Romance*. It tells of savage tribes of fish eaters in northern India who dressed in animal skins and ate their food without cooking it, preferring to dry it in the sun. Readers are regaled by the account of Alexander's search for the fountain of life and his crossing over into

a dark and dangerous area that teemed with monstrous creatures . . . giant-sized humans with hands and feet like saws; other giants with lion heads, hairy bodies, and red scalps; and a creature bristly as a pig, which, when caught and given a woman for its enjoyment, carried her away and proceeded to eat her. When set upon again, the creature let out a shriek, whereupon its fellows appeared on all sides, barking like dogs as they attacked the Greek soldiers.[8]

One of the most influential of the medieval Latin versions of the *Romance* was compiled by Archpresbyter Leo in the tenth century. The monkey with fur like a pig is called "a large wildman," *magnus homo agrestis*. The Indian giants are described as vegetarian wild men who live in the woods and pick fruit from the trees for sustenance. Later versions of the *Romance* continue to perpetuate the ancient stereotypes of monstrous wild men. There is even a wild woman, "huge and bristly and forebidding; she eats humans, with the teeth of a wild boar, a long tail, and a covering of 'fur' like an ostrich or a camel." The influence and deep penetration of the *Romance*'s accounts of fabulous races extend throughout numerous historical works and encyclopedias of the Christian medieval era.[9]

Christian writers frequently referred to pagan geographical texts and travel literature in ways that supplemented, reinforced, and confirmed their worst stereotypes and beliefs about distant tribal peoples untouched by the word of God. The geographical accounts contained in the texts of Roman encyclopedists like Pliny describing fabulous Wild Men were preserved and embellished by a succession of medieval Christian writers; Martianus Capella in the fifth century, Isidore of Seville in the seventh century, and Honorius of Auton in the twelfth century. Illustrations of Wild Men in distant locales also appear as supplements to the medieval encyclopedias. A manuscript from the turn of the millennium shows the Wild Men of India as naked creatures, standing upright without fur. A series of English manuscripts of the late tenth through twelfth centuries entitled *Marvels of the East* shows fish-eating Wild Men who appear as "repulsive naked giants with long beards, and hair that falls to the ground."[10]

One of the most famous, though spurious, texts from the Middle Ages confirms these fantastic accounts of savage Wild Men in the East as reported by the ancient sources. The letter, supposedly written by Prester John, a legendary ruler of a great kingdom in the East, was addressed to the Byzantine Christian emperor Manuel Comnenus (1143–1180). Prester John describes himself in this letter as a Christian ruler of a rich kingdom that happens to include "the terrestrial paradise of Christian tradition," along with a mythical assortment of "centaurs, fauns, satyrs, satyresses, pygmies, cynocephali, cyclopes, giants," and, of course, "wild men."[11]

Embassies were sent to the East in response to the letter, and Prester John's help was counted on in the fight against the Saracen infidels who were terrorizing the Holy Lands. The letter's influence spread throughout the travel and geographic literature of medieval Europe. Roger Bacon, for example, in his influential thirteenth-century work, *Opus Magnus,* starts his discussion of India and Central Asia with an account of Prester John that includes a description of a "hairy creature of human form, but of ape-like behavior, whom the native hunters overcome by the device of intoxicating him" in the high rocks.[12]

Christian writers helped keep alive the most dehumanized aspects, literally and figuratively speaking, of the Classical idea of the savage, by injecting the demons and spirits of Greek and Roman mythology into their biblical commentaries on Wild Men. Hairiness, as we have seen, is one of the paradigmatic stereotypes of savage countenance in Classical literature, art, and philosophy. Christian writers relied directly on the Classical language of savagery in their commentaries on hairiness as a telltale sign of demonic wildness in the Bible.

As Professor Richard Bernheimer describes, St. Jerome, in his Latin translation of the Bible from the Hebrew, rendered a phrase used by the prophet Isaiah to describe the demons who had incurred God's wrath roaming through the deserted ruins of Palestine as *et pilosi saltabunt ibi,* meaning "and the hairy ones will dance there." The Hebrew equivalent of Jerome's *pilosi* was *Se'irim,* a Jewish folklore term for a type of demon. Jerome's commentary explains: "When in the following it is said the 'the hairy ones will dance here,' we must understand this to mean either incubi or satyrs or a certain kind of wild men whom some call *fatui ficarii* and regard as of the nature of demons."[13]

As Bernheimer explains, *fatui ficarii* "were satyrs known for their insatiable lasciviousness and thus closely akin to incubi, the professional ravishers of mortal women."[14] Jerome simply borrowed and extended the pagan myth to flesh out his commentary on Isaiah's prediction of the desolation and chaos that would result from the Lord's wrath: *et pilosus clamabit at alterum,* "and one hairy creature will shout to the other." St. Augustine similarly categorizes fauns and sylvans as incubi, noting that both "desire women and act carnally with them."[15]

Christian dogmatists throughout the Middle Ages perpetuated the iconography of the Wild Man by keeping these ancient pagan myths of hairy demonic beings alive. Isidore of Seville describes *pilosi qui Graece Panita Latine Incubi appellantur*—"hairy ones called Pans in Greek and Incubi in Latin." Bartholomaeus Anglicus in his *De proprietatibus rerum* (On the Properties of Things), in the thirteenth century, devotes a chapter to fauns and satyrs, describing them as *homines silvestres,* wild men, much like the centaurs and other monstrosities. John Wycliffe rendered Jerome's Latin term "pilosi" into Middle English as "wodewose" or "wild man."[16]

This absorption of the most negatively imagined, dehumanizing aspects of the Classical idea of the savage into the biblical image of the Wild Man finds its way out to the common folk, of course. Wild Men and Wild Women are encountered throughout the folklore, legends, and festival rites of secular European society during the Middle Ages. They appear in myriad different guises and costumes, all sharing similarities and, in many instances, a common derivation from pagan myths and remnant religious traditions not wholly stamped out by the Church. They live in the woods or caves. They are typically large and hairy or small and fairylike, sexually deviant, lawless, and untamed savage beings.

The centaurs, satyrs, fauns, and other ancient woodland divinities remained alive among the peasantry in the yearly calendar of agricultural festivities. In the twelfth and thirteenth centuries, the satyrs and fauns flourished in the encyclopedias and bestiaries along with the general revival of learning and interest in ancient lore.

The *Wilder Man,* as the Germans labeled their version of the Wild Man, was a hairy, unclothed, violently disposed child of untamed nature, living alone in the wilderness. He represented an amorphous, ambiguous being, half human and animal. Ignorant of civilization and its constraining laws, morality and institutions, the Wilder Man lived a miserable, beastly life. A hunter of animals who foraged and grubbed for plants to supplement his rude diet, he lived accursed and apart from civilized Christian society in woods and caves.

The existence of these miserable creatures was etched in stone on the buildings and sculpted monuments of the Middle Ages. Satyrs, gorgons, and fauns can still be seen on the massive public and religious buildings constructed during the medieval era throughout Christian Europe. Bernheimer describes how the Arthurian legends of the Middle Ages, with their codes of Christian chivalry and tales of errant knights, freely borrowed from the Classical language of dark-sided savagery in their accounts of Merlin's birth.

In "Lestoire de Merlin," a young damsel loses her way on her return from market and falls asleep under a tree. A Wild Man appears and ravishes her. The child born out of this illicit union is Merlin, endowed with the traits of a sorcerer magician.

This late-thirteenth-century version is only slightly different from Geoffrey of Monmuth's *Historia regum Britanniae* (History of the Kings of Britain), written around 1137. In this rendition, Merlin's father is an incubus: "that is, a faun or satyr." Even before that, in the twelfth century, Robert of Boron's "Merlin" described a conspiracy by the devils in hell to produce the Anti-Christ by a virgin birth, assigned to undo Christ's work on earth. The plan failed because the virgin damsel had too much native goodness in her to bring forth such unmitigated evil. Her offspring turned out to be Merlin, who uses his magical powers as a sorcerer over nature to restore moral order among humans.[17]

Pagan myths and legends of demonic possession, sorcery, and witchcraft fit well into the biblical image of the Wild Man as eluding Christian norms and the established framework of Christian society. Women who refused to follow the rules laid down by the Church had to be particularly careful in the Middle Ages. In the hysteria of the papal Inquisitions, charges of witchcraft, sorcery, and demonic possession were applied to those "Wild Women" who lived outside Christian society, in the woods or a cave, beyond the control and surveillance of the Church.

The literature and legends of pagan antiquity that tell of witches and sorceresses who controlled demonic spirits and the forces of nature strongly reinforced this tendency of the medieval Church to persecute those females who did not follow the normal rules of sexual behavior and feminine submissiveness. Pagan myths often depicted sorceresses and witches as sexually seductive temptresses or nubile nymphs with magical powers who enjoyed coupling with humans when their satyr boyfriends were not around.

The West's first literary encounter with a sexy sorceress fits the stereotype perfectly. Circe, the witch-goddess of magic in ancient Greek mythology, was known for her ability to tame lions and wolves and transform any man who offended her into a beast through her knowledge of drugs and herbs. Her status as a witch who could exert total control over men doubly contributed to her demonic counterimage as the opposite of everything the

Greeks thought a virtuous, civilized woman should be: docile, obedient, and compliant.

In Homer's *Odyssey,* Circe turns Odysseus's men into pigs, but the immortal Greek warrior-hero is able to use his superior knowledge to overcome her potions. Ultimately she is made to have sex with Odysseus on his terms, thus confirming the superiority of Homer's hero over the sorceress and her mythical magic powers.

Nymphs were the hypersexualized earth goddesses of ancient Greek myth and legend who practiced their own forms of witchcraft and sorcery in controlling the hidden life forces of nature. They were known to cavort with satyrs: half-human, half-goat savage beings of unbounded sexual energy. In the Christian medieval era, these Classical earth goddesses were associated with the Devil himself. Nymphs were also notorious for their amorous liaisons with naive humans.

Homer's famous story of the beautiful nymph goddess Calypso is the first such recorded encounter with the mythical sprites in Classical Greek literature. Calypso had sex with Odysseus for seven years on her magical island before he got tired of her affections and decided to return home to his faithful wife, Penelope, spinning away at her fabled loom.

The Greeks imagined their nymph goddesses living among lush mountains, groves, and forested grottoes, or beside cooling springs and rivers, in wild and abundant nature. Like all the sexy savages of ancient Greek mythology, they were the antithesis of the idealized virtuous wives and chaste daughters of the Greek polis.

In the early Middle Ages, the Church's position on witchcraft and sorcery was that such things did not exist. Christian writers blamed the delusions on the stubborn persistence of pagan belief systems over the ages or plain old human horniness. In any event, the Church had no trouble associating magic with the old pagan rites of divination, reading of entrails, and other forms of ancient sorcery.

In the later Middle Ages, Christian writers began to more closely associate reports of witchcraft, nymphs, satyrs, and other demonic forces at work in the world, particularly where women and sex were involved, with Satan's influence. As the delusion of witchcraft spread throughout Christian Europe in the later Middle Ages, Church theologians like Thomas Aquinas and St. Bonaventure codified a theory of the "incubus and the succubus," which assumed that the Devil could take on either a male or a female form to substitute for a human being during sexual intercourse.[18]

Women, however, seemed to be the Devil's preferred form of appearance. By the late Middle Ages, the papal Inquisition began to focus on magical practices and witchcraft as evidence of heresy. In 1320, Pope John XXII authorized the Inquisition to take action against sorcerers, and in 1484, at the close of the medieval era, Pope Innocent VIII issued the infamous papal bull *Summis desiderantes affectibus* (Desiring with supreme ardor), responding positively to a Dominican inquisitor's request to prosecute witchcraft in Germany. Shortly after this bull, the infamous *Malleus Maleficarum* (the Hammer of the Witches) appeared in print in Germany. Written by two Inquisitors of the Church, Heinrich Kramer and Jacob Sprenger, the treatise affirmed the reality of witchcraft as shown in the Bible and discussed the appropriate punishments to be doled out by ecclesiastical and secular courts. The reproduction of the book in the late fifteenth century, thanks to the introduction of the printing press in Europe, has been credited with leading to the notorious witch hunts and persecutions of women during the European Renaissance centuries.

The Classical stereotypes and images associated with witchcraft, nymphs, and other demonic forces of nature proved highly useful to the Church in defining the norms and social mores governing appropriate female behavior in good Christian society. The sexy savages of ancient Greek mythology—exotically imagined, overly aggressive, mysteriously empowered, and hypersexualized—were appropriated by medieval Christian writers anxious to reinforce Church teaching and dogma on the identifying characteristics of the Wild Woman so that she could be properly burned at the stake.

## THE HOLY WAR TRADITION
## AND THE WILD MAN

The medieval Christian idea of the savage as embodied in the biblical image of the unredeemed Wild Man, the Church's disdain for pagan heretics, and the colonizing desires of European Christian monarchs and warlords can all be seen at work in Christianity's centuries-long tradition of holy wars against pagan peoples, culminating in the Crusades to the Holy Lands in the eleventh through thirteenth centuries. Early in the Church's institutional history as the official religion of the Roman Empire, theologians had condoned the idea of a holy war waged against pagan barbarians as righteous and just campaigns in defense of the faith.

St. Ambrose (ca. 339–397) had been a Roman imperial official prior to his conversion to Christianity. As Bishop of Milan, he pressed the emperor Theodosius to issue his infamous decrees declaring war on the pagan religion (see chapter 7). He combined Roman law and Cicero's authority with examples of the Hebrews' divinely sanctioned wars from the Old Testament to show that military campaigns could be lawfully waged by imperial authorities to protect religious orthodoxy and defend the empire from barbarian invaders and heretics. Addressing the emperor, Ambrose explained:

> Just as all men who live under Roman rule serve in the armies under you, the emperors and princes to the world, so too do you serve as soldiers of almighty God and of our holy faith. For there is no sureness of salvation unless everyone worships in truth the true God, that is, the God of the Christians, under whose sway are all things. For he alone is the true God, who is to be worshiped from the bottom of the heart, "for the gods of the heathen," as Scripture says, "are devils."[19]

Augustine's thinking on holy war closely followed that of his mentor, Ambrose, in holding that a war could be legitimately waged by the secular arm at the behest of the Church against its heretical enemies. As Bishop of Hippo, Augustine was forced to ask imperial authorities to supply the armed force necessary to persuade unruly groups of heretics and schismatics to cease in their unreason and rejoin the fold. The scriptural command, "compel them to come in" (Luke 14:16–24), in Augustine's reluctant view, justified a holy war against heretics who had fallen away from the Church but were nonetheless subject to its discipline.[20]

Throughout the Middle Ages, Christian princes and warlords carried on numerous holy wars "sanctioned by God" against unredeemed enemies of the faith. Their campaigns of terror, territorial expansion, and forced conversions against nearby pagan neighbors were approved by Christian writers and theologians who used the Church's idea of the savage as embodied by the Wild Man to justify these conquests.

Charlemagne's military campaigns to convert the pagans of Saxony (772–804) were among the most notorious of the Christian holy wars launched against the barbarian tribes of Europe in the Middle Ages. Charlemagne's efforts at military conquest, colonization, and conversion would serve later as examples and inspiration for the Church's announcement of the first Crusade against the infidels and heathen followers of Islam in the Holy Lands.

The Saxons were a German tribe, and, as has been mentioned in earlier chapters, the Germans had been notoriously stereotyped by Classical-era writers. They were well known to ancient writers as fierce, war-loving savages, dishonorable thieves, drunken louts, and wanton violators of any law they found not to their liking, human or divine. They sacrificed their captives in war and practiced numerous other abominations that revealed their base form of savagery.

Things had not changed much in terms of the Saxons' behavior or reputation by the early Middle Ages. As described by Charlemagne's chroniclers, they were still a barbarian race of savages and extremely hostile to conversion to the Christian faith. The embodiment of the Church's idea of the savage, they were regarded as Wild Men, unredeemed by God. Good Christian princes therefore could wage holy wars against them to secure either their sworn conversion to the community of the faithful or their complete annihilation as godless pagans. And then, of course, their lands could be seized and colonized.

Charlemagne's long series of violent military actions against the Saxons began in 772. Invading tribal villages, destroying sacred idols and altars, and forcing mass sworn conversions to Christianity, he carried on his war against the Saxons for more than 30 years. Along the way, he terrorized large swaths of Germany, issued decrees and edicts intended to destroy Saxon resistance, and executed anyone who continued the old pagan practices or violated the king's peace.

An entry for the year 782 in the Royal Frankish Annals, as one notorious example, records that after losing two envoys, four counts, and some 20 nobles in one battle against the Saxons, Charlemagne responded by summarily executing 4,500 Saxon prisoners in what has been called the Massacre of Verdun. As with the ancient Greeks and Romans, to the devout Christian European warlords of the Middle Ages, the normal rules of civilized warfare did not apply to barbarian tribal savages.

Even at this relatively early point in the development of Christian European state practice respecting holy wars against pagan tribes, we can see the usefulness of the Classical language of dark-sided savagery in constructing the Saxons as Wild Men. The king's chronicler employs a set of familiar inflammatory Classical stereotypes of Germanic savagery to describe the Saxons' fierce and stubborn resistance to Charlemagne's conquest, conversion, and colonization of their entire race: "[As to the Saxon War] no war ever undertaken by the Franks was waged with such persistence and bitterness, or cost so much labor, because the Saxons, like almost all Germans, were a ferocious folk, given over to devil-worship, hostile to our Faith, and they did not consider it dishonorable to transgress and violate all law—be it human or divine."[21]

Charlemagne persisted in his holy wars against the pagan tribes of Central Europe in some fifty campaigns of conquest, colonization, and conversion. Along the way, he slaughtered thousands of Saxons as well as Danes, Slavs, Dalmatians, and other barbarian peoples whose names are lost to Western history, in order to facilitate the missionary activities of the Church and new colonial settlements in formerly held pagan lands.

## THE CRUSADES

Christian writers throughout the Middle Ages asserted the basic religious thesis justifying holy wars against enemies of the faith as divinely directed campaigns against savage Wild Men who resisted the saving grace offered by the Church and its missionaries. Canon lawyers and popes justified military operations as diverse and far flung as the papally commissioned Reconquista of the Iberian peninsula by the Catholic kingdoms of Lisbon, Castile, and Aragon and William the Conqueror's Norman invasion of Britain as holy wars in defense of the faith against pagans, heretics, and infidel nonbelievers.

Pope Urban's call for the first crusade against the infidel Turks in the Holy Lands in 1095 was a natural outward extension of the Church's holy war tradition beyond the boundaries of Christian Europe. Urban, in fact, cited to Charlemagne's conquests of the Saxons as precedent; those pagan and infidel peoples who would not accept the authority of the Church were outside the pale of salvation and could be vanquished in a holy war waged in defense of the rights of the Christian faith. As one chronicler reported the pope's speech to the Franks calling for the first crusade to the Holy Lands: "Let the deeds of your ancestors move you and incite your minds to manly achievements; the glory and greatness of king Charles the Great, and of his son Louis, and of your other kings, who have destroyed the kingdoms of the pagans, and have extended in these lands the territory of the holy church."[22]

The series of Crusades to the Holy Lands launched by Urban's call represented the first large-scale effort by Western Christendom to implement the Church's idea of a holy war over non-Christian peoples outside Europe. In making his call, Urban invoked the cadenced biblical images and clichéd stereotypes associated with the Wild Man to depict the infidel Turks as "an accursed race, a race utterly alienated from God, a generation forsooth which has not directed its heart and has not entrusted its spirit to God." He described the infidels as mercilessly invading Christian settlements in the Holy Lands with "sword, pillage and fire." They lead away their captives to the cruel fate of slaves or, even worse, murder them by "cruel tortures." Their savage crimes against humanity are beyond forgiveness and redemption:

> They destroy the altars, after having defiled them with their uncleanness.
> They circumcise the Christians, and the blood of the circumcision they
> either spread upon the altars or pour into the vases of the baptismal font.
> When they wish to torture people by a base death, they perforate their
> navels, and dragging forth the extremity of the intestines, bind it to a
> stake; then with flogging they lead the victim around until the viscera
> having gushed forth the victim falls prostrate upon the ground. Others
> they bind to a post and pierce with arrows. Others they compel to extend
> their necks and then, attacking them with naked swords, attempt to cut
> through the neck with a single blow. What shall I say of the abominable
> rape of the women?

Urban completes his rather devastating portrait of these accursed Wild Men with a sly reference to one of the favored markers associated with the idea of the savage in the Christian medieval and Classical eras. He calls on the Franks "to humble the hairy scalp of those who resist you."[23]

Christian dogmatists and theologians throughout the medieval crusading era vigorously defended the Church's holy wars against the hairy-headed infidel Turks by citing their lack of faith and belief in the Christian God as proof of their irredeemable nature. For some of the most extreme canon lawyers who sought to elevate the papacy to a position of unchallengeable preeminence over all earthly rulers, the infidels' Wild Man status was reason enough for the pope to order their property confiscated by good Christian princes. Those crusading princes, of course, got to keep that property under conditions ordered by Rome, backed by the threat of excommunication of any other Christian ruler who dared to interfere with these papally conferred privileges.

One of the most influential legal thinkers of the late Middle Ages, the Italian canonist Hostiensis (1200–1271), held that as grace was a precondition of ownership and dominion over property, pagan infidels possessed no rights to their lands that Christians had to recognize under Church law. According to Hostiensis, "It seems to me that with the coming of Christ every office and all government authority and jurisdiction was taken from every infidel lawfully and with just cause and granted to the faithful through Him who has the supreme power and who cannot err."[24] The influential English canonist Alanus Anglicus, writing at about the same time, stated flatly that "none except those who believed in the true God had a right to the sword; nor do infidel rulers have it nowadays."[25]

## THE CHRISTIAN HUMANIST
## REACTION TO THE MEDIEVAL
## CHURCH'S IDEA OF THE SAVAGE

Vigorous defenders of the universal Christian commonwealth like Hostiensis and Alanus show us how the medieval Church was able to use the language of savagery associated with the biblical Wild Man to justify an unconditional and unprovoked holy war against the pagan peoples of the

Holy Lands. This extreme, dehumanized version of the medieval Christian idea of the savage came under close scrutiny by early Christian Humanist writers such as Albert the Great and Thomas Aquinas. Albert and Thomas were both influenced by the "new" Aristotle of Averröes and the works of the ancient Roman jurists that began circulating in European universities in the thirteenth century. Working with the new Classical concepts that came into vogue in the later Middle Ages, they focused their attention on human reason and our universal capacity for making informed judgments. They found it difficult to accept that infidels lacked rights, given the principles they were exploring and expounding, such as *ius naturale* (natural law) and *ius gentium* (the law of nations).

Aquinas, as we have seen, played a major role in harmonizing the "useful" parts of the Aristotelian corpus with Christian speculative thought. His influential synthesis of the Humanist strains in pagan philosophy and Church orthodoxy is reflected in his argument that conversion must be voluntary, not coerced, in accordance with humankind's rational nature and ability to conceive of the principles of natural law.

By far, the most important of the medieval Christian Humanists to directly address the thorny philosophic and theological issues raised by the Church's involvement in holy wars against pagans and infidels was Pope Innocent IV (r. 1243–1254). Innocent had served as a renowned canonist and lecturer at the University of Bologna, where the famous Latin scholar Irnerius had revived the study of Roman law in the late eleventh century. Innocent's own influential writings, along with his firm grounding in canon law and Christian doctrine, also reflected the eclectic absorption of a wide variety of pagan sources and philosophical texts.

Innocent's most important work on the topic of the legal status and rights of non-Christian societies is contained in his commentary on a papal decretal issued by his influential predecessor, Pope Innocent III (r. 1198–1216), *Quod super his*. In his commentary, Innocent asked, "[I]s it licit to invade a land that infidels possess or which belongs to them?"[26]

Innocent was careful in his legal analysis to preserve the Church's assertions of universal authority over non-Christianized pagan peoples while conceding their rights as human beings under natural law. According to his Christian Humanist–inspired analysis, even infidels shared in universalized reason common to all humankind. Thus, under natural law, they were free and rational beings made for God and possessed of the same rights as Christians. Christians could not confiscate their lordship and property solely on the basis of their nonbelief in the Christian God.

But Innocent reasoned that, as rational beings, infidels, like Christians, were responsible for their conduct under natural law. Any excessive or outrageously regarded breaches of the universalized dictates and norms of the Church's Christianized version of natural law indicated a lack of reason that required remediation by the pope as shepherd of all of God's flock on earth.

Innocent's novel assertion—the pope in Rome could order Christian armies to enforce the rationalized dictates of natural law against deluded pagan peoples anywhere in the world under his divinely mandated responsibility for all the sheep of God's human flock—brilliantly reformulated the legal basis of the Crusades on the naturalistic premises favored by Humanist-inspired Church theorists of the thirteenth century. The infidels' failure to follow the dictates of natural law, as interpreted and enforced by the pope, justified Christian holy wars of conquest, colonization, and conversion against them.

> [T]he pope has jurisdiction over all men and power over them in law but not in fact, so that through this power which the pope possesses I believe that if a gentile, who has no law except the law of nature [to guide him], does something contrary to the law of nature, the pope can lawfully punish him, as for example in Genesis 19 where we see that the inhabitants of Sodom who sinned against the law of nature were punished by God. Since, however, the judgments of God are examples for us, I do not see why the pope, who is the vicar of Christ, cannot do the same and he ought to do it as long as he has the means to do so. And so some say that if they worship idols [the pope can judge and punish them] for it is natural for man to worship the one and only God, not creatures. Also, the pope can judge the Jews if they violate the law of the Gospel in moral matters if their leaders do not punish them.

Innocent had rigged the game for pagan infidels right from the start; as far as he was concerned, their failure to admit Christian missionaries so they could listen to the word of God and exercise their rational faculties was a violation of natural law as defined by the Church. The pope in such circumstances, as Innocent explained, can therefore "order infidels to admit preachers of the Gospel in the lands that they administer, for every rational creature is made for the worship of God." According to Innocent, "the Pope has jurisdiction over all men and power over them in law but not in fact."

The pope's jurisdiction to enforce natural law against pagans could be exercised for any violation defined as serious enough by the Church to require papal intervention. Failure to permit Christian missionaries into their lands to preach was only one of several serious offenses that could authorize the pope to declare a crusade against them. If left unpunished by the infidels' rulers, sodomy and other forms of sexual perversions, for instance, would naturally necessitate papal intervention.

Like the good Christian theologian he was, Innocent held that God's will, interpreted through the pontifical office, expressed a far more perfect rationality than that possessed by imperfect human beings. According to Innocent, "[t]here is only one right way of life for mankind, and . . . the papal monopoly of this knowledge makes obedience to the Pope the only means of salvation."[27] The manifest irrationality of heathens and infidels who rejected the pope's message demonstrated their need for papal remediation. They were deluded peoples, Wild Men in the medieval Christian system of thought. The pope's divinely instituted mandate from Apostle Peter to build Christ's universal Church on earth required him to call on Christian princes to raise armies to punish their serious violations of natural law. And what if the infidels resist the pope's authority? According to Innocent, "they ought to be compelled by the secular arm and war may be declared against them by the Pope and not by anybody else."[28]

Innocent's influential efforts at harmonizing the Church's teachings on universal papal power with the naturalistic philosophy of the ancient Greeks and Romans will exercise a profound and directive influence on the relations of Christian Europe with the non-Christian world from this point forward. Numerous Christian legal theorists would subsequently elaborate on his influential legal opinions written as pope and infallible authority on Church canon law and doctrine. According to Professor James Muldoon, Innocent's discussion of the natural law rights and obligations of infidels, pagans, and heathens represented an important step in the development of European notions of international law. Innocent was quoted, for example, as undoubted authority in the sixteenth-century debates over the rights of the American Indians in the Spanish conquest of the New World.[29] Centuries prior to Columbus's voyages to the New World, this thirteenth-century canon lawyer-pope sought to reconcile medieval Christianity's idea of the savage as embodied in the biblical Wild Man with Classical Humanism's natural law tradition. The basic stereotypes and imagery the West had used for thousands of years to identify those non-Westernized peoples irrationally opposed to its expansion-minded form of civilization could now be used by the Church to justify its universal jurisdiction over all humankind.

# NINE

# THE RENAISSANCE HUMANIST REVIVAL OF THE CLASSICAL LANGUAGE OF SAVAGERY

We have seen how the biblical Wild Man came to embody the idea of the irreconcilable savage during the medieval Christian era. Subsuming earlier Classical pagan notions of savagery's ambiguous, dual-sided aspects, the Wild Man represented a wholly negative, bellicose, dehumanized interpretation of the possibility of redemption outside the Church. Even in its Christian Humanist form as articulated by Pope Innocent IV, the same basic set of negative stereotypes and categorical behaviors incorporated into the biblical image of the Wild Man from Classical Antiquity's dark-sided language of savagery served to justify the Church's crusading holy wars against pagan nonbelievers according to natural law.

During the European Renaissance (roughly from the fourteenth to sixteenth centuries), the Classical idea of the savage was rehabilitated. The language of ennobled savagery was recovered from centuries of Christian oppression. The Legend of the Golden Age once again assumed its role as a powerful form of social critique and protest against the vices of modernity.

The recovery of many of the lost and suppressed works of Greek and Roman antiquity from the monastic libraries of Europe happened just early enough in the Renaissance to dramatically recast the image of the savage, just in time for the West's first encounters with distant tribal peoples in the New World. Once the American Indian was "discovered" by Europeans, the biblical Wild Man was forced to share the New World stage with the Noble Savage, revived as part of a new emphasis on Classical learning and scholarship in the West. Taking on all the conflicting stereotypes and images that Europeans had been using for thousands of years to imagine and represent their worst fears and nightmares and their highest and best hopes for humanity, the American Indian became the real-life embodiment of the idea of the savage in the Renaissance.

## THE RENAISSANCE HUMANISTS

The story of the West's recovery of the full scope of the Classical idea of the savage begins with a group of pious Christian scholars and Churchmen who helped to inaugurate the Italian Renaissance in the large trading metropolises of Florence, Venice, Milan, Genoa, Rome, and other independent and often warring city-states of the peninsula. Among the most famous and influential of this notable group of Renaissance Humanist scholars are Francisco Petrarcha, better known as Petrarch (1304–1374), Giovanni Boccaccio (1313–1375), and Poggio Bracciolini (1380–1459). Their extraordinary biographies tell us a good deal about the spirit and temper of the revolutionary movement that begins in Italy in the fourteenth century and that will come to define the intellectual culture of much of Christian Europe for the next several centuries.

These three leading figures of the Italian Renaissance were all ordained Catholic priests. They were also all very able and talented scholars, knowledgeable on most matters pertaining to Christian doctrine and faith. And all three became intimately familiar with a large number of pagan works and authors that had been suppressed by the Church during the "Dark Ages."

The "Dark Ages" was a term invented by Plutarch, perhaps the greatest and most widely accomplished of the Renaissance Humanists. He coined the term to characterize the preceding centuries of darkness dominated by the Church's ignorance and suppression of pagan literature and knowledge. Renaissance men like Petrarch, Boccaccio, and Poggio did not share in the Church's institutional fear of works by such pagan authors as Aristotle, Lucretius, and Ovid. They believed that their recoveries of the long-suppressed genius of Classical Antiquity, which had been hidden away by the Church, would effect a renewal of the true light of the faith throughout the universal Christian commonwealth—a renaissance of the true faith, as it were, for this still deeply religious and devout era in the history of the West.

Pious Christians and good scholars, they recognized that Christian civilization's knowledge of the world had suffered greatly during those dark, dismal ages for humanity. Their tireless searches throughout the monastic libraries of Europe for lost pagan works were driven by the belief that many of the ancient manuscripts had not been literally "lost" to the ages. They had been stored away, unread, unappreciated, and ignored for centuries, guarded by ignoramus monks and overzealous prelates. Petrarch, Boccaccio, Poggio, and other like-minded Renaissance Humanists felt completely justified in "recovering" these long-neglected and suppressed works for humanity. They were not pilfering pagan treasures from the Church; they simply were restoring those treasures to light after centuries of darkness.

In 1345, Petrarch discovered the letters written by Cicero to his friend Atticus, his brother Quintus, and Marcus Brutus, Caesar's assassin, supposedly "lost" for centuries. The discovery so moved Petrarch that he wrote a personal letter to Cicero: "I heard you saying many things, lamenting many things."[1] What he discovered was not the Cicero who had been viewed for centuries by Christian writers as simply a good talker and able translator of approved Greek texts into Latin. The Cicero in these letters was one of the great, underappreciated philosophers and political animals of ancient Rome. Cicero's calls for active engagement in the world according to our true, human social natures resonated deeply with Petrarch, who served as an advisor to princes in the tumultuous Italian city-state politics of his day.

Giovanni Boccaccio, the great Italian Humanist scholar and author of the *Decameron*, was a close friend of Petrarch. Like his comrade, he served as a priest in the Church. He was one of the Renaissance's greatest discoverers of lost classical texts. Whatever we have of Tacitus's invaluable corpus of historical works we owe to Boccaccio. Professor Peter Gay tells the story of how Boccaccio liberated the great Roman historical writer from the Benedictine library of Monte Casino for the good of humanity. During a visit to the library, he found the manuscripts "covered with dust, torn and mutilated." When he asked what had caused the damage, Boccaccio was told "that the monks would tear off strips of parchment, to be made into psalters for boys or amulets for women, just to make a little money."[2]

Despite his profound regret over the Church's treatment of such great literary treasures, Boccaccio, like Petrarch, remained a pious Catholic and true to the faith throughout his life. In his literary works, he sought to reconcile the noblest impulses of pagan antiquity with Christian Humanist thought and sentiments. His magnificent *Decameron,* one of the first great books in Western Europe penned in the vernacular (in Boccaccio's case, Italian), rails at vile monks and clerical corruption. In his influential retellings of Ovid's *Metamorphoses,* he explains away the eroticism of the poem as an allegory of the Trinity and the seven virtues.

Like Petrarch and Boccaccio, Poggio Bracciolini was a pious Catholic, serving in the Church hierarchy as apostolic secretary of the Council of Constance from 1414 to 1418. The Council involved itself in, among other politically and theologically charged issues of the day, the infamous case of the Teutonic Knights' holy wars of conquest and conversion against the pagan Lithuanians. The Council also was responsible for punishing various heresies infecting Catholic society in the turbulent decades leading up to the Protestant Reformation.

Poggio also was a dogged and highly successful discover of "lost" classical texts. The long interludes between conciliar sessions and travel attendant to his papal appointment gave Poggio plenty of time and the access he needed to visit monasteries and libraries throughout Europe. He copied or surreptitiously took away what he could, and once admitted to bribing a monk to abstract a text by the revered Roman historian Livy.

Following his trips to monastic libraries in Switzerland, southern Germany, and eastern France, Poggio would return to Italy laden with invaluable manuscripts and haunting memories of indescribable neglect. In 1415, Poggio discovered Cicero's *Pro Cluentio, Pro S. Roscio, Pro Murena, Pro Milone,* and *Pro Cælio* at the monastery in Cluny. Two years later, at Langres, France, he recovered a number of other lost works of Cicero, including *Pro Rabirio, Pro Roscio Comœdo,* and *In Pisonem.* At St. Gallen, a monastery situated on a steep, almost inaccessible slope in present-day Switzerland, Poggio found the first complete Quintilian, the incomparable Roman polymath and rhetorician.[3]

In embracing the great intellectual treasures of Classical Antiquity and literally running out the door with them, Poggio and his fellow Renaissance Humanists were not rejecting the Christian worldview or even any particular elements of Christian belief, knowledge, or power. These leading lights of the Italian Renaissance were a part of the Church hierarchy of educated elites and also respected scholars. They saw themselves as carrying out a special mission of reconciling Church teachings with Classical knowledge for the improvement of Christian society here on earth.

## RENAISSANCE HUMANISM AND THE RECOVERY OF THE FULL SCOPE OF THE CLASSICAL IDEA OF THE SAVAGE

The Legend of the Golden Age represented one of the Renaissance's most important recoveries from pagan literature. The Renaissance Humanists often turned to the legend in thinking about the problems of improving and spreading the true message of the Gospel and Christ on earth. They were particularly fond of reworking and adapting the ancient legend's cyclic theory of history and applying it to their own turbulent era of wars, famines, plague, and political unrest. Blessed by exciting new discoveries and the widespread revival of Classical learning, some Renaissance Humanists fancied that they too might be on the verge of a Golden Age for Christian civilization in the West.

Others were less optimistic, adopting a contrarian approach, brilliantly drawing on the anciently derived language of familiar stereotypes and iconic imagery associated with the Legend of the Golden Age for inspiration. They used the Classical language of noble savagery to imagine far-off locales free from the ills that plagued Christian society in their own day.

Some drew on pagan authors such as Lucretius, Plato, and Aristotle, writers who had opposed the Golden Age legend's idealized vision of primitive humanity's easy way of life, to celebrate the achievements of the Renaissance. They used the idea of the savage in new and novel ways to illustrate the brutish, nasty, and short life of humanity in the primitive state of nature in contrast to the unparalleled achievements and excellence of their own age.

The hopes, fears, and anxieties of the Renaissance Humanists for their troubled yet exciting times is poignantly captured by a 1517 letter written by the great Dutch scholar-priest Erasmus (1466–1536). The author of *In Praise of Folly* and compiler of the first printed Latin translation of the New Testament based on original Greek language manuscripts, Erasmus invokes the notion of a "golden age" to describe a world enlightened by the rediscoveries of antiquity but still guided by the true knowledge of Christ. He writes that "at the present moment I could almost wish to be young again, for no other reason but this, that I anticipate the near approach of a golden age."[4] But he reveals an anxious, depressing thought that possesses his mind about this possibility: "I am afraid that, under cover of a revival of ancient literature, paganism may attempt to rear its head—as there are some among Christians that acknowledge Christ in name but breathe inwardly a heathen spirit—or, on the other hand, that the restoration of Hebrew learning may give occasion to a revival of Judaism. This would be a plague as much opposed to the doctrine of Christ as anything that could happen."[5]

Such anxieties and pessimism were characteristic of Erasmus. Like many Renaissance Humanists, he could be downright gloomy at times, lamenting the failures of contemporary society to live up to his high Christian ideals: "Who being a good man indeed, does not see and lament this marvelous corrupt world? When was there ever more tyranny? When did avarice reign more largely and less punished? When did our iniquity so largely flow with more liberty? When was ever charity so cold?" Writing in the wake of the "disaster" for Christendom brought on by Martin Luther, whom he vigorously opposed, Erasmus lamented the "irremediable confusion of everything" engendered, in large part, by the intellectual forces released by the very Renaissance of ancient learning that he had helped to lead.[6]

For Erasmus and other Renaissance Humanists like him, the Classical conceit of a "golden age" captured all their "hopes and strivings," their "doubts and disillusionments," and their own self-awareness of the uniqueness and "irremediable confusion" of their times.[7] They used the Legend of the Golden Age just as the Greeks and Romans had used it: as a way of thinking and talking about their own civilization's virtues and vices. Some even cited the greatest ancient Roman poet of the Augustan Age, Virgil, who prophesied a "'new beginning of the great sequence of the ages,' the return of the maid Justice and the restoration of Saturn's reign."[8] They hoped, by their efforts, to restore the great traditions of learning and knowledge in Western civilization that had begun with the ancient Greeks and Romans. By going back to the Classical virtues of the Golden Age, they aspired to bring coherence and order out of the confusion of their own troubled and anxious times.

But, characteristic of the era, they found themselves at odds over exactly what the Golden Age and its virtues represented for their own time or whether the concept applied at all. Some used the term to imagine a peaceful and orderly society, ruled by devout princes, illuminated by a pure Christian faith and informed by the love of the classics—Utopia, in other words, a popular theme in the Renaissance, even before the Renaissance Humanist Thomas More imported the term from the Greeks.

Others, seeking to revive the spirit and life of early Christianity, saw in the simple and austere faith of the primitive Church a golden age they hoped to restore. Still others, looking to nature rather than to Classical reason or Christian faith, longed for an age of freedom from custom, convention, and law. In reviving the full scope of the Classical language of ennobled savagery embedded within the Legend of the Golden Age, the Renaissance Humanists restored complexity, nuance, subtlety, and, most important, life to a vital form of social critique and protest borrowed and adapted from the ancient Greeks and Romans. They found themselves connected to a powerful literary tradition, one that still resonates strongly within the storytelling modalities of contemporary Western civilization. Simply watch the film *Avatar* or *Dances with Wolves* for an Academy Award–winning rendition of one of the Western world's most familiar storylines, revived by the Renaissance Humanists.

The great French Humanist Rabelais (1494–1553) invoked the broad visionary utopian themes of the legend in describing the fictional Abbey of Théléme in his romance, *Gargantua*. The abbey's motto of "Do what you will" expressed the Renaissance Humanist's hope of creating a world where men might enjoy all good things. A renowned Greek scholar, Rabelais describes the residents of the abbey as living like the noble savages of the Golden Age, enjoying a carefree, happy, and virtuous life:

> All their life was spent not in laws, statutes, or rules, but according to their own free will and pleasure. They rose out of their beds when they thought good; they did eat, drink, labour, sleep, when they had a mind to it, and were disposed for it. None did awake them, none did offer to constrain them to eat, drink, nor to do any other thing; for so had Gargantua established it. In all their rule and strictest tie of their order, there was but this one clause to be observed:

> ## DO WHAT THOU WILT.

> Because men that are free, well-born, well-bred, and conversant in honest companies, have naturally an *instinct* and spur that prompteth them unto virtuous actions, and withdraws them from vice, which is called *honour.*[9]

The Renaissance Humanists adopted a variety of approaches to Ovid's *Metamorphoses* and its uninhibited celebration of the Golden Age as a simpler time of nobler human virtues and free sex. The poet Torquato Tasso (1544–1505) simply reworked Ovid's account into a mournful ode for the good old days:

> O lovely age of gold!
> Not that the rivers rolled
> With milk, or that the woods wept honeydew;
> Not that the ready ground
> Produced without a wound,
> Or the mild serpent had no tooth that slew.[10]

Reprising the essential elements of the Hesiodic tradition, Tasso described the Golden Age for humanity as being free from war and the "insolent ships" that brought it from afar. The only law that bound its souls, "nursed in freedom," was "that law of gold," written by Nature's own hand: "What pleases is permitted."[11]

The poem ends on a note of profound remorse for the progressive degradation of humankind:

We here, a lowly race,

Can live without thy grace,

After the use of mild antiquity.[12]

Some Renaissance Humanists refused to adopt the legend's pessimistic view of human history as a cycle of inevitable decline, turning to other Classical writers and texts to express their aspirations and hopes for their troubled age. A long line of influential Classical thinkers and writers, including Protagoras, Plato, Aristotle, and Cicero, had turned the legend on its head, so to speak, by using the idea of the savage to illustrate the deprived condition of humanity in a primitive state and the superiority of an expansion-minded, resource-consuming form of civilization. This Classically inspired version of the idea proved to be the perfect vehicle for Humanist writers who wanted to celebrate the excellence and potentiality of their own age.

Marsilio Ficino (1433–1499) was one of the most influential intellectual figures of the early Italian Renaissance. Author of the Renaissance's first translation of Plato's complete extant works into Latin, Ficino picked apart the Legend of the Golden Age and reconstructed it in Platonic fashion in order to celebrate the great achievements of his Florentine imperial city-state in advancing the cause of civilization. "What the poets once sang of the four ages, lead, iron, silver, and gold, our Plato in the *Republic* transferred to the four talents of men, assigning to some talents a certain leaden quality implanted in them by nature, to others iron, to others silver, and to still others gold."[13] From this reworking of the legend, Ficino derives a classificatory principle for human talents: "If then we are to call any age golden, it is beyond doubt that age which brings forth golden talents in different places." He then goes on to list the "illustrious discoveries" made just in contemporary Florence, which in Ficino's century alone "like a golden age, has restored to light the liberal arts, which were almost extinct: grammar, poetry, rhetoric, painting, sculpture, architecture, music, the ancient singing of songs to the Orphic lyre, and all this in Florence. Achieving what had been honoured among the ancients, but almost forgotten since, the age has joined wisdom with eloquence, and prudence with military art."[14]

The influence of Lucretius's "hard," dark-sided language of savagery to describe primitive humanity's way of life in *De Rerum Natura* inspired the works of several important Renaissance Humanists. Lucretius's relentless Epicurean-brand of humanism and his pagan creed of science over religion made his work a marked text throughout the Middle Ages. The poem had been "practically unknown for many centuries," apparently surviving the Christian millennium in a single manuscript, housed away at the monastery of St. Galen, where it was rediscovered by Poggio in 1417.[15]

Even then, *De Rerum Natura* was not printed until the latter part of the fifteenth century, many decades after its initial recovery. In an age when the Inquisition was still a meaningful and menacing institution in the lives of pious Christians, the good Renaissance Humanist had to maintain a safe distance from Lucretius's more infamous pagan heresies.

The poem, once it did became more widely circulated, exercised a profound effect on the Renaissance and would exercise an even more profound effect on the European Enlightenment centuries (roughly from the sixteenth to the eighteenth centuries). Many of the Humanist writers were attracted to Lucretius's pessimistic account of human regress and decline through the ages, feeling it an appropriate model for understanding the chaos and confusion of their own times.

One of the more extensive works employing the Lucretian-inspired cyclic theme of declining ages is by Loys Le Roy (1510–1577), a French scholar of comparative cultural history. Characteristic of the pessimism of many of the Renaissance Humanists, Le Roy's tract, titled *The Excellence of This Age*,[16] represents an extended Lucretian-styled meditation on the ultimately doomed and nothing-you-could-do-about-it fate of Western civilization.

Le Roy begins by praising "we here in the West," who for the last two hundred years had "recovered the excellence of good letters and brought back the study of the disciplines after they had long remained as if extinguished." He then goes right to the Legend of the Golden Age, appropriating it for his own celebratory purposes. He first praises the many learned men whose scholarly work "has led to such success that today this our age can be compared to the most learned times that ever were." Then follows an amazing catalog of the ancient knowledge restored by his age and the heroes who performed these great deeds for humanity. Great men like Petrarch and "his disciple" Boccaccio had opened up libraries that had long been closed and removed the dust and the filth from the ancient writers. Le Roy then dutifully lists nearly two dozen other notable figures of the Renaissance and an even longer list of the accomplishments of his age, which far exceeded those of antiquity in his opinion. "For the ancients scarcely understood half of the heavens, the earth and the sea."

After this extensive chronicle on the unparalleled rise and greatness of Christian civilization in the West that has led to the excellence of his own age, Le Roy suddenly launches into an extended Lucretian-styled meditation on that same civilization's inevitable pattern of decline. Having gone through "the vicissitude in all human affairs, arms, letters, languages, arts, states, laws and customs, and how they do not cease to rise and fall, growing better or worse alternately," Le Roy predicts what is to follow this Golden Age for "the West": "For if the memory and knowledge of the past serve as instruction to the present and warning to the future, it is to be feared that since they have now arrived at such great excellence, the power, wisdom, disciplines, books, industry, works, and knowledge of the world may in the future decline as they have done in the past and be destroyed; that the order and perfection of today will be succeeded by confusion, refinement by crudity, learning by ignorance, elegance by barbarism." Le Roy ends by evoking a grand apocalyptic finish to Western civilization, conjuring up hordes of barbarian invaders, "strange in form, colour and habits, pouring in upon Europe," likening them to the Huns, Vandals, and Saracens of old, who burned libraries and discarded "customs, laws, languages and religion."

He concludes on an even more pessimistic note with dire prophecies of not only wars but pestilence, famine, and earthquakes: "And I foresee the universe approaching its end through the one or other form of dislocation, carrying with it the confusion of all things and reducing them to their former state of chaos."

As Le Roy shows us, the Renaissance Humanists found in the ancient pagan Legend of the Golden Age a perfect vehicle to express all their anxieties, hopes, and fears about the turbulent state of Christian civilization in their own times. Some writers, however, saw the need to lighten things up a bit. One of the most memorable and beloved uses of the legend is found in the late Renaissance masterpiece *Don Quixote* by Miguel de Cervantes (1547–1616), regarded as the first great novel of Western civilization. After Don Quixote, our knight errant, has stuffed himself on the simple fare laid out on the sheepskins of a group of rustic goatherds, he waxes eloquent over—what else?—acorns:

> Happy the age and happy those centuries to which the ancients gave the name of golden, and not because gold, which is so esteemed in this iron age of ours, was then to be had without toil, but because those who lived in that time did not know the meaning of the worlds "thine" and "mine." In that blessed era all things were held in common, and to gain his daily sustenance no labour was required of any man save to reach forth his hand and take it from the sturdy oaks that stood literally inviting him with their sweet and seasoned fruit.[17]

Don Quixote drones on in this rapt manner, dreaming his impossible dream of the Golden Age in this Classical language of ennobled savagery. He reminisces about a time when clear-running waters quenched man's thirst and the bees provided free-flowing honey. All was peace and concord, the plow had never "pried into the merciful bowels of our first mother." Thoughts of love "were set forth as simply as the simple hearts that conceived them," "[j]ustice kept its own domain," and "[m]aidens in all their modesty . . . went where they would and unattended." This was the age—and here Don Quixote improvises on Ovid in his long speech to his shepherd hosts—"that the order of knights-errant was instituted, for the protection of damsels, the aid of widows and orphans, and the succouring of the needy."

While our hero literally constructs his mission in life out of the Legend of the Golden Age, the narrator of this humorous tale, Sancho Panza, tells us his impressions of this absurd scene: "This long harangue on the part of our knight—it might very well have been dispensed with—was all due to the acorns they had given him, which had brought back to memory the age of gold." The goatherds had listened in "open-mouthed wonderment, saying not a word," and Sancho had been wise enough to keep quiet, munching his acorns and paying a visit "to the second wine bag, which they had suspended from a cork tree to keep it cool."

## THE INVASION OF THE CANARIES

The Renaissance Humanists' full-scale revival of the Legend of the Golden Age and other celebratory themes and concerns connected to the Classical idea of the savage helped to engender new and novel ways of looking at the world throughout Christian Europe. But still, as we have seen, the Christian system of thought as handed down from the Middle Ages continued to play a vital, defining role in the way that the pagan works of Classical Antiquity were interpreted and used by Europeans of the Renaissance.

As the historian Ronald Sanders notes, the Renaissance may have been more secular than the age of the Crusades before it, due in large part to its Humanist influences and the revival of Classical learning and knowledge. But the age of the Protestant and the Catholic Reformations was also one of the most intensely religious in the history of Western civilization.[18] This religious impulse and the recovery of the full scope of the Classical idea of the savage are both clearly reflected in the way that non-Christian pagan peoples are habitually described by Christian Europeans on their voyages of discovery, colonization, and conquest throughout the Renaissance. The use of a language of savagery to justify holy wars against pagan tribes outside Europe in the Renaissance begins with Portugal's efforts to colonize the Canary Islands off the coast of Africa in the fourteenth century.

As Professor Immanuel Wallerstein explains, Portugal was ideally suited to launch this new era of European overseas territorial expansion. Perched on the Atlantic maritime frontier, Portugal's Reconquista against the Moors on the Iberian peninsula had followed the same basic pattern of territorial expansion that characterized the history of Christian European colonization on much of the continent up until that time.[19]

Throughout the Middle Ages, Christian European monarchs and warlords, feeling the pressures of population and the need for new lands to settle, invaded nearby lands of pagan tribal peoples inside Europe or those of infidel followers of the prophet Muhammad in the Near East whenever they felt they needed to or could get away with it. They justified their marauding activities as holy wars against pagan and infidel savages, designed to extend the boundaries of the true Christian faith.

Once the crusading Christian monarchs of Portugal had succeeded in expelling the Moors from the country's western perch on the Iberian Peninsula, they had nowhere else to go, at least within continental Europe. Neighboring Christian monarchs in Aragon and Castile stood as formidable obstacles to further colonial expansion on the peninsula. So, the Portuguese looked westward, out into the vast Atlantic Ocean, and decided to invade the Canary Islands off the coast of Africa.

They would take some Italians along with them on their maiden Renaissance voyage of overseas discovery and conquest of non-European tribal peoples. Driven out of the Holy Lands by the Seljuk Turks following the collapse of the crusading movement in the thirteenth century, many of the Italians involved in the maritime trade of the Levant picked up stakes and their boats and moved to Portugal. The crown in Lisbon, hemmed in on all sides but one, welcomed them with open arms and privileges, seeking to utilize their unique skill set as overseas colonizers and suppressors of any local pagan resistance fighters to start building up its own overseas empire.

The tiny group of islands in the Atlantic off the northwestern coast of Africa was perched on the near horizons of European civilization. Throughout the Middle Ages, the Canaries often were associated with the mythical Fortunate Islands of the Greeks and Romans. So perhaps it is unsurprising that Giovanni Boccaccio, the same Renaissance Humanist who was so inspired by Ovid's *Metamorphoses*, drew on the Legend of the Golden Age to describe the primitive but peaceful peoples of the Canaries in his account of the Portuguese and Italian military joint venture to conquer the islands in 1341. Although Boccaccio apparently did not go on the trip himself, his work has left us with a vivid portrait of the expedition and the Canarians. It is one of the earliest Renaissance uses of the stereotypes and categorical markers associated with the Classical idea of the savage applied to African tribal peoples.

Two ships left Lisbon on July 1, 1341, with "horses, arms, and warlike engines for storming towns and castles, in search of those islands commonly called the 'Rediscovered.'"[20] The heavy military armaments were not uncharacteristic for the times, particularly considering Portugal's recent history in the Reconquista against the Moors. Its relations up to that point with non-Christian societies outside Europe had not been very amicable. The custom of the times was to go heavily armed into infidel-held territory, particularly if one intended to stay a while.

As the historian Ferdinand Braudel notes, horses, arms, and warlike engines were normal parts of the invasionary apparatus of Renaissance-era armies. Artillery and firearms radically transformed the nature of warfare and economic life in Europe during this period. Warfare became enormously expensive; now only the wealthiest monarchies and prosperous city-states could bear the cost of carrying on an extended campaign of conquest and occupation. In 1588, Spain used the profits from its New World empire to launch an armada of more than one hundred ships against England. The huge military force carried 2,471 cannons, 7,000 arquebuses, 1,000 muskets, enough gunpowder for 123,790 bullets and shot, and a huge army of sailors and soldiers to feed.[21]

The arms race on the European continent helps explain the outward, seaborne trajectory of European colonization activities during the Renaissance as well. As the price of warfare with their neighbors skyrocketed, European states sought to maximize their technological advantages in those parts of the world where artillery and heavy armaments had not yet been introduced or invented.

The Canaries were just such a place. The first natives to be discovered, as described by Boccaccio, lived on an island populated by goats (much like the island discovered off the Cyclopean coast in Homer's *Odyssey*). He describes the natives as a race of "naked men and women, who were like savages in their appearance and demeanor."[22]

Boccaccio's account of the next island, most likely the Grand Canary, describes an encounter with "a great number of natives of both sexes, all nearly naked." A few "were covered with goats' skins." On one island, the expedition came upon a crude "chapel or temple." One of the pagans' idols was formed of stone into a statute of a man, "otherwise naked" except for an apron of palm leaves, holding a ball. The statue, Boccaccio reports, was carried back to Lisbon, along with four of the Canarians.[23]

Boccaccio's detailed and vivid description of the natives brought home as prize specimens from the reconnaissance voyage suggests that he had seen them himself. The men were barefoot and wore nothing but "a sort of apron made of cord, from which they hung a number of palm or reed fibers of one and a half or two hairs' breadth." Married women wore aprons like the men, "but the maidens went quite naked, without consciousness of shame."[24]

Although unable to converse in the several languages spoken to them, Boccaccio tells us the Canarians could decipher hand signs. Overall, they were "gay and merry" and "very intelligent." They "sang sweetly" and danced "almost as well as Frenchmen." He takes a swipe at Portugal's neighbor and colonial competitor on the Iberian peninsula in commenting that the Canarians are "much more civilized than many Spaniards." Intelligent, with fine singing voices, their young women going around naked in all their fine bodily glory, everyone gay and merry as can be, dancing like the French, and much smarter than your average Spaniard, the Canarians were everything an Italian Renaissance Humanist could desire to see in the flesh: a noble savage living as if in the Golden Age, as told by the ancient poets.[25]

Boccaccio freely draws from the legend's themes of noble savagery as his template for describing the Canarians. "Wheat and barley they ate in plenty, as well as cheese and meat, which was abundant in the islands, and of good quality." They lived in simplicity, with no beasts of burden submitted to their will. While there were no oxen, camels, or asses to be found on the islands, there were "plenty of goats, sheep and wild hogs." The Canarians cared not for property, knowing nothing of gold and silver money. They were also unaware of the luxuries taken for granted by European civilization. They did not even spice their food. "Rings of gold and vases of carved work, swords and sabers, were shown to them, but they seemed never to have seen such things and did not know how to use them." Their moral code, or what could be determined of it, proved them to be far more virtuous than most Christian Europeans: "They showed remarkable faithfulness and honesty, for if one of them received anything good to eat, before tasting it, he divided it into portions which he shared with the rest."[26]

According to Sanders, Boccaccio's lively and detailed account of the primitive Canarians serves as the introductory text in the Renaissance Humanist literature of European overseas discovery, importing a familiar host of Classical themes, devices, and imagery.[27] This act of literary borrowing from the ancients by the renowned Renaissance Humanist, however, could not have happened at a worse time for the Canarians, historically speaking. Under Pope Innocent IV's thirteenth-century theory of infidel rights under the Christian system of natural law, casting these pagan peoples as noble savages meant that, for their own protection and salvation, they could be lawfully conquered, colonized, and converted by Christian princes acting on the authority of the pope.

## THE PAPALLY DECLARED HOLY WAR
## ON THE CANARY ISLANDS

The 1341 Portuguese colonizing expedition to the Canaries provided a basis for Portugal's claims to the islands in the next century in the first legal dispute of the Renaissance Discovery era between two European colonizing nations over who had the rights to conquer, colonize, and convert these happy-go-lucky pagan savages to Christianity. The conflicting desires of Spain to control the islands led to violent attacks on the Canarians, some of whom had been converted to the faith by Church-sponsored missionaries.

Upon hearing of the attacks on the natives, Pope Eugenius IV (r. 1431–1447), acting on his asserted universal jurisdiction as affirmed by Innocent IV over the endangered pagan souls and bodies of the Canarians, issued a series of papal bulls. Both Portugal and Spain were banned from entering the Canaries on pain of excommunication.

This action upset King Duarte (r. 1433–1438), Portugal's reigning monarch. He appealed the ban in 1436 with a document undoubtedly drafted by the crown's canonistically trained legal staff, who were fully aware of all the ins and outs of Church doctrine on the rights of infidels under natural law. Duarte's lawyers specifically appealed to the papacy to lift the ban on Lisbon so that the king could continue his righteous conquest of the Canaries on behalf of Christianity. Not surprisingly, the king's legal brief in this novel case relied heavily on the natural law approach to infidel rights and status of the famous canon lawyer-pope, Innocent IV.

Importantly, Innocent's position on those rights had been affirmed less than two decades earlier by the Council of Constance (1414–1418) in the case between Poland and the Teutonic Knights, one of the most infamous crusading priestly orders of the Middle Ages. Their constitution was modeled along the lines of other famous crusading orders, such as the Knights Templar. With the ouster of the crusading orders in the Levantine regions in the early thirteenth century, the Knights relocated to Germany and began to utilize their colonizing skills against their pagan neighbors. They acquired an extensive empire in central Europe, sanctioned by the papacy through holy wars of Christian conquest and forced conversion of nonbelievers bordering their territory.

The Constance Council had rejected the Knights' claims to wage a holy war on Christian Poland and pagan Lithuania for being insufficiently Christianized and had expressly affirmed Innocent IV's position that even pagan savages like the Lithuanians held natural law rights to territory and property. According to the Council, the Lithuanians' property and lordship could be taken away by Christian princes only for violations of natural law, on orders from the pope; the Knights had not met their burden of proof on that all-important legal issue pertinent to their case.

All of this helps to explain why Duarte's lawyers were so precise and careful in detailing how the Canarians were literally "wild" men, living as brute savages who required Christian guidance and remediation through the hands of papally authorized Christian princes committed to extending the faith to all the sheep of Christ's universal flock. They were, according to the king,

> not united by a common religion, nor are they bound by the chains of law, they are lacking normal social intercourse, living in the country like animals. They have no contact with each other by sea, no writing, no kind of metal or money. They have no houses and no clothing except for coverlets of palm leaves or goat skins which are worn as an outer garment by the most honored men. They run barefoot quickly through the rough, rocky and steep mountainous regions, hiding . . . in caves hidden in the ground.

As explained by the king's lawyers, according to Innocent's theory of infidel rights and obligations under Church law, because the Canarians were violating natural law—"living in the country like animals," for instance—the pope had to take quick remedial action by placing them under the benevolent care and control of the Christian king of Portugal.[28]

To add further emphasis to his pleas on their behalf, Duarte contrasted these wild Canarians, who lived a savage life under no form of law, government, or religion, with the natives who had been converted by the Portuguese. They were now loyal subjects of the Christian king, who had provided them with "civil laws and an organized form of society. . . . Where the name of Christ had never been known, Christ is now worshiped."[29]

In response to Duarte's carefully framed appeal, the pope issued the bull *Romanus Pontifex,* a legal edict modeled after the crusading bulls of the Middle Ages. Per form, the bull was made binding on all Christian monarchs and enforced by the Church's penalty of excommunication, which still meant something in those pre-Protestant Reformation days. By this and a series of subsequent confirming bulls, the pope granted Portugal exclusive rights to colonize not only the Canaries but all other parts of Africa, using the Christian Humanist idea of the savage to justify this extraordinary grant of territorial title and rights to a European sovereign:

> The Roman Pontiff, successor to the bearer of the keys of the heavenly kingdom and Vicar of Jesus Christ, looking with paternal interest upon all the regions of the world and the specific natures of all the peoples who dwell in them, seeking and desiring the salvation of every one of them, wholesomely orders and arranges with careful consideration those things which he perceives will be pleasing to the Divine Majesty and by which he may bring the sheep divinely committed to him into the one fold of the Lord, and may acquire for them the reward of eternal happiness, and may obtain pardon for their souls.[30]

Thus, the Christian Humanist language of savagery utilized in *Romanus Pontifex* gave Lisbon a monopoly over Christian colonization of the African continent and the inside position in the African slave trade that it would use to its advantage throughout the Renaissance Discovery era.

But the pope's use of the idea of the savage in justifying the conquest, colonization, and conversion of the Canarians set down a highly favorable precedent for other European Christian monarchs to follow. *Romanus Pontifex* meant that Spain would have to avoid Africa and sail westward out into the Atlantic Ocean in search of lands not occupied by any other

Christian people. The stereotypes and identifying markers that Europeans had used since the time of the ancient Greeks and Romans to describe those peoples it regarded as savages would now most assuredly be used wherever Christian Europeans went in search of distant lands occupied by strange and alien-seeming peoples. The idea of the savage had become integral to Western civilization's understanding of its legal reasons and justifications for conquering, colonizing, and converting pagan tribal peoples wherever they were encountered in the world.

# TEN

# THE RENAISSANCE DISCOVERY ERA AND THE IDEA OF THE SAVAGE

## COLUMBUS AND THE IDEA OF THE SAVAGE

Spain was forced to look farther westward now that the pope had given all of Africa to Portugal, its Iberian rival. In 1492, Ferdinand and Isabella took up the offer of an Italian navigator named Christopher Columbus to discover distant lands occupied by pagan tribes of savages and claim them on behalf of the Spanish Crown.

The Genoan sailor had approached the Spanish monarchs earlier with his proposed westerly directed "Enterprise of the Indies." After a junta of priests and theologians approved the plan, Columbus received royal backing and support for three ships to sail westward to the Indies, avoiding Portugal's African monopoly to the south. His intent was to discover lands unoccupied by other Christian princes and develop them into prosperous colonies, potential trading posts, and, most important, gold and other mining operations at a later time.[1]

We know from his own journals and personal library that Columbus was familiar with a number of Classical sources, medieval maps, Renaissance encyclopedias, and the typical Italian navigator's knowledge of the geography and peoples of Europe and limited parts of Asia and Africa. Beyond that, he was also familiar with the popular myths, legends, and travelers' tales about the edges of the world that traced back to the ancient Greeks and Romans.

Columbus's own belief in the possibility of a shorter westward sea route to the East Indies was supported by his reading of Aristotle's reported statement that the Atlantic could be crossed in just a few days. He also was fond of quoting the prophecy of the Roman Stoic poet Seneca in *Medea:* "An age will come after many years when the ocean will loose the chains of things, and a huge land will be revealed." Add all this to the prophecy contained in Psalms 22:8 that the Savior "shall have dominion also from sea to sea, and from the river into the ends of the earth," and you can begin to get a sense of the types of pagan, Christian, and heterodox sources of inspiration that helped to propel Columbus's westward trek across the uncharted reaches of the Atlantic.[2]

Pierre d'Ailly's great Renaissance Humanist-inspired work, *Imago Mundi* (World Images), was one important source of travel information for Columbus on what might lie to the west. Ailly's work, with Columbus's annotations, was part of Columbus's own library. Ailly (1350–1420) was a French cardinal well known and admired in the Catholic Church for his prominent role in the reforms debated at the Council of Constance. Like all the great Renaissance Humanists, the scholarly Ailly had absorbed a broad range of Classical literature and ideas connected to the idea of the savage, along with the usual medieval legends, folklore, and travelers' tales. A good deal of this knowledge is laid out in splendid detail in *Imago Mundi.* His account of the fierce tribal primitives and monsters in the far-off lands of the frigid North and tropical South of the westernmost parts of the northern hemisphere is typical of his method and style throughout his book. The inhabitants of these locales, he writes, are "savage men who eat human flesh and have depraved and frightening faces. . . . [T]hey are base in manner and savage in speech, and there are men or beasts in these places who present such a dreadful aspect, that one can tell only with difficulty whether they are men or beasts."[3]

Columbus was clearly influenced by the anciently derived legends and myths Ailly had collected that told of distant places where humans could enjoy a Golden Age–type existence. According to Ailly, the description of

the blissful climate said to exist in certain distant regions of the West suggests that the "terrestrial paradise is like this and perhaps even the place
which authors call the Fortunate Islands is like this." Columbus entered his
own note at this point in the text: "Terrestrial paradise perhaps is the place
which authors call the Fortunate Islands."[4]

Another source familiar to Columbus, *The Travels of Sir John Mandeville*,
related the existence of dog-headed human creatures, some with a single eye
in the middle of their foreheads, others with no heads and eyes in their
shoulders, and still others with flat faces with no nose or mouth. According
to this popular and widely translated mid-fourteenth-century work, all of
these creatures were to be found in the vicinity of Java, which Columbus
would have been delighted to come upon during his journey. Columbus
inscribed the vivid impressions left by such accounts of fierce, monstrous
savages on the edges of the earth in a journal entry dated April 11, 1492.
He writes that he expects to find "men with one eye, and others with dogs'
heads" on his journey to the Indies. He also jots down rather casually that
he saw "three mermaids who rose very high from the sea" and makes note of
a province to the west called Avan, where "the people are born with tails."[5]

Columbus's own language in describing the peoples of the islands he
discovered on his first voyage to the New World in 1492 is quite similar in
tone and emphases to that used by Boccaccio in his Classically inspired account of the peaceful, primitive natives of the Canaries. It is the language
of savagery developed by Europeans over the course of their colonial encounters with tribal peoples dating back to the ancient Greeks. Believing he
has discovered his conjectured shorter sea route to the Indies, he naturally
calls the first people he encounters *los Indios*—Indians—and claims their
island for the Spanish Crown. As Professor Robert Berkhofer, Jr., explains,
"Regardless of whether Columbus thought he had landed among the East
Indies or among islands near Japan or even elsewhere near the Asian continent, he would probably have used the same all-embracing term for the natives, because *India* stood as a synonym for all of Asia east of the river Indus
at the time and *Indies* was the broadest designation available for all the area
he claimed under royal patent."[6]

Columbus paints a vivid picture of a Golden Age–type existence among
the Indians he encounters on his voyage by running through all the familiar

categories and stereotypes of the noble savage derived from the Classical poets. They "gave as they received," Columbus wrote in his journal, "with the utmost pleasure." They were "very poor in every respect," go about "naked as when their mothers bore them," and were "well formed" with handsome bodies and faces.[7] "They are the best people in the world and the most peaceable." They are "so good-hearted" that he does not believe that "there are better men any more than these are better lands." "For anything at all we give them, without ever saying it is too little, they immediately give whatever they possess."[8]

These good Indians are noble savages in the fullest Classical sense; they lack in "artifice" and are "generous" to a fault. "I could not learn if they possess private property, but I seemed to discern that all owned a share of what one of them owned, and particularly with regard to victuals."[9] Columbus's description of their primitive material culture and pacifist natures strongly echoes the Classical language of noble savagery: "They do not carry arms or even know what they are; we showed them swords and they grabbed them by the blades and cut themselves in their ignorance. They do not have any iron; their spears are wooden sticks without iron, some of them having a fish's tooth at the tip, or other things of that sort."[10]

Columbus had been lucky to run into these noble savages first on his misdirected enterprise to the Indies. Cooperative and good-natured, they warned him about some cannibals on the north coast of present-day Cuba: "men with one eye, and others with dogs' noses, who ate men, and that when they took a man, they cut off his head and drank his blood and castrated him."[11]

Collecting other tales along the way, Columbus hears more dark-sided accounts of fierce savage peoples. He even hears of an island of women warriors who live like the Amazons, alone, without need of men.

Columbus was able to confirm these reports of wild men and women who ate human flesh on his second voyage to the New World. One of his reconnaissance boats landed on the island of Guadeloupe on November 4, 1493, where a half-dozen bones or so of human origin were found in a deserted village. "On seeing these," wrote Dr. Alvarez Chanca of Seville, one of the physicians on the expedition, "we suspected that we were amongst the Caribbee islands."[12] A group of women who had been held by the Caribs as forced concubines told of cannibals that "use them with such cruelty as would scarcely be believed." They ate their men as prisoners and then the children they bore their cruel masters. "When they capture little boys" in their raids on other islands, "they dismember them, and make use of them until they grow up to manhood, and then when they wish to make a feast they kill and eat them."[13]

The most significant consequence of all the conflicted, ambiguous stereotypes, images, and identifying markers from the language of savagery used by Columbus to describe these Indians was that these primitive, naked savages appeared to live without laws, religion, or government. They therefore were in violation of natural law, according to Church teachings and dogma. Under the law of the Church on infidel and pagan rights, as savages, they could be conquered and colonized for violations of natural law and ease of their conversion to the Christian faith by Spain.

Columbus confidently informs the Spanish crown that the peaceful Indians he has discovered can be encouraged to "adopt our customs and our faith." They are also inclined "to be made to build cities, to be taught to wear clothes, and to adopt our customs."[14] They have no real religion, "but they all believe that power and good are in the heavens and were firmly convinced that I, with these ships and men, came from the heavens, and in this belief they everywhere received me after they had mastered their fear."[15] As for the Indians who are cannibals, he is certain that even they could be saved if they could just hear the word of God brought to them by Spanish missionaries and preachers. Of course, he notes, these bad man-eating Indians would need to be made slaves first, "under the care of the most competent persons to teach them the language, giving instructions, at the same time, that they may be employed in useful occupations; and that by degrees more care be bestowed upon them than would be given to other slaves."[16]

On the basis of an appeal to Pope Alexander VI (who in 1492 just happened to be the Spaniard, Rodrigo Borgia) by the Spanish crown containing Columbus's account of the distant tribal peoples he had discovered, Spain received a grant to colonize what would turn out to be most of the New World, under the same basic terms that Portugal had received for Africa. The Indians of the New World were savages, but as human beings blessed with a soul and possessing rational capacity, under principles of Christian natural law, were capable of receiving the word of God. They therefore had been entrusted by the pope's authority over all the sheep of Christ's universal flock to the care and direction of the Spanish crown. By this papal grant of extreme privilege, the Indians of the New World became the embodiment of the idea of the savage in the Renaissance Discovery era, endowed by God with natural rights, and subject to conquest, colonization, and conversion for violating a higher law enforced by the warrior-heroes of a superior form of civilization—in this case, Conquistadores from Christian Spain.

## THE IDEA OF THE SAVAGE AND THE RENAISSANCE DISCOVERY– ERA TRAVEL LITERATURE

The first European impressions of the peoples of the New World, called Indians by Columbus, come from the early chroniclers of his voyages and those of other European travelers to different parts of the New World and beyond. It is impossible to canvass this huge corpus of literature, illustrated maps, drawings, engravings, and other media that all worked to reinforce the stereotypes and images of primitive savagery that Columbus had first used to describe the Indians. The most popular and influential of these works, however, suggest the quick penetration, wide diffusion, and unquestioning acceptance of a Classically inspired language of savagery to describe the Indians of the New World in the early decades of Europe's Renaissance Discovery era.

Peter Martyr of Anghera was an Italian historian who chronicled the first accounts of European explorations in Central and South America, including Columbus's expeditions. He was the first European writer to call the lands discovered by Columbus the "New World." Born in 1457 near Anghera, Italy, Martyr had received a well-rounded, Classical education at one of the celebrated Humanist academies of the day in Rome.

Martyr follows Boccaccio and Columbus in freely drawing on a Classically derived language of noble savagery associated with the Legend of the Golden Age to describe the Indians' desperate need and potential for conversion to the Christian faith. "And surely if they had received our religion," Martyr writes, they would be the "most happy of all men."

A few things content them, having no delight in such superfluities, for the which in other places men take infinite pains and commit many unlawful acts, and yet are never satisfied, whereas many have too much, and none enough. But among these simple souls, a few clothes serve the naked: weights and measures are not needful to such as know not skill or craft and deceit and have not the use of pestiferous money, the seed of innumerable mischiefs. So that if we shall not be ashamed to confess the truth, they seem to live in that golden world of which old writers speak so much: wherein men lived simply and innocently without enforcement of laws, without quarreling judges and libels, content only to satisfy nature, without further vexation for knowledge of things to come.[17]

Martyr's stereotype of the Indians of the New World as fully formed examples of human savagery in its primitive state and in dire need of conversion and civilizing influences is echoed throughout the early travel literature of the Renaissance Discovery era. A Dutch pamphlet published in English in the early sixteenth century stated authoritatively that the Indians of the New World have "no king or lord nor their god[.] But all things is commune/the people goeth all naked. . . . These folk live like beasts." Cannibalism, the most extreme form of human savagery, was portrayed as being pervasive among the New World's tribal peoples: "[T]hey eat also one another[.] The man eateth his wife[,] his children/as we also have seen and they hang also the bodies of persons flesh in the smoke."[18]

Publication on the new printing presses of Europe of Americo Vespucci's influential accounts of his five voyages of discovery on behalf of both Spain and Portugal between 1497 and 1504 did much to add fuel and fire to these early reports of the New World as full of flesh-eating, barbarous savages with no laws, manners, or civilized religion. According to Vespucci's authoritative-sounding first-person narrative of his voyages, the natives of the New World lived for hundreds of years (like those long-lived noble savages of ancient legend) and cured themselves with roots and herbs. They also engaged in constant warfare.

Typical of the Italians, Vespucci took note of their few good points, which he framed in a familiar Classical language of ennobled savagery. Unlike greedy Europeans, they did not seek to enlarge their dominions or yearn "for the increase of riches, because they are content with their own commodities." "As for gold," Vespucci reported, "pearls, precious stones, jewels, and such other things which we in Europe esteem as pleasure and delicates, they set naught by."[19]

Such widely read and disseminated accounts suggest some of the ways the Indian could be whatever type of savage the Christian European of the Renaissance Discovery era might want him or her to be. It really did not matter in the end; all these accounts agreed on one essential fact: The Indians of the New World were stereotypical savages, which meant that Christian Europeans could conquer and colonize them for their violations of natural law, as authorized by the pope in Rome.

Even in the famous debate between Bartholomew de Las Casas and Juan Ginés de Sepúlveda at Valladolid in 1550 on the question of the Spanish crown's rights to rule over the Indians of the New World, the two disputants were in agreement on this one essential fact: The Indians of the New World were savages, as defined by Classical *and* Church authorities, and therefore subject to Christian control.

Sepúlveda was a learned authority on Aristotle and on the Christian theory of just wars. He had been asked to make a statement before a council called by the Spanish emperor, Charles, to consider whether the Spaniards' wars against the Indians were just. Sepúlveda asserted in the strongest terms that the wars indeed were just, basing his argument on the Aristotelian notion that certain men (such as savages and barbarians) were by nature slaves. Sepúlveda, who had never been to the Indies, argued that the law of nature, represented by the *ius gentium* (law of nations), was honored and understood only among the wisest and most prudent of the higher races. The Indians, being savages, did not live by the law of nature, and thus they were by nature slaves. They therefore could be justly conquered by Spain and made to serve as slaves for their own good, the good of the crown, and the good of the Church.

That seemed like a winning argument to many Spaniards in the New World. Las Casas, who had been there and had witnessed firsthand the inhumane treatment of the Indians by the Conquistadores and their enslavement in the name of the crown in the mines and sugarcane fields, took the opposing side. He countered with the Dominican Humanist–inspired argument that started with the Indians' rational capacity as human beings, though savage, to apprehend the Gospel. Of this, Las Casas had firsthand experience through his extensive missionary work in the Indies, after he had renounced his former life as an Indian slave owner himself.

Las Casas won the debate. The pope issued a bull that backed his position on Indian rights under natural law and the law of the Church. But in the end, for the Indians, it did not matter. The colonizing form of civilization that invaded the New World had defined them as the embodiment of the idea of the savage, and therefore fit subjects for conquest and conversion by Christian princes, as authorized by the Papacy in Rome.

## THE ENGLISH PROTESTANT REFORMATION AND IDEA OF THE SAVAGE

Compared to Catholic Spain, Protestant England followed a much different path of colonial growth and development in the New World, as did English Protestantism's use of the idea of the savage. The basic language of Classically derived stereotypes and clichéd images used to describe the American Indians as savage peoples starts out much the same as in Spain. Henry Cabot's late-fifteenth-century discoveries on behalf of Henry VII in North America had generated a buzz in England with reports of brutish, primitive peoples. Real-life specimens had been brought back to prove those claims. The stereotyping of the North American "savages"—the favored term used by the English (derived from the old Norman French *salvage,* meaning "wild, savage, untamed," originally from the Latin *salvaticus,* literally meaning "of the woods," from *silva,* "forest, grove")—throughout the Renaissance and Enlightenment eras flourished from that point onward in the English travel literature.

Martin Frobisher, one of the early English discoverers to search for the Northwest Passage to Asia by attempting to sail through the cold, uncharted northern waters of North America, reported that the savages he encountered were primitive brutes; they plucked up grass for food, "not daintily." They ate their food "without either salt, oils, or washing." They were like "brute beasts" devouring their rough fare without benefit of a "table, stool, or table cloth for comeliness." They even used their tongues to lick their knives clean.[20] Other early travelers' accounts described how the Indians "live in Caves of the earth, and hunt for their dinners or prey, even as the bear or other wild beasts do," daring to do "anything that their consciences will allow, or courage of man may execute."[21] They are, in other words, your basic stereotypical savages.

The sixteenth-century Protestant Reformation in England had only minor effects on the way Englishman used the idea of the savage, as can be sensed in reading Christopher Carleill's 1583 pamphlet, "A Brief and Summary Discourse upon the Intended Voyage to the Furthermost Parts of America." Carleill argues for English colonization of the New World by appealing to "Christian Charity," which "doth as greatly persuade the furtherance of this action, as any other that may be had before us, in as much as thereby we shall do . . . a most excellent work in respect of reducing the savage people to Christianity and civility."[22]

In religious terms, the only thing English Protestantism changed with regard to the indigenous peoples of North America was that the English crown, denominated as head of the English Protestant Church, took on the responsibilities of authorizing the conquest and conversion of savages for a competing brand of Christianity. The younger Richard Hakluyt, a close associate of the vigorously Protestant Sir Walter Raleigh, wrote an influential treatise that Raleigh presented to Queen Elizabeth in 1584. It was pointedly titled "A Discourse of Western Planting" and argued strongly for the Virgin Queen's support of Raleigh's Roanoke colony in North America. Hakluyt cited as one of the principal benefits of the enterprise the planting of the seeds of faith and civility among the country's "simple people." The English would lead these poor savages out of "error" and into the "right and perfect way of their salvation."[23]

The 1606 patent issued to the Virginia Company by King James continued this practice of deploying a Protestantized language of savagery to defend the English crown's authority to conquer, colonize, and convert the indigenous tribal peoples of North America. Raleigh had been unable to maintain a colony at Roanoke, so his rights granted by Elizabeth were now controlled by King James. James's historic grant, establishing the first permanent English colony in North America, specifically cited the Virginia Company's earnest desire to plant colonies that would spread the true Christian faith of the Church of England to the savages of the New World. The "propagating of *Christian* religion to such people, as yet live in darkness, and miserable ignorance of the true knowledge and worship of God," the king's patent declared, "may in time bring the infidels and savages living in those parts, to human civility and to a settled and quiet government."[24]

## ENGLISH PROTESTANTISM AND
## THE CRUSADING TRADITION

There were other slight differences between the language of savagery used by Catholic Spain and that developed by English Protestants in their respective conquests of pagan and infidel lands in the New World during the Renaissance Discovery era. Sir Edward Coke's famous opinion as Chief Justice for the Court of the King's Bench in *Calvin's Case* (1608) suggests a more thorough absorption of the medieval Christian crusading tradition and its highly negative views on pagan and infidel rights into England's common law tradition. Infidels, Coke stated in his famous *dicta* in the case, were regarded at law as perpetual enemies (*perpetui inimici*) of a Christian kingdom. Thus, they had no rights under English common law: "But a perpetual enemy (though there be no wars by fire and sword between them) cannot maintain any action, or get anything within this realm. All infidels are in law *perpetui inimici*, perpetual enemies, (for the law presumes not that they will be converted, that being *remota potentia*, a remote possibility), for between them, as with devils, whose subjects they be, and the Christian, there is perpetual hostility, and can be no peace."[25]

Coke went on to discuss the consequences of a Christian king's conquest of an infidel kingdom. Once that kingdom is brought under subjection by the king, "there *ipso facto* the laws of the infidel are abrogated, for that they be not only against Christianity, but against the law of God and of nature, contained in the decalogue [the Ten Commandments]." Upon conquest, therefore, the king, according to the highly influential legal authority of Chief Justice Coke, must establish laws among the infidel "and judge their causes according to natural equity." In other words, the king could do whatever he thought was just in his treatment of the infidels under the Christian law of conquest in holy war.

Coke's assertion of the king's absolute prerogative powers in infidel territories acquired by conquest essentially adopted the medieval Catholic

Church's crusading-era idea of the unredeemable savage and Protestantized it. Without any of the Christian Humanist flourishes by which Pope Innocent IV had recognized the natural law rights of non-Christian peoples, Coke vested the power to enforce a higher law of a superior civilization over pagan savages in the head of the English Church, who also happened to be the English king.

In the Enlightenment Age of the eighteenth century, Lord Mansfield, in another celebrated case in the English common law tradition, *Campbell v. Hall*,[26] would reject Coke's position on infidel rights in *Calvin's Case*. Lord Mansfield called it a piece of the "mad enthusiasm" for the crusades. But if Coke was mad when he wrote his opinion in *Calvin's Case*, so were other prominent jurists, philosophers, and legal thinkers of the English Protestant Reformation. They uniformly relied on the idea of the savage to justify the king's rights of conquest over infidel pagans who violated "the law of God and of nature" or any other English notions of a higher law.

The influential Italian Protestant exile Alberico Gentili (1452–1608) was a highly respected law professor at Oxford and one of the Renaissance era founders of the modern West's international law tradition. In his treatise, *The Law of War in Three Parts*, Gentili used the same bellicose language of savagery as Lord Coke to justify a religious crusade against pagans who violate natural law. The Oxford don declared that if a conquering Christian monarch assumed sovereignty over peoples "who are alien to humanity and to all religion, these he may most justly compel to change conduct which is contrary to nature."[27]

## THE LANGUAGE OF SAVAGERY IN THE ENGLISH RENAISSANCE DISCOVERY ERA

A number of well-known works by English writers during the Renaissance Discovery era freely draw on this Protestantized, dark-sided language of savagery with its anciently derived stereotypes and images of beastly, primitive peoples. William Shakespeare, in his last and some critics say greatest play, *The Tempest*, used a dark-sided, Classically inspired language of savagery when he created the immortal monster Caliban, the evil brute slave to the wizard Prospero. The Bard describes Caliban as the misalliance of an incubus and the witch Sycorax, "a devil," "a born devil," a "demi-devil," a "thing of darkness," a pagan idolator who worships Setebos, the Patagonian god. As depicted in *The Tempest*, Caliban is your basic stereotypical, dark-sided, Classical savage brought to life in monstrous form on the English Renaissance Discovery–era stage.[28]

The monster imagery and the paradisiacal themes of the New World tropical isle setting of the play draw on Shakespeare's familiarity with a number of Classical sources and authors. We know he was fond of Ovid, for example; the famous burlesque scene of Pyramus and Thisbe in *A Midsummer Night's Dream* is found in Book VI of the *Metamorphoses*. Shakespeare's early poem, "Venus and Adonis," reflects an obvious Ovidian influence. Prospero's invocation of the spirits of magic in *The Tempest* borrows heavily from the seventh book of the *Metamorphoses*, where Medea's incantations are described.

Shakespeare's monstrous creation also owes a good deal to the French Humanist Michel de Montaigne's (1553–1592) influential essay, *On Cannibals*, which drew on a vast archive of Classical sources and references to describe the Indians of the Amazon. Montaigne described these savages as having received "very little form and fashion from art and human intelligence," living still very close to their "original simplicity," with

> no manner of traffic, no knowledge of letters, no science of numbers, no name of magistrate or political superiority; no use of service, riches or poverty, no contracts, no successions, no dividends, no properties, no employments, but those of leisure, no respect of kindred, but common, no clothing, no agriculture, no metal, no use of corn or wine; the very words that signify lying, treachery, dissimulation, avarice, envy, detraction, pardon, never heard of.[29]

Shakespeare also appears to have been familiar with the early English travel literature, with its images of biblical Wild Men in desperate need of Christian remediation to save their damned souls. Most Shakespeare scholars believe that *The Tempest* was heavily indebted to William Strachey's 1612 poem, *History of Travel into Virginia Britania*. Strachey drew heavily on Classical sources in making his argument that the English were intended to conquer, colonize, and convert the savages of the New World. The English themselves, Strachey writes, "might yet have lived overgrown satyrs, rude and untutored, wandering in the woods, dwelling in caves, and hunting for our dinners," were it not for the civilizing influence of the conquering Romans over "our barbarous island." "Wild as they are, accept them so were we," Strachey says, commending the Romans for establishing colonies of old soldiers throughout England, building castles and towns, "and in every corner teaching us ever to know the powerful discourse of divine reason." Light was brought to the heathen barbarian then, so why not now, asked the poet, for the Indians were surely as barbarous as the ancient Britons once had been. Thus, "by a gentle and faire entreaty," Strachey reasons, "we may win them to be willing to hear and learn of us and our preachers."[30]

## THE LANGUAGE OF SAVAGERY AT JAMESTOWN

Strachey did not elaborate on what would happen if a "gentle and faire entreaty" failed to work in winning over the savages of Virginia to Christianity and civility. But other early English colonizers of North America did not hesitate to follow up on his Protestantized language of savagery and its militant analogies to the empire-building Romans. The Virginia Company hired the Reverend Robert Gray in England to justify Protestant England's intended territorial encroachments on Virginia's natives. In a sermon delivered in 1609, Gray preached that the English had been given license by their charter from King James to invade North America and spread the word of the true Christian gospel to the savages there. Thus, the Virginia Company, according to the popular preacher, "may lawfully make war" on the savages of Virginia because they "live under no lawful or warrantable government."[31]

Based on their depravity and backwardness, Gray proclaimed that it was England's Christian duty "to reclaim and reduce those savages from their barbarous kinds of life and from their brutish manners to humanity, piety, and honesty." The English, according to Gray, had a biblically imposed obligation to seize the earth from "wild beasts" and "brutish savages," which "by reason of their godless ignorance and blasphemous idolatry are worse than those beasts." Invoking the shades of the medieval Christian

Wild Man, lurking in the dark forests of the New World, Gray went even further in his Protestant-inspired discourse: It was a sin against God to allow the earth to remain in "the hands of beasts and brutish savages, which have no interest in it, because they participate rather of the nature of beasts than men." To Gray, the reports of the New World from European explorers confirmed that

> these savages have no particular propriety in any part of parcel of that country, but only a general residency there, as wild beasts in the forest; for they range and wander up and down the country without any law or government, being led only by their own lusts and sensuality. There is not *meum* and *tuum* [mine and thine] amongst them. So that if the whole land should be taken from them, there is not a man that can complain of any particular wrong done unto him.[32]

Gray's bellicose, Protestantized language of savagery was used widely by Englishmen during this early period of English colonization efforts in Jamestown. In his *Nova Britannia* (1609), Richard Johnson used this same basic language of anciently derived, dark-sided stereotypes and identifying markers when he wrote of a land "inhabited with wild and savage people, that live and lie up and down in troupes like herds of Deer in a Forrest: they have no law but nature, their apparel skins of beasts, but most go naked: the better sort have houses, but poor ones, they have no Arts nor Science."[33]

Captain John Smith, in charge of military affairs during the early years of the Jamestown colony, drew on this same basic language in one of the early, on-the-ground reports of the Indians of Virginia in his *1612 Map of Virginia*. Smith is typical of many of the English Protestant Renaissance soldiers who went to the New World during the early colonizing period. Before his arrival in Virginia in 1607, Smith had fought against the infidel Turks and Tartars in eastern Europe. An adept storyteller, he claimed to have been wounded, captured, and sold into slavery in Constantinople and Tartary in 1603, managing to escape through Russia by beating his owner to death with a threshing flail.

Smith's highly popular *Map* described the country's Indians as being "all *Savage.*" While there was "yet in *Virginia* no place discovered to be so *Savage* in which the savages have not a religion," the main deity worshipped by the Indians "is the Devil."[34]

This rather routine demonization of the Indians of Virginia as biblical Wild Men, without hope or prayer of Christian redemption, had been going on since the Jamestown landing, and the medievally derived themes had penetrated deeply into the language used by English Protestant writers to describe the native inhabitants of the colony.

In his 1613 tract, *Goode Newes from Virginia*, Alexander Whitaker, a minister in Henrico, Virginia, described the Indians of the Tidewater region as "naked slaves of the divell" who acknowledge "a great good God, but know him not." He has heard how they sometimes sacrifice their own children to the devil and notes that their priests "are no other such as our English witches are." They "live naked" and "esteem it a virtue to lie, deceive and steal as their master the devil teacheth to them."[35]

Such notions of irredeemable savagery, witchcraft, and demonic possession were significantly reinforced in 1622 with the outbreak of war between the Jamestown colony and the natives. Rapid colonization of Indian land between 1619 and 1621 had resulted in nearly 3,500 new colonists arriving. Chief Opechancanough convinced the Tidewater tribes to launch an all-out surprise attack on the colony or risk cultural extermination by the English invaders of their lands.

Opechancanough's warriors succeeded in killing nearly 350 English settlers at Jamestown, sending the Virginia Company's hopes of establishing a permanent and profitable colony in North America into a tailspin. The Company commissioned its secretary, Edward Waterhouse, to write a pamphlet on the massacre and drum up support for all-out war against the heathen savages. His pamphlet, based on information collected from eyewitnesses and the colony's officials, describes how the Indians descended on the innocent colonists, killing without mercy, "not sparing either age or sex, man, woman or child." Heads were cut off, brains were beat out, corpses were mutilated, and other cruelties were committed by the savages, "unbefitting to be heard by any civil ear."[36] This treachery by the Indians demanded an appropriate response:

[O]ur hands which before were tied with gentleness and fair usage, are now set at liberty by the treacherous violence of the savages, not untying the knot, but cutting it: So that we, who hitherto have had possession of no more ground than their waste, and our purchase at a valuable consideration to their own contentment, gained; may now by right of war, and law of nations, invade the country and destroy them who sought to destroy us.

As Waterhouse explains in a language of savagery that was becoming increasingly pervasive back in England and on the ground in Jamestown, the massacre was actually "for the good of the Plantation." Now, he wrote, "their cleared grounds in all their villages (which are situated in the fruit-fullest places of the land) shall be inhabited by us, whereas heretofore the grubbing of woods was the greatest labor." Other benefits arose from the massacre as well:

Because the way of conquering them is much more easy than of civilizing them by fair means, for they are a rude, barbarous, and naked people, scattered in small companies, which are helps to victory, but hinderances to civility: Besides that, a conquest may be of many, and at once; but civility is in particular, and slow, the effect of long time, and great industry.

Backed by Waterhouse's legal analysis and following Coke's dicta in *Calvin's Case,* the Indians, as savage infidels, were effectively declared *perpetui inimici* of the Jamestown colony. Only their children were to be spared for conversion; the rest were to be destroyed. Jamestown's governor was instructed from London to set "upon the Indian in all places." All trade with the natives was prohibited. Superior English arms and a coordinated campaign of raids and theft of the Indian corn supplies eventually wore Opechancanough's alliance down. Remnants of the tribes that had sided with him in his rebellion were rounded up and herded onto a tiny reserve territory, safely out of the way of English settlement.[37]

The Reverend Samuel Purchas, who edited Richard Hakluyt's highly popular English-language voyaging narratives in the seventeenth century, ably cataloged the litany of stereotypes and clichés confirming that the savages of Virginia were perpetual enemies to the colonizing, expansion-minded form of civilization the English sought to plant in the New World;

they were "bad people, having little of Humanity but shape, ignorant of Civility, of Arts, of Religion: more brutish then the beasts they hunt, more wild and unmanly then that unmanned wild Country, which they range rather than inhabit; captivated also to Satan's tyranny in foolish pieties, mad impieties, wicked idleness, busy and bloody wickedness." According to the Renaissance Discovery–era idea of the savage as translated by Purchas, the lands of the Indians of America were thus ripe and ready for Christian conquest: "All the rich endowments of Virginia, her Virgin-portion from the creation nothing lessened, are wages for all this work: God in wisdom having enriched the Savage Countries, that those riches might be attractive for Christian suiters, which there may sowe spirituals and reap temporals."[38]

# ELEVEN

# THE ENLIGHTENMENT IDEA OF THE SAVAGE AND THE FOUNDERS' FIRST INDIAN POLICY

Jean-Jacques Rousseau (1712–1778) was one of the most important literary figures of the eighteenth-century European Enlightenment. The Genevan *philosophe* who wrote *The Social Contract,* invented the modern biography with his *Confessions,* and helped incite the French Revolution with his incendiary writings is also notorious for having advocated the simple, primitive lifestyle of the noble savage as the antidote for the ills that plagued contemporary society.

The problem is that Rousseau never used the idea of the savage in quite this way in any of his writings—that is, as an argument for returning to a benignly imagined state of nature. His ideas on the savage and the Classically inspired language that he used were far more complex and nuanced and drew from a diverse range of sources, although he was particularly influenced by the pessimistic, dark-sided language of primitive humanity's "hard" mode of existence found in Lucretius's *De Rerum Natura.*

Rousseau first became famous in the Paris salons by winning an essay contest on the topic of whether the development of the arts and sciences had morally benefited humanity. Taking a Lucretian-themed, contrarian approach to his topic, Rousseau's prize-winning 1750 essay showed that the arts and sciences were actually responsible for humanity's moral decline. We were basically good by nature, Rousseau explained. Society and its love of property were what really corrupted us.

After adapting one of Western civilization's oldest contrarian ideas and updating it to win an essay contest, Rousseau found himself catapulted into public notoriety. He decided to try his hand at another writing competition in 1754 that allowed him to further develop his earlier prize-winning theme.

This second essay, the famous incendiary tract of 1754 titled *Discourse on the Origin of Inequality*, did not take the prize that year, but it did win Rousseau even greater notoriety. The *Second Discourse*, as it is sometimes called, represents one of the Enlightenment's most important, stimulating, and still-relevant works of political philosophy. Rousseau's provocative essay addressed this loaded question floating around pre-Revolutionary French intellectual circles: "What is the origin of inequality among men, and is it authorized by natural law?"[1]

Rousseau sought to demonstrate that inequality is not something "natural" to humanity but rather is produced by society. It is the "spirit of society," Rousseau asserted, "and the inequality which society produces, that thus transform and alter all our natural inclinations." Echoing a familiar theme from the Classical literature of protest and social critique inaugurated by Hesiod's retelling of the Legend of the Golden Age, Rousseau declared that it is society itself that causes humanity's present state of unhappiness.

To prove his controversial thesis that society produces the inequality that alters our true nature and makes us miserable human beings in the process, Rousseau sought to describe our "natural," unadorned state. Although he does not directly cite *De Rerum Natura*, his rather pessimistic picture of humanity in the state of nature at the very beginnings of time closely resembles that drawn by Lucretius,[2] whose rejection of superstition and religion in favor of science and atoms was extremely popular with Enlightenment philosophers, writers, and intellectuals.

Rousseau invokes a number of defining elements from the Lucretian language of hard savagery in describing primitive humanity's desperate mode of existence: "Solitary, indolent, and perpetually accompanied by danger," primitive humans, Rousseau explains, wander "up and down the forests," "without speech, and without home, an equal stranger to war and to all ties." Humanity in this primitive condition, as he observes it, is without morals, virtues, or vices. There is nothing noble about it. Although the natives are healthier and stronger than those of us who live in civilized society, this brutish life in the state of wild, untamed nature is made up of chance sexual couplings and perpetual life-and-death struggles with wild beasts and the forces of brute nature.

Throughout his essay, Rousseau supplements his Classically inspired language of savagery with frequent references to accounts of primitive tribal peoples taken from contemporary travel literature. His clichéd use of familiar stereotypes and categories of identification suggests that the idea of the savage as received by the Enlightenment philosophers from the Renaissance era had remained remarkably stable and consistent in Western intellectual circles at least. Nakedness, odd sexual behaviors, and the usual list of exotic customs and manners top Rousseau's list as the primary identifying marks of the lowest form of savagery. The "Caribs of Venezuela," he writes, go about "almost naked" and "expose themselves freely in the woods, armed only with bows and arrows." They have "as yet least of all deviated from the state of nature, being in fact the most peaceable of people in their amours, and the least subject to jealousy, though they live in a hot climate which seems always to inflame the passions."

Relying on the "narratives of travelers" to "savage nations," Rousseau's state of nature updates and confirms the age-old stereotypes of primitive human beings possessed of superior physical qualities in comparison to civilized city dwellers. There are the reports, for example, of native peoples who possess "sight, hearing, and smell exceedingly fine and subtle":

It is there no matter for surprise that the Hottentots of the Cape of Good Hope distinguish ships at sea, with the naked eye, at as great a distance as the Dutch can do with their telescopes; or that the savages of America should trace the Spaniards, by their smell, as well as the best dogs could have done; or that these barbarous peoples feel no pain in going naked, or that they use large quantities of pimento with their food, and drink the strongest European liquors like water.

Rousseau is careful to make the point that the hard, primitive way of life he illustrates represents the lowest stage of humanity's development. In the second part of the *Second Discourse,* he tells us of an "intermediate" stage of humanity's progress and development over time, a stage that followed the most primitive stage. According to Rousseau, this intermediate state of human development was brought about by the creation of tools for hunting and fishing, the construction of huts, the development of language, and advances in other simple arts.

In describing this intermediate stage, Rousseau freely adopts the language of noble savagery associated with the ancient Greek Legend of the Golden Age to imagine a time of few laws or constraints on human freedom. This ancient time, Rousseau explains, was the "happiest and most stable of epochs" for humanity, "the least subject to revolutions, and altogether the very best man could experience." It was so wonderful that the only way we would ever have abandoned it was through "some fatal accident, which, for the public good, should never have happened." Once again, to support his account of this slightly more advanced primitive stage of development, Rousseau points to the example of the various races of savage peoples encountered by Europeans around the world in his own day, "most of whom have been found in this state."

Following this digression from his major thesis, Rousseau goes back to the dystopian, Lucretian-styled language of hard savagery and its historical thesis of cyclic decline to describe what comes next for humanity: "[A]ll subsequent advances have been apparently so many steps towards the perfection of the individual, but in reality towards the decrepitude of the species." What then follows is a rather concise statement of the Enlightenment era's idea of the ennobled savage:

> So long as men remained content with their rustic huts, so long as they were satisfied with clothes made of the skins of animals and sewn together with thorns and fish-bones, adorned themselves only with feathers and shells, and continued to paint their bodies different colours, to improve and beautify their bows and arrows, and to make with sharp-edged stones fishing boats or clumsy musical instruments; in a word, so long as they undertook only what a single person could accomplish, and

confined themselves to such arts as did not require the joint labour of several hands, they lived free, healthy, honest, and happy lives, in so far as their nature allowed, and they continued to enjoy the pleasures of mutual and independent intercourse.

Echoing a language of contrarian social critique that can be traced back to Hesiod, Lucretius, and other Classical poets and philosophers, Rousseau explains that this happy state for humankind was lost the moment "property was introduced." From that point on, it was all toil and woe for humanity; "work became indispensable, and vast forests became smiling fields, which man had to water with the sweat of his brow." He directly cites the tradition of protest poetry that extends from Hesiod to make his point: "The poets tell us it was gold and silver, but, for the philosophers, it was iron and corn, which first civilized men, and ruined humanity." Rousseau finishes this distressing thought by pointing to a familiar (and highly inaccurate) stereotype of the American Indian as a primitive hunter-gatherer with Stone Age tools. Metallurgy and agriculture, he writes, "were unknown to the savages of America, who for that reason are still savage."

Rousseau, as I noted at the beginning of the chapter, is frequently misunderstood as having proposed the way of life lived by the mythical noble savage in a state of nature as an antidote to eighteenth-century European civilization's degrading and corrupting influences on human personality.[3] But as his *Discourse* shows, Rousseau's views on humanity in the state of nature were far more complex than that. He recognized that once the institution of property had been introduced, returning to a state of nature was impossible for humanity. His oft-quoted opening lines of the second part of his *Second Discourse* reflect that sad awareness in a language of ennobled savagery that traces back directly to the Legend of the Golden Age:

The first man, who, having enclosed a piece of ground, bethought himself of saying "This is mine," and found people simple enough to believe him, was the real founder of civil society. From how many crimes, wars, and murders, from how many horrors and misfortunes might not any one have saved mankind, by pulling up the stakes, or filling up the ditch, and crying to his fellows: "Beware of listening to this impostor; you are undone if you once forget that the fruits of the earth belong to us all, and the earth itself to nobody."

Like most of the major eighteenth-century Enlightenment philosophers who used the idea of the savage as a centerpiece of their work on the failings of contemporary society, Rousseau was not all that interested in returning to a state of nature. Far from it; believing in human perfectibility, he wanted his contemporaries to understand our true human nature, which can only be revealed and understood, according to Rousseau, through a language of savagery.

## THE ENLIGHTENMENT-ERA
## IDEA OF THE SAVAGE

Professor Ronald Meek has called attention to the fact that Rousseau's picture of humanity is a complete abstraction, totally disconnected "from society and its institutions."[4] The state of nature in the *Second Discourse* is a pure invention, an intellectual exercise constructed for a writing contest with a nice prize and some notoriety attached at the end.

Rousseau himself is careful to note that his picture of primitive man is one "which no longer exists, perhaps never did exist, and probably never will exist." Even the most primitive peoples yet discovered, like the "savages of America," Rousseau explains, have evidently already advanced far beyond this picture, proving that the primordial state of nature he hypothesizes in his essay is irretrievable. The conceit of portraying a nonexistent savage state of nature allows Rousseau to construct his picture of primitive humanity unimpeded, "laying all facts aside, as they do not affect the question."

The idea of the savage in a state of nature had been familiar to Western civilization in one form or another since the time of the Greeks and Romans; it was a fanciful conceit that Renaissance writers had fully revived and made popular throughout European literary culture. Rousseau's notion that the Indians of America could be used as a living model of human development in its more savage, less civilized stages was a vital and animating part of a new science of society that was being developed and refined by Enlightenment philosophers and political thinkers of the eighteenth century.

This new science of society grew out of the efforts of towering Enlightenment figures like Rousseau to demonstrate or deny the "perfectibility" of humanity in a Westernized mode of social existence.[5] Those who helped contribute to this new type of social science transformed the Indians of America into the primitivized antithesis of their own "civilized" society. For writers and theorists who were obsessed with using the "state of nature" to prove their theories of human nature and society, the Indian was as close to that natural state as you could get in the world: an ideal stand-in for humanity's first, primitive, backward stage of social development. As such, the Indian was regarded as deserving of close study and attention.

In creating this new version of the Indian as a paradigm of humanity in a savage state of nature, Enlightenment era writers sharpened and refined the Classical categories and markers into a finely calibrated language of measurement and differentiation. As the Indian became transformed into a "living model" of humanity in its most primitive, savage state of existence, superstitions derived from the medieval Christian era's idea of the savage as the biblical Wild Man were discarded or subsided into the background.[6] Reliable descriptions derived from actual travelers' accounts and first-hand observations supported by Classical references and authors were what mattered most to the new science of society.

The idea of the Indian as a living model of humanity in the state of nature emerged at an early point in the major legal and political writings of the European Enlightenment. In developing his influential theory on property, Hugo Grotius (1583–1645), the Dutch lawyer and founder of modern international law in the West, relied on Dicaearchus of Messana, the fourth-century B.C. Peripatetic philosopher and student of Aristotle who adopted the Hesiodic time frame in his influential history of the Greeks (see chapter 2).

Grotius begins his legal history of property with the primitive hunter-gatherer state, described precisely according to the Classical language of ennobled savagery derived from the Legend of the Golden Age. But along with his Classically derived references and stereotypes of barbarian savage tribes like the ancient Scythians to illustrate how "primitive man" lived "in great simplicity" on the fruits of the earth, Grotius also points to "some races of America" who practice a kind of "community of goods" and have done so for centuries "without inconvenience." According to Grotius, this form of primitive common ownership had been abandoned by Europeans, who were not content to dwell in caves, go naked, and live life among the wild and ravenous animals. They wanted "a pleasanter way of life," characterized by individual property ownership.[7]

The great English political philosopher Thomas Hobbes disagreed with the Dutch lawyer Grotius's views on a number of important theoretical points. He was in full agreement with the Dutchman, however, on the appropriateness of using the Indians of America as a perfect, real-life example of humanity in its most primitive stage of social development, without any property or laws for protection from the savage forces of nature. For both Hobbes and Grotius, the critical, civilization-defining institution of property differentiated the savage state from the more advanced stages of society. In his monumental *Leviathan*, published in 1651, Hobbes, without any of the cumbersome supporting Classical references that Grotius often used, described "the naturall condition of mankind" as a perpetual "condition of warre," where every man "is Enemy to every man." According to Hobbes's infamous account, humanity in the state of nature must

> live without other security, than what their own strength, and their own invention shall furnish them withall. In such condition, there is no place for Industry; because the fruit thereof is uncertain: and consequently no Culture of the Earth, no Navigation, nor use of the commodities that may be imported by Sea; no commodious Building; no Instruments of moving, and removing such things as require much force; no Knowledge of the face of the Earth; no account of Time; no Arts; no Letters; no Society; and which is worst of all, continuall feare and danger of violent death; And the life of man, solitary, poore, nasty, brutish, and short.[8]

Without property and the security it brings, in Hobbes's view, civilization is impossible. Hobbes, of course, is echoing an ancient theme in Western political philosophy, tracing back to the language of hard savagery first used by Cicero, Aristotle, and Plato. But, characteristic of other Enlightenment thinkers, Hobbes does not stop there in sketching out this theoretical construct. Fearing that he has tested his reader's credulity with his highly distressing, theorized narrative of man's precarious, anxious existence in the state of nature, Hobbes feels compelled to illustrate this philosophical construct with a familiar and stabilizing point of real-world reference: the Indians of America. "It may peradventure be thought, there was never such a time, nor condition of warre as this; and I believe it was never generally so, over all the world: but there are many places, where they live so now. For the savage people in many places of *America*, except the government of small Families, the concord whereof dependeth on naturall lust, have no government at all; and live at this day in that brutish manner, as I said before."[9]

This use of the American Indian as a near perfect model for a universal first stage of primitive social development surpassed by a far more advanced European form of property-owning civilization is a central animating device in a number of influential philosophical works of the Enlightenment era. John Locke (1632–1704) described his hypothetical state of nature in his *Two Treatises of Government* (1690) with this oft-quoted declaration: "In the beginning all the World was America."[10] And America, he next says to underscore the point that this is a prior, earlier stage of human development, "is still a pattern of the first Ages in Asia and Europe."

Much in the same manner as Rousseau, Grotius, and Hobbes, Locke uses the example of the American Indian, "nourished by Fruit or Venison" and knowing "no inclosure," to illustrate the harsh conditions of deprivation characterizing primitive humanity's life in the state of nature. His clichéd stereotypes and grossly inaccurate caricature of the Indian's savage, hunter-gatherer state defined a life of irredeemable hardship and irremediable want compared to the highly civilized state of humanity in an advanced agricultural society. In this higher form of human society, labor was mixed with nature's bounty to create individualized private property.

> There cannot be a clearer demonstration of anything, than several Nations of the Americans are of this, who are rich in Land, and poor in all the Comforts of Life; whom Nature having furnished as liberally as any other people, with the materials of Plenty, i.e., a fruitful Soil, apt to produce in abundance, what might serve for food, rayment, and delight; yet, for want of improving it by labour, have not one hundredth part of the Conveniences we enjoy: And a king of a large fruitful Territory there feeds, lodges, and is clad worse than a day Labourer in England.

This Enlightenment-era idea of the American Indian as a living, breathing, real-life model of the savage state is featured most prominently in the famous four-stages theory of the Scottish Enlightenment's "conjectural" historians.[11] Lecturing from universities in Glasgow and Edinburgh during the latter part of the eighteenth century, writers such as William Robertson, Lord Kames, Adam Ferguson, and Adam Smith fleshed out a richly detailed, spuriously documented, but highly dynamic interpretation of humanity's rise and progress through four distinct stages of development. The stages moved on their own, from primitive rudeness to civilized complexity, and all were marked by a society's relation to private property. They also were all elaborated in a rather standardized classically grounded language of savagery.

From the eighteenth-century Enlightenment era onward, as Meek explains in the leading study of the Scottish School's writings on socioeconomic development, the four-stages theory became of "crucial significance in the subsequent development of economics, sociology, anthropology, and historiography, right down to our time."[12] As we shall see, the Scottish School's contributions to the Enlightenment era's perpetuation of the ancient stereotypes and categorical markers associated with the Classical idea of the savage to describe the American Indian were especially influential among the Founding Fathers of the United States.

In developing their theory, the Scots relied heavily on Baron de Montesquieu (1689–1755), whose monumental *Spirit of the Laws* (1748) remains one of the most influential works of political thought and philosophy in the history of the Western world. The French baron's comparative approach to history, based on the assumption of a universal human nature, sought to show that social change could be understood in terms of a historical process that eventually affected every human society. The customs of a nation, he writes, "have a very great relation to the manner in which the several nations procure their subsistence. There should be a code of laws of a much larger extent for a nation attached to trade and navigation than for people who are content with cultivating the earth. There should be a much greater for the latter than for those who subsist by their flocks and herds. There must be a still greater for these than for such as live by hunting."[13]

Peoples who do not cultivate the land, the great baron writes, "can scarcely form a great nation. If they are herdsmen and shepherds, they have need of an extensive country to furnish subsistence for a small number; if they live by hunting, their number must be still less, and in order to find the means of life they must constitute a very small nation." And what makes a great nation, according to the baron, is the institution of private property. "The division of lands is what principally increases the civil code," he explains. "Amongst nations where they have not made this division there are very few civil laws." Where there are very few civil laws, there is no security of property, and property is what makes civilization possible. "The culture of lands," he writes, "requires the use of money."

Significantly refining the baron's descriptions of the successive stages of man's social development, the Scots deployed what they regarded as a "scientific" form of discourse that rigidly classified the savage state of existence as the lowest and most backward form of human social organization imaginable. From "savagery," which was characterized by its precarious reliance on hunting and gathering as a mode of subsistence, human society progressed toward "the Age of Shepherds" and a reliance on the more secure food supplies allowed by the nomadic herding of flocks of cattle and sheep. Then, in the "Age of Agriculture," men discovered the advantages of domesticating barnyard animals and growing crops. Only at that stage of development could it be said that human society had become "civilized." Finally, as surpluses were produced, human society progressed to its highest stage of development and perfectibility, the "Age of Commerce," characterized by a complex division of labor, sophisticated mechanisms of finance and exchange, and the production of luxuries and cultural refinement. This highest point of social development, not coincidentally, was the stage that the Scots believed Christian European civilization—that is, their form of society—had recently entered.[14]

To the Scots, this course of progressive development over time furnished conclusive, irrefutable evidence that as we humans progressed upward, we became more "social." To live fully in society was our highest aim and destiny. History proved that the good life for humanity was the life of a rich and complex society, through which we achieve the perfectibility of our true original nature.

The Scots' "scientific" discourse uniformly pointed to the familiar stereotypes that had been used since Europe's discovery of the New World to isolate the Indians of America as paradigm examples of savage hunter-gatherer societies. As William Robertson explained in his 1777 *History of America*, a landmark in the development of modern cultural anthropology and a highly influential text for late-eighteenth- and early nineteenth-century understandings of American Indian society and culture on both sides of the Atlantic: "In America, man appears under the rudest form in which we can conceive him to subsist. . . . That state of primeval simplicity, which was known in our continent only by the fanciful description of poets, really existed in the other."[15]

All societies, the Scots inferred from the evidence of history, normally proceeded through several phases of organization, from "rude" simplicity to "civilized" complexity. Their society had arrived at the highest stage of man's social development, the Age of Commerce, first. Therefore, they confidently concluded, their society was unqualifiedly superior to all others. In terms of security, safety, comfort, and the cultural refinements that led to human sociability and therefore human perfectibility, there was no comparison between human life in the savage state, as exemplified by the Indians of America, and the superior quality of life secured by European civilization's own advanced stage of social organization. Despite its destruction of the savage virtues of simplicity, martial ardor, and primitive egalitarianism, according to the Scots, civilization had put something "higher and greater in their place."[16]

Adam Smith's influential version of the four-stages theory typifies the Scots' "scientific" language of savagery applied to the Indians of America. By way of irrefutable contrast, Smith's belief in the ultimate superiority of the higher, more advanced stages of man's development points repeatedly to the American Indian's savage state of existence.

In Smith's socioeconomic theory, which was heavily influenced by his thorough grounding in the works of Grotius, Hobbes, Locke, and Montesquieu and an incredibly rich and erudite array of Classical sources, the elaboration of ever more sophisticated forms of private property becomes the most important and progressive step for humanity. This process of change occurs as society moves from one state of social organization to the next higher state.

According to Smith, the savage state is the lowest stage of society, and the Indians of America are a more retrograde form of society than anything ever encountered in the literature of Classical Antiquity. "Among the northern nations which broke into Europe in the beginning of the 5th century, society was a step farther advanced than amongst the Americans at this day. They are still in the state of hunters, the most rude and barbarous of any." There is, according to Smith, "almost no property amongst them," which accounts for their lack of sophisticated laws or regulations in comparison to more advanced societies. "The more improved any society is and the greater length the several means of supporting the inhabitants are carried, the greater will be the number of their laws and regulations necessary to maintain justice, and prevent infringements of the right to property." The governments of "the savage nations of America," Smith says, are unsophisticated and weak; lacking any forms of private property. Such societies have no need for a government strong enough to preserve the wealth of the rich from "the attacks of the poor," which naturally occur in the more advanced forms of society.[17]

Smith sought to demonstrate the ultimate inferiority of the savage state in comparison to the higher stages of civilization by conjecturing on the material forces that would lead to changes in the mode of subsistence for a society of hunters. Like other Scottish proponents of the four-stages theory, Smith believed that increasing population along with the institution of private property was a key determinant of social change. He speculated that the members of a hunter-gatherer society "would find the chase too precarious for their support" as their numbers multiplied. "In the age of hunters it is impossible for a very great number to live together. As game is their only support they would soon exhaust all that was within their reach." Faced with an increasing population, they would therefore, out of necessity, have to contrive "some other method whereby to support themselves."

Smith's theory clearly implied that in cases where the expansion of a more advanced form of society that could support greater numbers on the land exerted pressure on a race of hunters, the latter would be deprived of the territory and game necessary to support its mode of subsistence. At that point, resistance to a more civilized society was futile. As Smith explained, it would be impossible for a savage race to form a very "formidable" force to repel the inevitable invasion by the higher, more advanced form of civilization. "The hunters cannot form any very great schemes, nor can their expeditions be very formidable." For evidence supporting this key proposition that proved the intrinsic inferiority of the savage state to more advanced societies, Smith pointed to travelers' stereotypical (and again highly inaccurate) accounts of the savages of North America, where a "scalping party seldom consists of above ten or twelve. So that there can be no great danger from such a nation."

The Classically inspired idea that the American Indian was a living model of humanity in the inferior savage state assumed tribalism's doomed fate in North America. The savage was destined to be surpassed by a superior form of civilization. This Scottish-inspired stereotype of the American Indian as doomed savage is found reflected in the writings of Smith, his fellow members of the Scottish School, and a good number of the major European Enlightenment philosophers.

The Scots' highly refined theory of successive stages in the development of human civilization defined by society's relation to property proved particularly influential in the United States following the Revolutionary War. The Founding Fathers, in fact, sought to translate this theory into action, in their first Indian policy for their new nation. Scottish theory was a driving force behind the Founders' policy goal of gradual territorial expansion achieved through treaties negotiated with tribes on the new nation's vulnerable western frontiers.

George Washington, Samuel Adams, Henry Knox, Thomas Jefferson, and virtually all the other Founders involved in the development and execution of that first policy spoke the same basic language of familiar stereotypes, categorical markers, and iconic images that Western civilization had been using for thousands of years to identify and isolate the savage as an irreconcilable enemy to civilization. By force of habit imported from the Old World, the Founders readily adopted that language, virtually unchanged from its ancient Greek roots, for their own invention of the United States of America.

## THE FOUNDERS' AND THE ENLIGHTENMENT-ERA IDEA OF THE SAVAGE

For the most part, the Founders were not overly concerned with constructing idealized states of nature when they thought about the difficult tasks of nation building on the North American continent. The Massachusetts Puritan and lawyer John Adams, one of the intellectual leaders of the Founding Generation, expressed his exasperation with Rousseau's method of "laying all facts aside" in the margin of his copy of the *Second Discourse*. Adams wrote, "Reasonings from a State of Nature are fallacious, because hypothetical. We have not facts. Experiments are wanting. Reasonings from Savage Life do not much better. Every writer affirms what he pleases. We have not facts to be depended on."[18]

Adams was one of the great polymaths of the British-American Enlightenment. His knowledge of and particularly his passion for Classical Antiquity was unrivaled in the British colonies. In his diary, he confessed to having declaimed aloud the Catilinarian orations of Cicero alone in his room at night at the age of 23. But like the other members of the Founding generation, he sought empirical facts when it came to developing the principles of government for a new nation.

When it came to the Founders' views on the American Indian, the facts were plainly stated in the 1776 Declaration of Independence. Thomas Jefferson, primary author of that famous founding text in American history, well understood the animating, organizing power invoked by the harrowing image of the Indian as a warlike, bloodthirsty savage when he incorporated it into the indictment against King George III. As one of the Founders' justifications for launching their revolution against Great Britain, Jefferson included the king's despicable endeavors "to bring on the inhabitants of our frontiers, the merciless Indian Savages, whose known rule of warfare, is an undistinguished destruction of all ages, sexes and conditions."

Given the virtually uninterrupted history of the British colonists' wars and unrelenting efforts at territorial dispossession of the savage tribes of North America, stretching all the way back to Jamestown, it is not too hard to understand why the Founders embraced the socioeconomic form of "scientific" discourse deployed by the Scots with such a passion. The facts of the Indians' savage status, as laid out by the Scots, provided an essential form of knowledge for solving one of the most pressing policy dilemmas of the United States: promoting peaceful white agrarian expansion onto the Indian-held lands of the western frontier.

According to the Scottish School, the Indians of the New World were among the most primitive, savage peoples ever to live on the face of the earth. Lacking the civilizing institutions of property, law, government, or acceptable religious belief, the Indians' incontestable savage nature presented a challenge and an obstacle that the Founders sought to overcome by promoting white settlement of the Indian-held "Western Country." The Western Country was the vast and fertile area between the eastern mountain ranges and the Mississippi River. The 1783 Treaty of Paris with Great Britain that ended the Revolutionary War granted this incredibly valuable piece of real estate to the United States, the principal landed prize of the war. From the Founders' perspective, the major problem the United States faced in the Western Country—a problem that would persist well into the nineteenth century—was that it was occupied by hostile Indian tribes that refused to surrender their lands for white expansion.

The Founders' basic approach to the problem of promoting peaceful white expansion onto Indian-held lands was firmly grounded in their Scottish-inspired belief that inferior tribes of savages would inevitably be forced to retreat before the advance of a superior form of agrarian-based civilization. As George Washington, writing as commander in chief, explained to Congress in his recommendations "relative to Indian Affairs" shortly after the signing of the treaty of peace in Paris:

> [P]olicy and economy point very strongly to the expediency of being upon good terms with the Indians, and the propriety of purchasing their Lands in preference to attempting to drive them by force of arms out of their Country; which as we have already experienced is like driving the Wild Beasts of the Forest which will return as soon as the pursuit is at an end and fall perhaps on those that are left there; when the gradual extension of our Settlements will as certainly cause the Savage as the Wolf to retire; both being beasts of prey tho' they differ in shape.[19]

Washington's advocacy of a policy of peaceful purchase of Indian-held lands was based on his firm, Scottish-inspired conviction that a war with the tribes was both futile and unnecessary. "In a word, there is nothing to be obtained by an Indian War but the Soil they live on and this can be had by purchase at less expense, and without that bloodshed, and those distresses which helpless Women and Children are made partakers of in all kinds of disputes with them."[20]

Washington's Americanized language of savagery and his conviction on "the expediency of being upon good terms with the Indians" by purchasing their lands through treaties reflected the pervasive influence of the Scottish School's scientific discourse of successive, identifiable stages of human social development on so many aspects of late-eighteenth-century political thought in America. Virtually every major policy-making figure of the Founding generation believed that the Indians' essential savage nature made costly military campaigns for tribal lands unnecessary and unwise; this view in fact became the Americanized translation of the Scottish School's idea of the Indian as doomed savage.

In the Americanized language of Indian policy spoken by Washington and his fellow Founders, wars for Indian-held lands were a waste of precious lives and resources, as the "Savage as the Wolf" would return soon after being expelled by any military force. The wiser policy was to permit white civilization to advance gradually and in an organized fashion on the frontier. The forests would be cleared, and the game on which the savage relied for subsistence would retreat westward. The hunter-gatherer tribes would follow, just as the Scots said they would, surrendering their asserted claims to their former lands relatively cheaply.

A Congressional Committee Report, adopting Washington's recommendations, in some of its crucial passages near verbatim, was sent to Congress in mid-October of 1783. Congress in turn quickly adopted Washington's recommendations on Indian policy, which became the foundation for the first US Indian policy for the Western Country. Washington's language of savagery and its founding stereotype of the Indian's doomed fate in competition with the white man in North America provided the architecture, direction, and tone for US relations with the tribes on the nation's frontiers for the next century.

Congress, per Washington's express recommendations, issued a proclamation forbidding and voiding settlement on Indian-claimed lands on the western frontier. By winter of 1783, tribes on that frontier were being informed of the US government's new policy toward them. The people of the United States had the right to treat them as conquered nations. But as former Revolutionary War General Philip Schuyler explained to one group of Indians during negotiations under this policy,[21] if the Indians agreed to sign treaties voluntarily surrendering their lands according to a US-dictated boundary line, Congress was "willing to forget the injuries and give peace." This Americanized language of Indian savagery invented by the Founders was now being used by Congress to limit and define Indian rights under US law.

## THE FOUNDERS' AMERICANIZED LANGUAGE OF INDIAN SAVAGERY

The idea that the Indians of America were doomed savages destined to be surpassed by a superior Anglo-American race of expansion-minded farmers was part of a language of savagery spoken by virtually all the Founders who played a significant role in managing Indian affairs in the post-Revolutionary period of nation building. It was a widely shared assumption among US policy makers that the Indians had to give up their savage way of life as hunter-gatherers and adapt to an agricultural way of life or be extinguished as a race.

Schuyler, the Revolutionary War general, was from one of the leading Dutch trading families in New York. Working closely with Washington and Congress, he was one of the principal architects of the nation's first Indian policy. His family connections to the Indian trade went back to the Dutch founding of New Amsterdam in the seventeenth century, and he had contacts among many of the major trading tribes of New York. Congress, in fact, appointed Schuyler to the presidency of the Commissioner for Indian Affairs of the Northern Department. He was charged with maintaining friendly relations with the powerful Iroquois Confederacy of tribes that served as the strategic military buffer between Great Britain in Canada and New York's northern and western frontiers. Like his close friend Washington, Schuyler advocated an orderly program of peaceful purchase of Indian-held lands based on the theory of the Indians' doomed savage fate:

> It will be little or no Obstacle to our future improving the very country
> they may retain, whenever we shall want it, for as our settlements ap-
> proach their country, they must, from the scarcity of game, which that

approach will induce to, retire farther back, and dispose of their lands, unless they dwindle comparatively to nothing, as all savages have done, who gain their sustenance by the chase, when compelled to live in the vicinity of civilized people, and thus leave the country without the expence of a purchase, trifling as that will probably be.[22]

The Founders' Scottish-inspired stereotypes and images of the Indian as a doomed form of human savagery were reinforced by their own interpretations of their experiences in dealing with the tribes of the frontier. Henry Knox, Washington's secretary of war, was one of the most eloquent and consistent advocates of the "civilization" program pursued by the United States as part of its post-Revolutionary-era Indian policy. He summarized the familiar lessons that all of the Founders knew and understood in his 1789 report to the Congress on Indian affairs: "[A]ll the Indian tribes, once existing in those states now the best cultivated and most populous, have become extinct." He blamed this regrettable state of affairs not on the Americans who were invading the Indians' lands and dispossessing them but on "the inevitable consequence of cultivation."[23]

For the Founders, the Scots' four-stages theory on humanity's progressive development over time excused them from any responsibility for the sad but unavoidable fate of the American Indian. Adherence to and belief in that theory also dictated a policy that would do nothing to hinder the inevitable process of Indian tribalism's disappearance from the continent.

This view of lack of culpability for the American Indians' ultimate savage demise was stated most famously by Thomas Jefferson, who authored the anti-Indian screed in the Declaration of Independence. Jefferson's views on philosophy and a broad range of other topics were indebted to his close reading of the Scots during the 1780s as he prepared his *Notes on the State of Virginia* (1784). During this period, he heavily annotated his personal copy of Lord Kames's *Principles of Morality and Natural Religion* (1751) and underscored its discussion of the moral sense of savages.

The *Notes* contained extensive commentary on American Indian culture and society. Consistent with his Scottish sources, Jefferson recognized that the Indian shared in the white man's essential humanity. The Indian's hunter-gatherer mode of subsistence determined the uniqueness of his culture, social structure, forms of expression, and achievements. The Indian's praiseworthy "eloquence in council, bravery and address in war,"[24] for example, were all traits produced by the unique "circumstances" of his social state, "which call for a display of particular talents only."[25]

In the inaugural address to Congress of his second presidential term in 1805, Jefferson summarized the major themes of the Americanized language of Indian savagery that had so inspired the Founders. Jefferson's lifelong dedication to the Scots' theory of social development displayed in the *Notes*, written two decades earlier, is plainly evident in the historical framework he elaborates for understanding the Indians' essential savage nature and fated destiny. The Jeffersonian stereotype of the American Indian as doomed savage is complimented in his presidential address by the special obligation of the United States to offer salvation to the tribes by encouraging them to adopt white civilization's agricultural mode of subsistence or perish from the face of the earth:

> The aboriginal inhabitants of these countries I have regarded with the commiseration their history inspires. Endowed with the faculties and the rights of men, breathing an ardent love of liberty and independence, and occupying a country which left them no desire but to be undisturbed, the stream of overflowing population from other regions directed itself on these shores; without power to divert or habits to contend against it, they have been overwhelmed by the current or driven before it; now reduced within limits too narrow for the hunter's state, humanity enjoins us to teach them agriculture and the domestic arts; to encourage them to that industry which alone can enable them to maintain their place in existence and to prepare them in time for that state of society which to bodily comforts adds the improvement of mind and morals.[26]

As Roy Harvey Pearce explains in his indispensable book, *The Savages of America*, "the American theory of the savage takes its clearest and most definite origins in Jefferson's thinking."[27] But Jefferson's Americanized version of the Scottish School's theory of humanity's progress from our rudest to our most civilized state of social development reflected the lessons taught by an all-encompassing form of knowledge, expressed in an anciently derived and continuously perpetuated language of savagery that all of the Founders embraced and understood. The Founders believed that their vision of Anglo-American Christian civilization's fated triumph in America made the disappearance of the Indian as savage an inevitable and desirable necessity.

According to their late-eighteenth-century perspective on the future of the nation they were inventing, there could be no remorse over the Indian's disappearance from the American frontier, the place where, as the historian Frederick Jackson Turner would write from his late-nineteenth-century perspective on that mythical space in the national consciousness, civilization met savagery. White Americans really were not to blame for the fact that the "Savage as the Wolf" was fated to be overwhelmed by a civilized society of cultivators who claimed a superior sovereignty and rights over the land of hunters and gatherers. The Founding Generation Americanized the Scottish School's socioeconomic discourse of human society's progress as part of a great national mythology. In the language of savagery embedded by the Founders into the United States' first Indian policy, this great American creation myth tells the story of Indian tribalism's ultimate doomed fate when confronted by an expansion-minded form of civilization.

# TWELVE

# SAVAGE ANXIETIES

## Indigenous Peoples' Human Rights in the Twenty-First Century

*When we examine psychoanalytic theory the burning question that should occupy our time should concern where the complex of ideas that constitute Western civilization originated, how they originated, and whether they have any realistic correspondence to what we can observe and experience in nature.*

—Vine Deloria, Jr., "The Trickster and the Messiah"

### THERAPEUTIC INTERVENTIONS

Even in the twenty-first century, Western civilization remains obsessed with the idea of the savage. By "obsessed," I am drawing on a language that is intimately familiar to most people throughout the West today—a language of therapy.

According to the most widely used psychiatric diagnostic tool in the United States, the Diagnostic and Statistical Manual of Mental Disorders, Fourth Edition, Text Revision: "*Obsessions* are persistent ideas, thoughts, impulses, or images that are experienced as intrusive and inappropriate and that cause marked anxiety or distress. . . . [T]he content of the obsession is alien, not within his or her own control, and not the kind of thought that he or she would expect to have."[1]

Empirical evidence suggests that the idea of the savage persists as an un-controllable obsession throughout the Western world, intruding into nearly every corner of twenty-first-century culture, politics, religion, and daily life. Take a step back and reflect on the language of savagery we encounter and use every day here in the West.

We are all familiar with a rich and varied archive of clichéd stereotypes, cultural markers, and identifying categories of strange and alien forms of primitivity and exoticism. Virtually all of these notions can be traced back to ancient Greek and Roman times and are deeply embedded in the history and foundations of Western civilization. By taking a step back, as we have in this book, my hope is that we can begin to see how the idea of the savage remains a persistent obsession in the West; a type of irrepressible response; a bad habit developed over the course of nearly three thousand years.

Think of all the different ways twenty-first-century politicians, military generals, and talking heads on cable news programs draw on a language of savagery to describe the West's violent, dangerously opposed enemies in the "primitive" mountain ranges and "tribally controlled" territories of Afghanistan or Pakistan. People over there are stuck in the "Stone Age"; they are possessed of a "medieval" mentality. A distinctively Westernized language of savagery, dating all the way back to the ancient Greeks and their civilization-defining conflicts with the "barbarian" hordes of the Persian Empire, might have something to do with where these mental pictures in our heads originated.[2]

The problem for Western civilization is that these mental pictures have little correspondence to the reality of the world we live in today. As just one telling example: Think of how the Western mainstream media, political establishment, intelligence analysts, and military experts all had a picture in their heads of Osama Bin Laden hiding in a cave in some mountainous, lawless, and inaccessible "tribal" region that marks off that alien and distant part of the world. All the time, he was holed up in that nice, comfortable, suburban compound with his family, less than a mile away from the Pakistan Military Academy.

By now we are all too familiar with the stereotypes and imagery of a language of savagery that has been a constant part of the contemporary West's unrelenting wars against terrorism, drugs, crime, undocumented immigrants, and other enemies of civilization. As I have seen myself, living in Tucson, Arizona, an hour's drive away from the Mexican border, the idea of the savage can be used to stereotype and demonize the most powerless of the powerless in our society—undocumented migrant workers and their children. "DREAM Act kids" have somehow been transformed into an insidious and dangerous threat to America's civilized values of law and order (and failed immigration policies of the past century).[3]

There is more to this obsession of course than just finding a way to express our distress about the threatening forces out there in the world perceived as irreconcilably opposed to Western civilization's continued existence. We all know how a language of savagery can be used, for instance, to talk about another anxiety-producing obsession in the West: sex.

The Greeks, as has been discussed (chapter 8), helped to define the basic shape and contours of what modern feminist scholars have called Western femininity, particularly through their mythical counterimages and stereotypes of exoticized, demonized, and eroticized sexy savages of the female variety. Encountered throughout the literature, art, philosophy, and public and private life of ancient Greece and Rome, these fertile and imaginative uses of a gendered language of savagery have made a profound impression on the way the non-Westernized woman has been imagined, represented, and regarded in the West.

Advertising and marketing campaigns in the West seek to evoke the forbidden allure of the sexy savage in addressing the obsessions, fantasies, and desires of both women and men. The noble savage theme, for instance, still resonates strongly in present-day France, centuries after Rousseau. Christian Dior's "classic" men's fragrance, Eau Sauvage, first marketed in 1969 and revived with a new ad campaign, was the third best-selling men's fragrance there for 2010.[4]

A language of savagery has become an indispensable part of the culture, ethics, and morality of consumption throughout the West today. Just ask Al Gore, who was widely caricatured as wanting to take Western civilization back to the Stone Age in even talking about the possibility of human-caused global warming.

Alex Shakar's best-selling 2001 novel, *The Savage Girl*, uses a language of savagery to brilliant and telling effect in satirizing the Western world's consumption-driven values, norms, and obsessions. A young but oddly somewhat naive "trendspotter," Ursula Van Urden, comes upon "the savage girl," a homeless woman dressed in pieces of clothing and accessories stitched together from discarded furs and animal bones.[5] Writes Shakar, "The sleeves and sides of her olive-drab T-shirt are cut out, exposing her flanks and opposed semicircles of sunburned back. . . . Her pants are from some defunct Eastern European army, laden with pockets, cut off at the knees. Her shins are wrapped in bands of pelt, a short brown fur. Her feet are shod in moccasins."[6]

Dorothea Löbberman's insightful twenty-first-century feminist deconstruction of Shakar's novel, "Fashion/ing Statements: Reading Homeless Bodies in Contemporary Fiction," tells us that Ursula is able to "read" the woman's dress "as a message of primitivism and anti-consumerism and starts the successful marketing campaign of a 'savage' trend." Ursula's marketing strategy uses a language of savagery that goes back to Juvenal and Lucian: The savage girl is "sick of modernity," "tries to live authentically," and "may be deeper than the rest of us. She may be superior."[7] Think of what Hesiod would say about this wonderfully apt reinvention of a familiar theme he developed thousands of years ago while battling it out in poetry contests with Homer in ancient Greece. Like many conservative social critics in the West today, he would likely say he longed for a return to the values of the Golden Age.

The ubiquity and deep penetration of the idea of the savage can be confirmed by turning on your TV set and watching a football game between the Kansas City Chiefs and Washington Redskins. You'll soon be besieged with commercials featuring Viking raiders dressed in furry pelts wielding primitive weapons to promote credit cards that give free airline miles to vacationing American families. Next come hypersensitive cavemen hawking easy-to-understand insurance policies for auto, home, and life. From Fred and Wilma Flintstone to *Survivor* and *Lost*, without the savage, what else would the West use to populate the empty wasteland of its favorite network television shows?

The movies, of course, are another ready example of the continued vitality and marketing potential of the idea of the savage in the twenty-first-century West. Just think for a moment about the cinematic vocabulary you are expected to know when you view Hollywood blockbusters like James

Cameron's *Avatar*, with its blue-skinned, supersexy, Amazonian-themed Na'vi warrior-woman in a lead romantic role. Young teenage girls throughout the Western world's movie houses and cinemas absorb an ancient primal language of fear and desire every time those sexy Native American teenage werewolves appear on screen in the *Twilight Saga* movies.

We immediately recognize that blockbuster Academy Award–winning films like *Dances with Wolves, Apocalypse Now,* and *Last of the Mohicans* are just reinventions of the "Hollywood Indian" of early twentieth-century American cinema. And that iconic stereotype is simply a reinvention of an idea that started with the ancient Greeks when they talked about the nomadic, horse-riding Scythians and other strange and alien savage tribes in distant lands located on the far edges of the earth.

## SAVAGE ANXIETIES: THE DOCTRINE OF DISCOVERY IN THE TWENTY-FIRST-CENTURY WEST

Contemporary psychological research suggests that the best way to break ourselves of any bad habit that has become an obsession over time is to focus our intention, attention, time, and effort.[8] The problem is that most people in the West are not even aware of their habitual use of the idea of the savage to stereotype indigenous tribal peoples in nearly all domains of their daily life.

As just one important example, in the legal systems of the most "advanced" Western settler states in the world today—the United States, Canada, Australia, and New Zealand—the idea of the savage as perpetuated by the Doctrine of Discovery is still being relied on to justify the denial of indigenous tribal peoples' fundamental human rights. This colonial era doctrine was utilized by all the major colonizing nations of the West to justify their legal and political claims to superior sovereignty and rights to the ancestral territories and lands owned and occupied by indigenous tribal peoples. Christopher Columbus, John Cabot, and all the European Discovery–era voyagers (see chapter 10) took possession of indigenously held territories in the names of their sovereigns under the doctrine. Typically, European sovereignty over these foreign lands was demonstrated by symbolic acts like planting a flag or reading a royal document to an empty forest or deserted beach.

One of the most notorious and oft-cited legal decisions upholding this racist doctrine is Chief Justice John Marshall's 1823 opinion for the US Supreme Court in the case of *Johnson v. McIntosh.*[9] *Johnson* represents the most influential legal opinion on indigenous peoples' human rights ever issued by a court of law in the Western world. All the major English-language-speaking settler states adopted Marshall's understanding of the Doctrine of Discovery and its principle that the first European discoverer of lands occupied by non-Christianized tribal savages could claim a superior right to those lands under the European Law of Nations.

Canada, Australia, and New Zealand all followed Marshall's opinion as a precedent for their domestic law on indigenous tribal peoples' inferior rights to property and control over their ancestral lands. Other Western settler states that traced their colonial legal foundations to Spain, Portugal, France, and Holland also adopted the basic principles of the doctrine vesting a European right of first discovery and occupation in indigenous tribal lands as laid out in *Johnson.*

According to Marshall's oft-cited words in *Johnson,* European "discovery" of Indian-occupied land in the New World gave title "to the government by whose subjects, or by whose authority, it was made, against all other European governments, which title might be consummated by possession." The Supreme Court held that under principles derived from European international law and customary practice of the time, the discovering European nation had "an exclusive right to extinguish the Indian title of occupancy, either by purchase or conquest." This power of unilateral extinguishment of Indian rights to property and self-determination in tribal lands is the most important aspect of the discovery doctrine. Once native rights were extinguished by the European sovereign, no matter what the theory or method (e.g., by purchase, conquest, or abandonment), every purchaser of land in the colony tracing from the crown had a vested interest in perpetuating the "complex of ideas"[10] that constituted the Doctrine.

Marshall himself was an important member of the Founding Generation, having served under George Washington at Valley Forge and then having been given the critical responsibility of securing the ratification of the Constitution from the key state of Virginia in 1787. Not surprisingly, Marshall relied heavily on the Enlightenment-era language of savagery associated with the Scots' four-stages theory (see chapter 11), familiar to all the leaders of the Founding Generation, to justify and ground his ruling in *Johnson*.

The savage, backward "character and religion" of the indigenous inhabitants of the New World, Marshall explained, "afforded an apology for considering them as a people over whom the superior genius of Europe might claim an ascendancy." The Indians "were fierce savages, whose occupation was war, and whose subsistence was drawn chiefly from the forest." As the white population advanced on the frontier, "the Indians necessarily receded. The country in the immediate neighbourhood of agriculturists became unfit for them. The game fled into thicker and more unbroken forests, and the Indians followed. The soil, to which the crown originally claimed title, being no longer occupied by its ancient inhabitants, was parceled out according to the will of the sovereign power."

Under the Doctrine of Discovery as interpreted by Marshall, American Indian "rights to complete sovereignty, as independent nations, were necessarily diminished, and their power to dispose of the soil at their own will, to whomsoever they pleased, was denied." The discovery of territory in the New World gave an "exclusive title" to the European discoverers. Marshall further held that once the savage tribes were "discovered," they became the "exclusive" concern of the European colonizing nation. In the language of savagery perpetuated by the doctrine and *Johnson v. McIntosh*, their rights, or lack thereof, as indigenous tribal peoples were to be determined solely by the laws of a more civilized nation.

## THE DOCTRINE AND INDIGENOUS PEOPLES' RIGHTS IN CANADA, AUSTRALIA, AND NEW ZEALAND

The major English-speaking settler states—Canada, Australia, and New Zealand—all adopted Marshall's decision in *Johnson*, incorporating the Doctrine of Discovery and its racist nineteenth-century colonial-era language of savagery into the foundations of their domestic law and policies respecting indigenous peoples' rights. *St. Catherine's Milling and Lumber Company v. The Queen* (1888), issued by the Privy Council in London, affirmed that Canada had been settled under the Doctrine of Discovery, and thus its indigenous peoples did not hold a fee simple interest (full ownership interest protected by the courts) in their ancestral lands. Lord Watson's opinion in the case cited directly to *Johnson v. McIntosh*, calling Chief Justice Marshall's holding "the leading case in the United States" on the question of the Indians' (called First Nations in Canada) diminished rights to property and sovereignty in their lands. First Nations' rights in the lands they had traditionally used and occupied for thousands of years in Canada, according to *St. Catherine's Milling and Lumbering Company*, amounted to "a personal and usufructuary right dependent upon the goodwill" of the Crown.[11]

Canadian judges followed the lead of the Privy Council in their decisions on Indian rights well into the twentieth century. In the notorious 1929 case *R. v. Syliboy*,[12] the Canadian court held that hunting and fishing rights guaranteed to the Indians of Nova Scotia by treaty with the crown were unenforceable because Indians did not have the capacity to conclude a valid treaty agreement as understood in international law. Judge George Patterson, writing for the court, relied on the foundational principles of the Doctrine of Discovery in dismissing the legal significance of Indian treaties under Canadian law in these terms:

> But the Indians were never regarded as an independent power. A civilized nation first discovering a country of uncivilized people or savages held such country as its own until such time as by treaty it was transferred to some other civilized nation. The savages' rights of sovereignty even of ownership were never recognized. Nova Scotia had passed to Great Britain not by gift or purchase from or even by conquest of the Indians but by treaty with France, which had acquired it by priority of discovery and ancient possession; and the Indians passed with it. . . . In my judgment the Treaty of 1752 is not a treaty at all and is not to be treated as such; it is at best a mere agreement made by the Governor and council with a handful of Indians giving them in return for good behaviour food, presents, and the right to hunt and fish as usual—an agreement that, as we have seen, was very shortly after broken.[13]

Australia adopted an even more extreme version of the doctrine as the foundation of its laws for defining the rights of its indigenous tribal peoples in their traditional lands. Under Australian law, beginning with the initial founding of the colony, indigenous peoples had no recognizable rights in their ancestral lands. Early reports back to England had described New South Wales as the "solitary haunt of a few miserable Savages, destitute of clothing,"[14] and thus subject to appropriation under the Doctrine of Discovery. English colonial officials believed that the native population was so backward and uncivilized that the entire continent could be regarded as *terra nullius,* empty land, with no owner. According to this racist language embedded into the foundations of Australian Aboriginal rights law, Australia was devoid of human inhabitants at the time of Captain James Cook's discovery of the continent on behalf of England—a legal position that had no correspondence to reality and was adhered to by Australia's highest court until the very last decade of the twentieth century.

In New Zealand, in 1840, the native Maori tribes had signed the Treaty of Waitangi with government officials recognizing Maori rights to property and self-determination over their traditional lands, territories, and resources.[15] But in *Wi Parata v. Bishop of Wellington,*[16] the New Zealand court, applying the Doctrine of Discovery as interpreted by *Johnson,* viewed the Maori as incompetent to exercise sovereignty under then-accepted principles of international law. The court declared the entire treaty a legal nullity.[17]

Influential Western writers and theorists on international law during this period also helped to perpetuate the Doctrine of Discovery and its central organizing idea of indigenous peoples as stereotypical savages with inferior rights as human beings. Leading books and treatises published during the late nineteenth and early twentieth centuries interpreted the doctrine's widespread acceptance as part of the domestic law of European-derived settler states like the United States, Canada, Australia, and New Zealand as evidence of the principles of a customary law of all "civilized" nations in dealing with indigenous peoples. According to these authorities, the only territorial titles recognized by international law are those held by "civilized" members of the family of Western nations.[18] "[O]nly such territory can be the object of occupation as is no State's land, whether entirely uninhabited, as *e.g.,* an island, or inhabited by natives whose community is not to be considered as a State."[19]

British publicist John Westlake was one of the most influential English-speaking international legal authorities of the late nineteenth century. He wrote at length on the topic of indigenous peoples' rights under then current views of international law. In his widely disseminated *Chapters on the Principles of International Law,* Westlake distinguishes between "civilised and uncivilised humanity." International law and society were concerned only with relations between "civilized" states—that is, those with European state forms of government.[20] As for the international legal status of indigenous peoples, Westlake had this to say:

> When people of European race come into contact with American or African tribes, the prime necessity is a government under the protection of which the former [European race] may carry on the complex life to which they have been accustomed in their homes, . . . which may protect the natives in the enjoyment of a security and well-being at least not less than they enjoyed before the arrival of the strangers. . . . The inflow of the white race cannot be stopped where there is land to cultivate, ore to be mined, commerce to be developed, sport to enjoy, curiosity to be satisfied. If any fanatical admirer of savage life argued that the whites ought to be kept out, he would only be driven to the same conclusion by another route, for a government on the spot would be necessary to keep him out. Accordingly international law has to treat such natives as uncivilized.[21]

## INTERNATIONAL LAW AND INDIGENOUS PEOPLE'S RIGHTS IN THE TWENTY-FIRST CENTURY

I imagine most people are simply unaware that this blatantly racist European colonial-era legal doctrine continues to be used by courts and policy makers in the West's most advanced nation-states to deny indigenous peoples their basic human rights guaranteed under principles of modern international law. The contemporary global movement for indigenous peoples' human rights is a direct response to the anxieties and distress caused by these types of dehumanizing legal principles adhered to by "civilized" states around the world today. The movement emerged out of the social and political activism of indigenous peoples throughout the world, protesting violations of their human rights by governments and resource development corporations. Through their activism, they sought to draw attention to and support their struggles for cultural survival against the governments, agents, and proxies of a highly urbanized, expansion-minded, resource-consuming form of civilization.

These efforts at broadening awareness of the human rights struggles of the world's indigenous tribal peoples led to important international conferences convened by the major human rights bodies within the United Nations, the Organization of American States, and other international organizations. Heightened attention from scholars and international nongovernmental organizations also helped to promote this broad-based human rights agenda and campaign. Indigenous peoples and their representatives began appearing before human rights bodies in increasing numbers and with increasing frequency, grounding their concerns on generally applicable human rights principles trumpeted by the West and the rest of the civilized world.

This new form of indigenous advocacy has resulted in a steady stream of important developments from the international human rights system responding to the concerns of indigenous peoples. Indigenous peoples prompted the International Labour Organization (ILO) to discard Convention No. 107, adopted by that organization in the 1950s, which was designed to promote the assimilation of indigenous peoples. In 1989, the ILO adopted a new multilateral treaty—ILO Convention No. 169. Ratified and accepted as binding by more than twenty nation-states around the world, many in Latin America, ILO Convention No. 169 recognizes indigenous peoples' rights to property and self-determination over their traditional lands and many other important human rights denied to "savage" and "uncivilized" peoples by the West under the Doctrine of Discovery.[22]

The establishment of the UN Working Group on Indigenous Populations in 1982 led to the ultimate passage of a formal UN Declaration on the Rights of Indigenous Peoples in 2007.[23] This important document of twenty-first-century international human rights law has focused even greater international attention on the human rights concerns of indigenous peoples. The declaration, built on a foundation of existing human rights principles applied generally throughout the international legal system, recognizes the human rights obligations of UN member states to recognize and protect indigenous peoples' rights to:

- Self-determination
- Determine and develop priorities and strategies for exercising their right to development
- Maintain and develop their own distinct political, economic, social, and cultural identities and legal systems
- Not be subjected to genocide or ethnocide, or actions aimed at or affecting their integrity as distinct peoples, their cultural values and identities, including the dispossession of land, forced relocation, assimilation, or integration, and the imposition of foreign lifestyles and propaganda

Most important, the UN Declaration has strong provisions recognizing and protecting indigenous peoples' property rights in their traditional lands and territories. Among the protective lands provisions of the declaration is Article 28, which directly contradicts the Doctrine of Discovery in recognizing that indigenous peoples possess basic human rights in their traditional lands. These rights include "the right to redress, by means that can include restitution or, when this is not possible, just, fair and equitable compensation, for the lands, territories and resources which they have traditionally owned or otherwise occupied or used, and which have been confiscated, taken, occupied, used or damaged without their free, prior and informed consent."

These new international standards have significantly influenced the work of international human rights bodies and other institutions throughout the UN system. The UN Human Rights Committee and the UN Committee on the Elimination of Racial Discrimination now regularly apply the principles of indigenous peoples' human rights reflected in the UN Declaration, drawing heavily on these norms and standards when they monitor human rights situations involving indigenous groups.

Even beyond the formal human rights process, this new language of indigenous human rights now affects the lending processes of the World Bank, the Inter-American Development Bank, the European Union, and the domestic legislation and policies and judge-made law of countries throughout the world. All of these important developments reflect the inventiveness and dedication of indigenous tribal peoples in negotiating the ever-increasing interdependencies, ever-improving communications technologies, and burgeoning international institutions that characterize the contemporary international legal system and its human rights regime of substantive norms and related procedures.

You might think that the most advanced nation-states in the West with their own significant indigenous tribal populations—the United States, Canada, Australia, and New Zealand—would be strong supporters of the UN Declaration on the Rights of Indigenous Peoples, particularly given its unequivocal rejection of the racist, colonial-era language of savagery perpetuated by the Doctrine of Discovery. You would be wrong. These four nations were the only ones in the entire UN General Assembly to vote against adoption of the declaration in 2007. All subsequently relented and reversed their positions after intense international pressure from the UN members that did vote for the declaration and from indigenous tribal peoples in their own countries and from around the world. But all four of these countries' governments continue to embrace and perpetuate the racist principles of the Doctrine of Discovery in asserting their legal privilege as superior sovereigns to extinguish indigenous peoples' rights in their traditional lands through the workings of their domestic legal systems. In other words, they can't let go of their obsession with the doctrine and its language of savagery no matter how hard they try.

## CANADA

Canada is one of the world's most prosperous countries, yet its record in protecting the most basic human rights of indigenous tribal peoples has been abysmal. The Canadian government's policies and laws on indigenous peoples' rights have been harshly and persistently criticized by well-known human rights advocacy organizations, such as Amnesty International; by numerous organs, bodies, and officials within the UN human rights system; and by the Inter-American Commission on Human Rights in a case in which I am involved as lead counsel, *Hul'qumi'num Treaty Group v. Canada*.[24]

According to the UN Development Programme, Canada has the second highest Human Development Index (a comparative measure of life expectancy, literacy, education, and standards of living for countries worldwide) in the Americas and the eighth highest in the world. Yet, one recent federal government analysis found a significant gap between indigenous and nonindigenous communities in four indicators of "community well-being": educational attainment, labor force participation, income, and housing. The study found that 96 of the 100 lowest-ranked communities in these areas of community well-being in Canada were First Nations.[25]

Concerns over these and other types of gross disparities in community health and well-being have been expressed by the UN Human Rights Committee, the UN Committee on the Elimination of Racial Discrimination, the UN Committee on the Elimination of Discrimination Against Women, the UN Committee on the Rights of the Child, the UN Special Rapporteur on adequate housing, and the UN Special Rapporteur on the rights of indigenous peoples. Major organs of the United Nations have recognized the critical relationship between First Nations' poverty in Canada and the state's failure to protect traditional lands, territories, and resources from environmentally destructive development. The facts, as found by all these bodies and experts, are that these social and economic disparities between indigenous and nonindigenous groups in Canada originate in and are exacerbated by the government's systemic failures to adequately protect the rights of First Nations peoples in their traditional lands, territories, and resources. As the UN Committee on Economic, Social, and Cultural Rights stated more than a decade ago, "The Committee views with concern the direct connection between Aboriginal economic marginalization and the ongoing dispossession of Aboriginal people from their lands."[26]

Instead of acting to address this human rights crisis for its First Nations' peoples, Canada's government continues to rely on the nineteenth-century colonial-era legal principles embodied in the Doctrine of Discovery to exercise its powers of extinguishment of First Nations' fundamental human rights in their traditional lands, as recognized under the UN Declaration and other international legal documents. Mineral and forestry development corporations are permitted to destroy the traditional lands used by First Nations' peoples for their subsistence, religious, and other cultural activities practiced for thousands of years. But under Canadian law and the Doctrine of Discovery, indigenous peoples are not compensated for the extinguishment of their property rights in these corporate-controlled lands. In fact, it has been impossible for First Nations to bring a successful legal case for recognition and protection of their rights to property in these traditional lands. No Canadian court decision has ever recognized the existence of indigenous peoples' property rights in their ancestral lands once granted to these private natural resource development companies. As the Inter-American Commission on Human Rights recently found in granting admissibility to a human rights complaint brought by the University of Arizona Indigenous Peoples Law and Policy Program by the Hul'qumi'num indigenous peoples in British Columbia challenging Canada's continued adherence to the Doctrine of Discovery and its racist legal principles, "there is no due process of law to protect the property rights" of First Nations in their traditional lands in Canada's courts.[27]

## AUSTRALIA

Like Canada, Australia, another of the Western world's most advanced and wealthiest nation-states, continues to perpetuate the Doctrine of Discovery and its racist language of savagery in its laws and policies defining the human rights of its indigenous tribal peoples. Government studies confirm that "indigenous Australians experience the worst health of any one identifiable cultural group in Australia," noting a seventeen-year gap in indigenous life expectancy compared to the nonindigenous population in Australia.[28] Indigenous peoples make up 24 percent of the total prison population, with a rate of imprisonment thirteen times higher than the nonindigenous population. Indigenous youth comprise more than 50 percent of persons in juvenile detention, a rate more than twenty times higher than for nonindigenous youth.[29]

Like Canada, Australia continues to apply the racist legal principles of the Doctrine of Discovery and its European colonial-era language of savagery in deciding the human rights of indigenous peoples. In 1992, in *Mabo v. Queensland* (No. 2), the Australian High Court reversed more than a century of Australian jurisprudence and official policy and finally recognized that, indeed, Australia was not *terra nullius* when it was discovered for England by Captain Cook in the eighteenth century. There were indigenous tribal peoples on the land as well as "native title": that is, a right of property based on indigenous peoples' customary land tenure. But even though the leading opinion in the case by Justice Gerard Brennan characterized the past failure of the Australian legal system to embrace and protect native title as being "unjust and discriminatory," the Court made it clear that the legal principles of the doctrine, particularly those affirming the government's power of unilaterally extinguishing rights in traditional lands, continue to define indigenous peoples' property rights under Australian law.[30]

The decision in *Members of the Yorta Yorta Aboriginal Community v. State of Victoria*[31] explains why the High Court's continued adherence to the Doctrine of Discovery causes anxiety and distress for Australia's indigenous peoples. The way the Doctrine is applied by courts in Australia threatens their continued cultural survival under twenty-first-century Australian law. The High Court in that case held that the ancestors of the present-day members of the Yorta Yorta community had somehow lost their traditional cultural connection to their land sometime before the end of the nineteenth century and therefore could not bring a claim for native title and property rights in Australia's courts. It had been effectively extinguished under Australian law. In so ruling, the High Court approved the trial judge's finding that the "tide of history has indeed washed away" the rights of the Yorta Yorta in their traditional lands, perpetuating a habit of resorting to a racist language of savagery that remains deeply embedded in twenty-first-century Australian law, despite the landmark *Mabo* decision.[32]

## THE UNITED STATES

In the United States, the Doctrine of Discovery, its underlying legal principles, and sometimes even its nineteenth-century racist language of savagery are still used by courts and policy makers to decide the basic human rights of American Indian tribes over their traditional lands and resources. A series of late-twentieth-century US Supreme Court decisions, beginning with then Associate Justice William Rehnquist's 1978 majority opinion in *Oliphant v. Suquamish Indian Tribe*,[33] highlights how justices on the highest court in the United States perpetuate the doctrine and its racist language of savagery to deny Indian tribal peoples their basic human rights as recognized under well-established principles of international law.

*Oliphant* denies Indian tribal governments the right to police their own reservations and protect their members from violent crimes committed by non-Indian offenders. The Supreme Court's subsequent decisions that have followed Rehnquist's opinion for the Court in *Oliphant* as binding precedent have significantly limited the civil and criminal jurisdiction of tribal governments over non-Indians on the reservation. As recognized by the Nobel Peace Prize–winning organization, Amnesty International, the Supreme Court's decisions limiting tribal jurisdiction in these cases is a significant contributing factor, along with the history of racist negative stereotyping of Indian women, to serious violations of the human rights of Indian women living in reservation communities.[34]

The Court's limitations on tribal criminal and civil jurisdiction over non-Indians (Congress has never voted on or approved these limits) make criminal prosecution for violence against Indian women who live in reservation communities throughout the United States particularly difficult. Human rights advocates cite to an "epidemic" of sexual and domestic violence afflicting Indian women nationwide. A US Department of Justice study found that more than one in three American Indian and Alaska Native women will be raped during their lifetime: The comparable figure for the United States as a whole is less than one in five. The Department also reports that in at least 86 percent of reported cases of rape or sexual assault against American Indian and Alaska Native women, survivors report that the perpetrators are non-Native men.[35]

In the language of savagery perpetuated by the Doctrine of Discovery in US law, Justice Rehnquist's 6–2 majority opinion for the Court in *Oliphant* held that Indian tribes, by virtue of their "diminished status," cannot punish the non-Indian perpetuators of these crimes that occur on the reservation. As Rehnquist explained, Indian tribes "come under the territorial sovereignty of the United States and their exercise of separate power is constrained so as not to conflict with the interests of this overriding sovereignty." As arresting and criminally prosecuting non-Indians who commit crimes of violence against members of the tribe on the reservation would "conflict" with the United States' overriding sovereign interests, under the principles of the Doctrine of Discovery, those specific tribal powers are extinguished.

The principle that tribes were unable to protect themselves from crimes committed by non-Indians, Rehnquist wrote, "would have been obvious a century ago when most Indian tribes were characterized by a 'want of fixed laws [and] of competent tribunals of justice.'" It should be "no less obvious today," he observed, despite the "dramatic advances" of some tribes in establishing their own tribal courts to take care of precisely these types of crimes on their reservations. It doesn't matter. The language of savagery per-petuated by the Doctrine of Discovery and the Supreme Court in *Oliphant* requires that Indian tribes have no power to try non-Indian citizens of the United States accused of raping and assaulting their female members, "ex-cept in a manner acceptable to Congress."

## SOMETHING TO BE ANXIOUS ABOUT: WESTERN CIVILIZATION WITHOUT THE IDEA OF THE SAVAGE

We are left with a "burning question"[36]: Why does the West still use a lan-guage of savagery originating with an ancient, blind Greek bard named Homer, who may have never existed, to justify its violations of the human rights of indigenous tribal peoples in the twenty-first century? I recognize that there is much more involved in the answer to that question than just a bad habit. As Chief Justice Marshall recognized in another of his famous Indian law opinions, "[P]ower, war, conquest, give rights, which, after pos-session, are conceded by the world, and which can never be controverted by those on whom they descend. We proceed then to the actual state of things, having glanced at their origin, because holding it in our recollection might shed light on existing pretensions."[37]

My simple hope in writing this book has been to shed light on a habit of thought and speech that has defined tribal peoples as irreconcilable sav-ages for close to three thousand years in the West, perpetually at war with civilization, and ultimately doomed to extinction. The best psychological research,[38] common sense, and human decency suggest that the "actual state of things" will likely be improved for indigenous peoples if the West can cure itself of its obsession with using a language of savagery perpetuated by racist legal principles like the Doctrine of Discovery to discuss and decide vitally important questions of contemporary tribalism's rights to cultural survival and flourishing in the twenty-first century. With intention, attention, time, and effort, it can be done. The burning question that should occupy our time then, I believe, is whether Western civilization will be able to reinvent itself and its law of indigenous peoples' human rights without using the idea of the savage.

# NOTES

## INTRODUCTION

1. *See, e.g.,* Patricia G. Devine, "Stereotypes and Prejudice: Their Automatic and Controlled Components," 65 *Journal of Personality and Social Psychology* 5 (1989); Patricia G. Devine et al., "Prejudice With and Without Compunction," 60 *Journal of Personality and Social Psychology* 817 (1991); Miles Hewstone, Klaus Jonas, and Wolfgang Stroebe, *An Introduction to Social Psychology* 93–118 (5th ed. 2012). *See also* Robert A. Williams, Jr., *Like a Loaded Weapon: The Rehnquist Court, Indian Rights, and the Legal History of Racism in America* 161–170 (2005).
2. *See* Walter Lippmann, *Public Opinion* 3 (1922).
3. Gordon Allport, *The Nature of Prejudice* 7 (1954).
4. 347 US 483 (1954).
5. *See* sources cited in note 1, *supra.*
6. Phyllis A. Katz, "The Acquisition of Racial Attitudes in Children," in *Towards the Elimination of Racism* 147 (Phyllis A. Katz ed. 1976).
7. *See, e.g.,* David L. Ronis et al., "Attitudes, Decisions, and Habits as Determinants of Repeated Behavior," in *Attitude, Structure and Function* 213, 218 (Anthony R. Pratkanis et al. eds. 1989).
8. *See* Percy Bysshe Shelley, "Preface" to *Hellas: A Lyrical Drama* viii–ix (Thomas James Wise trans., Reeves and Turner, 2d ed., 1886) (1821).
9. Sarah Iles Johnson, *Religions of the Ancient World: A Guide* 633 (2004). *See also* Margalit Finkelberg, "Homer as a Foundation Text," in *Homer, the Bible, and Beyond: Literary and Religious Canons in the Ancient World* 30 (Margalit Finkelberg and Guy G. Stroumsa eds. 2003).
10. Vine Deloria, Jr., "The Trickster and the Messiah," in *Spirit and Reason: The Vine Deloria, Jr. Reader* 30 (Barbara Deloria, Kristen Foehner, and Sam Scinta eds. 1999).

## CHAPTER 1: HOMER AND THE IDEA OF THE SAVAGE

1. All quotations for the *Iliad* are taken from Homer, *The Iliad* (A. T. Murray trans., Loeb Classical Library No. 170, 1924).
2. See, e.g., Merryl Wyn Davies, Ashis Nandy, and Ziauddin Sardar, *Barbaric Others: A Manifesto on Western Others* 27 (1993).
3. All quotations for the *Odyssey* are taken from Homer, *The Odyssey* (A. T. Murray trans., Loeb Classical Library No. 104, 1919).
4. The numbers quite frankly are all over the place, compounded by the fact that Homer, as a historical personality and author, might not have existed. For

consistency's sake, I follow Richard Janko's linguistic analysis of the poems, which concludes that the *Iliad* was composed between 750 and 725 B.C. and the *Odyssey* between 743 and 713 B.C. Richard Janko, *Homer, Hesiod and the Hymns: Diachronic Development in Epic Diction* 228–231 (1982).

5. See Milman Parry, *The Making of Homeric Verse: The Collected Papers of Milman Parry* (Adam Parry ed. 1971).

6. In Book IX of *The Odyssey*, the giant one-eyed Cyclops blinded by Odysseus is also named Polyphemus, but here in Book I of the *Iliad*, Nestor is apparently referring to a wholly different character, a "shadowy" figure in Greek mythology linked with the Argonaut expedition. See Virginia Knight, *The Renewal of Epic: Responses to Homer in the Argonautica of Apollonius* 130 (1995).

7. I follow the Loeb edition, *see supra*, this chapter. Homer's Greek phrasing, Φηρσὶυ ὀρεσκώοισι, is translated by Samuel Butler in his translation of the *Iliad* as "the fiercest tribes of mountain savages." Homer, *The Iliad* (Samuel Butler trans. 1999). Nestor's listing of the heroes traditionally associated with the Centauromachy makes it clear that the "savages" he is referring to are the mythical centaurs. Arthur O. Lovejoy and George Boas note in their essential text, *Primitivism and Related Ideas in Antiquity* (1935), that the phrase, which they translate as "wild men who dwell in the mountains," has traditionally been rendered simply as "with the centaurs." *Id.* at 23, n. 2. W. H. D. Rouse, in his version of the *Iliad*, translates the term as "monsters of the mountains," with a footnote indicating that Nestor is referring to the centaurs. Homer, *The Iliad* (W. H. D. Rouse trans. 1938).

8. Victor Alonso, "War, Peace, and International Law in Ancient Greece," in *War and Peace in the Ancient World*, 212–213 (Kurt A. Raaflaub ed. 2007).

9. James S. Romm, *The Edges of the Earth in Ancient Thought: Geography, Exploration, and Fiction*, 19–26 (1992).

10. *Id.* at 10–11.

11. *Id.* at 22–24.

12. As described by Hesiod in *Theogony:* "the savage, the bronze-barking dog of Hades, fifty-headed, and powerful, and without pity." Hesiod, *The Works and Days, Theogony, the Shield of Herakles*, 141 (Richard Lattimore trans. 1959).

13. Robin Sowerby, *The Greeks: An Introduction to Their Culture* 15 (1995).

## CHAPTER 2: THE LEGEND OF THE GOLDEN AGE AND THE IDEA OF THE SAVAGE

1. Perry Anderson, *Passages from Antiquity to Feudalism* 28 (1974) (emphasis supplied).

2. Mary E. White, "Greek Colonization," 21 *Journal of Economic History* 443, 445 (1961).

3. All quotations from *The Works and Days* are taken from Hesiod, *The Works and Days, Theogony, The Shield of Herakles* (Richard Lattimore trans. 1959).

4. On the language of savagery used to describe indigenous tribal peoples in modern-day Western nation-states like the United States of America, *see* Robert A. Williams, Jr., *Like a Loaded Weapon: The Rehnquist Court, Indian Rights, and the Legal History of Racism in America*, xxv–xxvii (2005).

5. All quotations from Dicaearchus's poem are taken from Arthur O. Lovejoy and George Boas, *Primitvism and Related Ideas in Antiquity* 94–96 (1935).

6. All quotations from Aratus's poem are taken from Arthur O. Lovejoy and George Boas, *supra* at 34–36.

7.  *See* James S. Romm, *The Edges of the Earth in Ancient Thought: Geography, Explo-ration, and Fiction* 49–52 (1992).

8.  All quotations from the *Odyssey* are taken from Homer, *The Odyssey* (A. T. Mur-ray trans., Loeb Classical Library No. 104, 1919).

9.  Romm, *supra* at 49–53.

10. All quotations from the *Iliad* are taken from Homer, *The Iliad* (A. T. Murray trans., Loeb Classical Library No. 170, 1924).

11. Thomas Bulfinch, *Bulfinch's Mythology* 178–179 (1979).

## CHAPTER 3: THE EMERGENCE OF THE CLASSICAL IDEA OF THE SAVAGE

1.  John E. Coleman, "Ancient Greek Ethnocentrism," in *Greeks and Barbarians: Es-says on the Interaction of Greeks and Non-Greeks* 189 (John E. Coleman and Clark A. Walz eds. 1997).

2.  Plutarch, "Convivial Questions," 621c, quoted in Alex T. Cheung, *Idol Food in Corinth: Jewish Background and Pauline Legacy* 35 (1999).

3.  François Lissarrague, "The Athenian Image of the Foreigner," in *Greeks and Bar-barians* 101–124 (Thomas Harrison ed. 2002).

4.  *See id.*

5.  *Id.*

6.  Edith Hall, *Inventing the Barbarian: Greek Self-Definition Through Tragedy* 9 (1989).

7.  *Id.* at 9–11.

8.  Coleman, *supra* at 178.

9.  Hall, *supra* at 101.

10. Coleman, *supra* at 189.

11. Hall, *supra* at 11.

12. *Id.* at 1.

13. *Id.* at 1.

14. Euripides, "Medea," in *Three Great Plays of Euripides:* Medea, Hippolytus, Helen 42 (Rex Warner trans. 1958).

15. Herodotus, *The Histories* xi–xii (Aubrey De Sélincourt and John Marincola trans. 1996).

16. Herodotus's reliability and methods as a historian are discussed in Detlev Feh-ling, *Herodotus and His "Sources": Citation, Invention, and Narrative Art* (J. G. Howie trans. 1989).

17. All quotations from the *Histories* are taken from Herodotus, *The Histories* (Au-brey De Sélincourt and John Marincola trans. 1996).

18. All quotations from the *Iliad* are taken from Homer, *The Iliad* (A. T. Murray trans., Loeb Classical Library No. 170, 1924).

## CHAPTER 4: THE CLASSICAL IDEA OF THE SAVAGE AND THE INVENTION OF WESTERN PHILOSOPHY

1.  *The Oxford Handbook of Plato* iii (Gail Fine ed. 2008).

2.  Kathleen Freeman, *Ancilla to the Pre-Socratic Philosophers* (1983).

3.  All quotations from the *Protagoras* are taken from Plato, *Protagoras* (Benjamin Jowett trans. 2009).

4.  Daphne O'Regan, *Rhetoric, Comedy and the Violence of Language in Aristophanes' Clouds* 6 (1992).

5. All quotations from the *Birds* are taken from Aristophanes, *The Birds of Aristophanes* 169–170 (Benjamin Bickley Rogers trans. 1906).

6. All quotations from the *Memorabilia* are taken from Xenophon, "Memorabilia," Book I, Section 4, in *Xenophon in Seven Volumes*, Vol. 4, Chapter 6 (E. C. Marchant ed. 1923).

7. All quotations from the *Republic* are taken from Plato, *Republic* 121 (Sir Henry Desmond Pritchard Lee trans. 1955).

8. Arthur O. Lovejoy and George Boas, *Primitivism and Related Ideas in Antiquity* 123 (1935).

9. Charles George Herbermann, ed., *The Catholic Encyclopedia* 582 (1913).

10. Lovejoy and Boas, *supra* at 117–123.

11. *Id.* at 118.

12. *See* Ronald L. Meek, *Social Science and the Ignoble Savage* 8 (1976); Plato, *The Laws* 55–61 (A. E. Taylor trans. 1960); Plato, "Laws," 676–682a, in *Plato in Twelve Volumes*, Vols. 10 and 11 (R. G. Bury trans. 1967); Lovejoy and Boas, *supra* at 162–166.

13. Lovejoy and Boas, *supra* at 180.

14. *Id.* at 175–177.

15. *Id.* at 179.

16. Aristotle, *The Politics of Aristotle* 6 (Benjamin Jowett trans. 1885).

17. Lovejoy and Boas, *supra* at 175–177.

18. *See generally* Wilfred Nippel, "The Construction of the 'Other,'" in *Greeks and Barbarians* 291–293 (Thomas Harrison ed. 2002); John E. Coleman, "Ancient Greek Ethnocentrism," in *Greeks and Barbarians: Essays on the Interaction of Greeks and Non-Greeks* 200–201 (John E. Coleman and Clark A. Walz eds. 1997).

## CHAPTER 5: THE IDEA OF THE SAVAGE AND THE RISE OF ROMAN IMPERIAL CIVILIZATION

1. All quotations from the *Gallic Wars* are taken from Julius Caesar, *The Gallic Wars* (W. A. McDevitte and W. S. Bohn trans. 1896).

2. Polybius, *Histories* Book II, Chapter 28 (quoted in Miranda Jane Aldhouse-Green ed., *The Celtic World* 53 [1995]).

3. Dionysius of Halicarnassus, *History of Rome* Book XIV, Chapter 9 (quoted in Miranda Jane Aldhouse-Green ed., *The Celtic World* 53 [1995]).

4. Lord Byron, *Childe Harold's Pilgrimage: Canto the Fourth*, stanza 140 (1818).

5. Frank Bigelow Tarbell, *A History of Greek Art* 261 (1907).

6. *See* Charles Norris Cochrane, *Christianity and Classical Culture: A Study of Thought and Action from Augustus to Augustine* 35 (2003).

7. Marcus Tullius Cicero, *Cicero's Brutus: Or a History of Famous Orators* 181 (Edward Jones trans. 1776).

8. Cheryl Glenn, *Unspoken: A Rhetoric of Silence* 150 (2004).

9. All quotations from the *Germania* are taken from Cornelius Tacitus, "The Germania," in *The Agricola and the Germania* (H. Mattingly trans. 1948).

10. Juha Pentikäinen, *Kalevala Mythology* 226 (Ritva Poom trans. 1999).

11. Arthur O. Lovejoy and George Boas, *Primitivism and Related Ideas in Antiquity* 357 (1935).

12. *Id.* at 357–358.

13. James S. Romm, *The Edges of the Earth in Ancient Thought: Geography, Exploration, and Fiction* 105 (1992) (quoting Book 7 of Pliny's *Natural History*).

## CHAPTER 6: PARALLEL LIVES

1. Quoted in Sallust, *Conspiracy of Catiline* 51.37–38 (John Selby Watson trans. 1867).
2. Charles Norris Cochrane, *Christianity and Classical Culture: A Study of Thought and Action from Augustus to Augustine* 104 (2003).
3. All quotations from *On the Nature of the Universe* are taken from Lucretius, *On the Nature of the Universe* (Ronald Latham trans. 1951).
4. Cochrane, *supra* at 43.
5. *Id.*
6. Peter W. Rose, "'The Conquest Continues': Towards Denaturalizing Greek and Roman Imperialisms," 96 *The Classical World* 409, 414 (2003) (quoting Cicero, *The Speeches: Pro Caelio; De provinciis consularibus; Pro Balbo* [R. Gardner trans. 1970]).
7. Arthur O. Lovejoy and George Boas, *Primitivism and Related Ideas in Antiquity* 244 (1935).
8. *Id.*
9. *Id.*
10. *Id.* at 251.
11. Quoted in Suetonius, *The Twelve Caesars* 61 (Robert Graves trans. 2003).
12. Cochrane, *supra* at 79.
13. *Id.* at 105–106.
14. *Id.* at 80.
15. See A. Bartlett Giamatti, *The Earthly Paradise and Renaissance Epic* 25 (1966) (quoting Virgil, Aeneid, Book VI ll. 791–795).
16. Lovejoy and Boas, *supra* at 58.
17. *Id.*
18. *Id.*
19. *Id.* at 46–47.
20. *Id.* at 46.
21. *Id.* at 47.
22. Ovid, "Tristia," 2.207, in *Tristia Ex Ponto* 71 (A. L. Wheeler trans. 1924).
23. Lovejoy and Boas, *supra* at 71.
24. *Id.*
25. *Id.* at 72.
26. *Id.* at 64.
27. *Id.* at 65.
28. *Id.* at 302.
29. *Id.*

## CHAPTER 7: THE MEDIEVAL CHRISTIAN CHURCH'S WAR ON THE CLASSICAL IDEA OF THE SAVAGE

1. Ernst Robert Curtius, *European Literature and the Latin Middle Ages* 22 (1991). I have relied extensively on this invaluable study by Professor Curtius, along with Peter Gay's prize-winning *The Enlightenment: An Interpretation: The Rise of Modern Paganism* (1966) and Charles Norris Cochrane's still-unsurpassed *Christianity and Classical Culture: A Study of Thought and Action from Augustus to Augustine* (1940), throughout this chapter.
2. Quoted in Curtius, *supra* at 40.
3. Quoted in Gay, *supra* at 219 (quoting Deuteronomy, XXI, 11–13) (1966).

4. *Id.* at 220.
5. *Id.* at 220.
6. *Id.* at 220–221.
7. 1 Corinthians 1:18–21, *The New Testament: A New Translation* (James Moffatt trans. 1919). See Walter M. Dunnett, "Scholarship and Spirituality," 31 *Journal for the Evangelical Study of the Old Testament* 1 (1988).
8. Tertullian, *Tertullian's Treatise on the Incarnation* 19 (Ernest Evans ed. and trans. 1956).
9. Gay, *supra* at 216.
10. Tertullian, *A Treatise on the Soul,* in *The Ante-Nicene Fathers: Latin Christianity: Its Founder, Tertullian. I. Apolgetic; II. Anti-Marcion; III. Ethical* 183 (Alexander Roberts, Sir James Donaldson, Arthur Cleveland Coxe, Allan Menzies, Ernest Cushing Richardson, Bernard Pick eds. 1903).
11. *Id.* at 183–184.
12. Quoted in Cochrane, *supra* at 244.
13. Tertullian, *A Treatise on the Soul, supra* at 183.
14. Quoted in Arthur O. Lovejoy and George Boas, *Primitivism and Related Ideas in Antiquity* 342 (1935).
15. *Id.*
16. *Id.*
17. Quoted in Curtius, *supra* at 22.
18. Quoted in Robert A. Williams, Jr., *The American Indian in Western Legal Thought: The Discourses of Conquest* 43 (1990).
19. Curtius, *supra* at 115.
20. *Id.* at 49.
21. Gay, *supra* at 223.
22. *Id.* at 219.
23. Helen Waddell, *The Wandering Scholars* 15 (1954). I have relied extensively on this invaluable book, along with A. Bartlett Giamatti's *The Earthly Paradise and Renaissance Epic* (1989), throughout this chapter in discussing the suppression of the idea of the savage in the medieval Christian era.
24. Waddell, *supra* at 16.
25. *Id.* at 18–19.
26. *Id.* at 20.
27. Giamatti, *supra* at 30–32.
28. *Id.* at 72.
29. *Id.* at 76.
30. Waddell, *supra* at 180.
31. *Id.* at 182–183.
32. *Id.* at 183–184.
33. *Id.* at 195.
34. *Id.* at 193.
35. *Id.* at 202.
36. *Id.* at 203.
37. *Id.* at 205.

## CHAPTER 8: THE WILD MAN AND THE MEDIEVAL CHRISTIAN IDEA OF THE SAVAGE

1. Hayden White, "The Forms of Wildness: Archaeology of an Idea," in *The Wild Man Within: An Image in Western Thought from the Renaissance to Romanticism*

12 (Edward Dudley and Maximilian E. Novak eds. 1972). I have relied on this leading essay by White and on Richard Bernheimer's invaluable *Wild Men in the Middle Ages: A Study in Art, Sentiment, and Demonology* 88–89 (1952) throughout this chapter.

2. White, *supra,* at 13.
3. *Id.* at 14 (emphasis in original).
4. *Id.* at 16.
5. *Id.* at 16 (emphasis in original).
6. *Id.* at 17–18.
7. *Id.* at 18.
8. Bernheimer, *supra.*
9. *Id.* at 89–90.
10. *Id.* at 91.
11. *Id.* at 92.
12. *Id.* at 93.
13. *Id.* at 96–97.
14. *Id.*
15. *Id.*
16. *Id.* at 97–98.
17. *Id.* at 99.
18. Bernheimer, *supra* at 101.
19. Ted Byfield, *Darkness Descends: A.D. 350 to 565, The Fall of the Western Roman Empire* 93 (2003).
20. Carl Erdmann, *The Origin of the Idea of Crusade* 8–11 (M. W. Baldwin and W. Goffart trans. 1977). *See also* Herbert A. Deane, *The Political and Social Ideas of St. Augustine* 154–220 (1963).
21. *Readings in Ancient History: Illustrative Extracts from the Sources,* Vol. 2, 374 (William Stearns Davis ed. 1913) (brackets in original).
22. *Urban and the Crusaders* 6 (Dana Carleton Munro ed. 1901).
23. *Id.* at 5–6.
24. James Muldoon, *Popes, Lawyers and Infidels: The Church and the Non-Christian World, 1250–1550* 16 (1979).
25. Brian Tierney, *The Crisis of Church and State: 1050–1300* 123 (1964).
26. All quotations from Innocent IV's Commentary on *Quod super hiis* are taken from Innocent IV, "Commentaria Doctissima in Quinque Libros Decretalium," in *The Expansion of Europe: The First Phase* 191–192 (James Muldoon ed. 1977) (hereinafter *The Expansion of Europe*).
27. M. J. Wilks, *The Problem of Sovereignty in the Later Middle Ages* 413 (1963).
28. *See The Expansion of Europe, supra* at 192.
29. *See* Muldoon, *Popes, Lawyers, and Infidels, supra* at 119.

## CHAPTER 9: THE RENAISSANCE HUMANIST REVIVAL OF THE CLASSICAL LANGUAGE OF SAVAGERY

1. Dennis Feeney, "Caesar's Body Shook," 33 *London Review of Books* 19, 19–20 (reviewing Peter White, *Cicero in Letters: Epistolary Relations of the Late Republic* [2010]).
2. Peter Gay, *The Enlightenment: An Interpretation: The Rise of Modern Paganism* 262 (1966).
3. *Id.* at 264.
4. James Bruce Ross and Mary Martin McLaughlin, *The Portable Renaissance Reader* 80 (1953).

5. *Id.* at 82–83.
6. *Id.* at 1.
7. *Id.*
8. *Id.* at 16.
9. François Rabelais, *The Works of Francis Rabelais,* Vol. 1, 342 (Sir Thomas Urquhart and Peter Anthony Motteux trans. 1807) (emphasis in original).
10. Ross and McLaughlin, *supra* at 89–91.
11. *Id.* at 89–90.
12. *Id.* at 91.
13. *Id.* at 79.
14. *Id.*
15. Gay, *supra* at 262.
16. All quotations from *The Excellence of This Age* are taken from Ross and McLaughlin, *supra* at 91–108.
17. All quotations from *Don Quixote* are taken from *id.* at 116–119.
18. Ronald Sanders, *Lost Tribes and Promised Lands: The Origins of American Racism* 16 (1992).
19. Immanuel Wallerstein, *The Modern World-System I: Capitalist Agriculture and the Origins of the European World-Economy in the Sixteenth Century* 38 (1974).
20. Pierre Bontier and Jean Le Verrier, *The Canarian, or, Book of the Conquest and Conversion of the Canarians in the year 1402* xiii–xix (Richard Henry Major trans. 1872, 1971).
21. Fernand Braudel, *The Structures of Everyday Life: The Limits of the Possible,* 395 (1979).
22. Quoted in Sanders, *supra* at 35.
23. *Id.* at 35–36.
24. *Id.* at 36–37.
25. *Id.* at 36.
26. *Id.* at 36–37.
27. *Id.*
28. Quoted in *The Expansion of Europe: The First Phase,* 54–56 (James Muldoon ed. 1977).
29. *Id.* at 55.
30. Quoted in *Church and State Through the Centuries* 142 (Sidney Ehler and John Morrall trans. and eds. 1967).

## CHAPTER 10: THE RENAISSANCE DISCOVERY ERA AND THE IDEA OF THE SAVAGE

1. Robert A. Williams, Jr., *The American Indian in Western Legal Thought: The Discourses of Conquest* 74–81 (1990). *See also* Arthur Nussbaum, *A Concise History of the Law of Nations* 62–63 (rev. ed. 1954); Samuel Eliot Morison, *The European Discovery of America: The Southern Voyages,* A.D. *1492–1616* 27–44 (1974).
2. Williams, *supra* at 76; Morison, *supra* at 27–54.
3. Quoted in Ronald Sanders, *Lost Tribes and Promised Lands: The Origins of American Racism* 100 (1992).
4. Quoted in Sanders, *supra* at 77.
5. Quoted in Tzvetan Todorov, *The Conquest of America: The Question of the Other* 15–16 (1999).
6. Robert Berkhofer, Jr., *The White Man's Indian: Images of the American Indian from Columbus to the Present* 5 (1979).

7. Quoted in Sanders, *supra* at 93–94.
8. Quoted in Todorov, *supra* at 36, 38.
9. *Id.* at 39.
10. Quoted in Sanders, *supra* at 94.
11. Quoted in Stanley L. Robe, "Wild Men and Spain's Brave New World," in *The Wild Man Within: An Image in Western Thought from the Renaissance to Romanticism* 44 (Edward Dudley and Maximilian E. Novak eds. 1972).
12. *Select Letters of Christopher Columbus, with Other Original Documents Relating to his Four Voyages to the New World* 25–31 (Richard Henry Major ed. and trans. 1847, 1961) [hereinafter *Select Letters*]; Peter Hulme, "Tales of Distinction: European Ethnography and the Caribbean," in *Implicit Understandings: Observing, Reporting, and Reflecting on Encounters Between Europeans and Other People in the Early Modern Era* 168 (Stewart B. Schwartz ed. 1994).
13. *Select Letters, supra* at 25–31.
14. Quoted in Todorov, *supra* at 43.
15. Christopher Columbus, *The Journal of Christopher Columbus* 194–200 (L. A. Vigneras ed. 1960).
16. *Id.* at 81–82.
17. Sanders, *supra* at 95.
18. *The First Three English Books on America* xxvii (Edward Arber ed. 1885) (some spelling modernized).
19. H. C. Porter, *The Inconstant Savage: England and the North American Indian, 1500–1660* 15 (1979).
20. Richard Hakluyt, *The Principal Navigations, Voyages, Traffiques and Discoveries of the English Nation*, Vol. 7, 224 (1904) (some spelling modernized).
21. Quoted in Roy Harvey Pearce, *The Savages of America: A Study of the Indian and the Idea of Civilization* 5 (rev. ed. 1965) (some spellings modernized).
22. *The Voyages and Colonizing Enterprises of Sir Humphrey Gilbert*, Vol. 2, 76–81 (David B. Quinn ed. 1940) (some spelling modernized).
23. *The Original Writings and Correspondence of the Two Richard Hakluyts*, Vol. 1, 231–232 (E. G. R. Taylor ed. 1935) (some spelling modernized).
24. "The First Charter of Virginia," in *Documents of American History* 8–10 (Henry Steele Commager 8th ed. 1968) (emphasis in original).
25. *Calvin's Case*, 77 Eng. Rep. 377, 378 (1608).
26. *Campbell v. Hall*, 1 Cowp. 204 (1774). *See also* Robert A. Williams, Jr., *The American Indian in Western Legal Thought: The Discourses of Conquest* 200 (1990).
27. Alberico Gentili, *De jure belli libri tres* 341 (J. Rolfe trans. 1964).
28. Bernard W. Sheehan, *Savagism and Civility: Indians and Englishmen in Colonial Virginia* 40–41 (1980).
29. Michel Eyquem de Montaigne, *The Essays of Michel Eyquem de Montaigne* 93–94 (Charles Cotton trans., W. Carew Hazlitt ed. 1952).
30. William Strachey, *Historie of Travaile into Virginia Britannia*, in *Dominion and Civility: English Imperialism and Native America, 1585–1685* 53 (Michael Leroy Oberg ed. 2004) (some spellings modernized).
31. Williams, *supra* at 210.
32. Williams, *supra* at 210–211.
33. Quoted in Roy Harvey Pearce, *The Savages of America: A Study of the Indian and the Idea of Civilization* 12 (rev. ed. 1965) (emphasis in original; some spellings modernized).
34. Quoted in *id.* at 14–15 (some spellings modernized).

35. Alexander Whitaker, *Goode Newes from Virginia* 24–27 (1613); quoted in Robert F. Berkhofer, Jr., *supra* at 19 (1978) (some spellings modernized).

36. All quotations from Waterhouse's text are taken from Edward Waterhouse, "A Declaration of the State of the Colony and Affairs in Virginia. With a Relation of the Barbarous Massacre in the Time of Peace and League, Treacherously Executed by the Native Infidels upon the English, the 22 of March Last. Together with the Names of those Massacred," in *The Records of the Virginia Company of London*, Vol. 3, 541–571 (Susan Myra Kingsbury ed. 1933).

37. Williams, *supra* at 216–218.

38. Samuel Purchas, *Hakluytus Posthumus, or Purchas His Pilgrimes*, Vol. 19, 231–232 (1906) (some spellings modernized).

## CHAPTER 11: THE ENLIGHTENMENT IDEA OF THE SAVAGE AND THE FOUNDERS' FIRST INDIAN POLICY

1. All quotations are taken from Jean-Jacques Rousseau, *The Social Contract and Discourses* (G. D. H. Cole trans., J. H. Brumfitt and J. C. Hall eds. 1973).

2. *See* Arthur O. Lovejoy, "The Supposed Primitivism of Rousseau's Discourse on Inequality," 21 *Modern Philology* 184–186 (1923); Arthur O. Lovejoy and George Boas, *Primitivism and Related Ideas in Antiquity* 239–242 (1935).

3. Lovejoy and Boas, *supra* at 240–241.

4. Ronald L. Meek, *Social Science and the Ignoble Savage* 77–78 (1976).

5. *Id.* at 80.

6. *Id.* at 17.

7. Hugo Grotius, *The Law of War and Peace*, Book II, 78–80 (Louise R. Loomis trans. 1949).

8. Meek, *supra* at 16–17.

9. *Id.* at 17 (emphasis in original).

10. All quotes from *Two Treatises on Government* are taken from John Locke, *Two Treatises on Government* (Peter Laslett ed. 1965).

11. Meek, *supra* at 81.

12. Meek, *supra* at 2.

13. All quotes from *The Spirit of the Laws* are taken from Baron de Montesquieu, *The Spirit of the Laws*, Vol. 1 (Thomas Nugent trans. 1949).

14. Meek, *supra* at 116–125.

15. *Id.* at 142.

16. Roy Harvey Pearce, *The Savages of America: A Study of the Indian and the Idea of the Civilization* 84–85 (rev. ed. 1965).

17. All quotes from Smith are taken from Meek, *supra* at 117–124.

18. Pearce, *supra* at 106.

19. "George Washington to James Duanne, September 7, 1783," reprinted in *Documents of United States Indian Policy* 1–2 (Francis Paul Prucha ed., 2nd ed., 1990).

20. *Id.* at 2.

21. Francis Paul Prucha, *American Indian Treaties: The History of an Anomaly* 42–44 (1994).

22. Maryly Barton Penrose, *Indian Affairs Papers, American Revolution* 292 (1981).

23. Walter Mohr, *Federal Indian Relations, 1784–1788* 171 (1933).

24. Quoted in Bernard W. Sheehan, *Seeds of Extinction: Jeffersonian Philanthropy and the American Indian* 76 (1973).

25. Quoted in Pearce, *supra* at 93–94.

26. *Inaugural Addresses of the Presidents of the United States: From George Washington, 1789 to George H. W. Bush, 1989* 20 (Joint Congressional Committee on Inaugural Ceremonies ed. 2008).

27. Pearce, *supra* at 95–96.

## CHAPTER 12: SAVAGE ANXIETIES

1. American Psychiatric Association, *Diagnostic and Statistical Manual of Mental Disorders* 457 (4th ed. Text Revision, 2000) (emphasis in original).

2. *See* Walter Lippmann, *Public Opinion* 3 (1922).

3. The Development, Relief, and Education for Alien Minors Act ("DREAM Act") was introduced on May 11, 2011, and would provide a pathway to citizenship for undocumented students graduating from high school. S. 952, 112th Cong. (2011); H.R. 1842, 112th Cong. (2011).

4. This ranking was provided by the NDP Group, a market-research company tracking department store sales. Michael Walker, "That Man Smells Familiar," *The New York Times* E3 (October 20, 2011).

5. Alex Shakar, *The Savage Girl* 4 (2001).

6. *Id.* at 3.

7. *Id.* at 97, quoted in Dorothea Löbbermann, "Fashion/ing Statements: Reading Homeless Bodies in Contemporary Fiction," *Expositions* 5.1 (2011): 62–69.

8. Patricia G. Devine, "Stereotypes and Prejudice: Their Automatic and Controlled Components," 65 *Journal of Personality and Social Psychology* 5, 16 (1989); Patricia G. Devine et al., "Prejudice With and Without Compunction," 60 *Journal of Personality and Social Psychology* 817, 817–819 (1991). *See also* Miles Hewstone, Klaus Jonas, and Wolfgang Stroebe, *An Introduction to Social Psychology* 96 (5th ed. 2012).

9. All quotations from Chief Justice Marshall's opinion are found in *Johnson v. McIntosh*, 21 U.S. 543 (1823).

10. *Spirit and Reason: The Vine Deloria, Jr. Reader* 30 (Barbara Deloria, Kristen Foehner, and Sam Scinta eds. 1999).

11. *St. Catherine's Milling & Lumber Co. v. The Queen*, [1888] 14 App. Cas. 46, 48 (J.C.P.C.).

12. [1929] 1 D.L.R. 307 (Co. Ct.).

13. *Id.* at 313–314.

14. Quoted in Stuart Banner, "Why Terra Nullius?" Anthropology and Property Law in Early Australia, 23 *Law and History Review* 95, 104 (2005).

15. *See generally* Michael C. Blumm, "Native Fishing Rights and Environmental Protection in North America and New Zealand: A Comparative Analysis of Profits A Prendre and Habitat Servitudes," 8 *Wisconsin International Law Journal* 1, 30–32 (1989).

16. 3 Jur. (N.S.) 72 (1877).

17. See Blumm, *supra* at 32–33.

18. *See generally* C. Hyde, *International Law Chiefly as Interpreted and Applied by the United States* Vol. 1, 320–330 (1945).

19. *See* Lassa Oppenheim, *International Law: A Treatise*, Vol. 1, Peace, 383 (Ronald F. Roxburgh, 3rd ed. 1920).

20. J. Westlake, *Chapters on the Principles of International Law* 136–140 (1894).

21. *Id.* at 141–143.

22. *See id.*

23. G. A. Res 61/295, U.N. Doc. A/RES/61/295 (September 13, 2007).

24. *Hul'qumi'num Treaty Group v. Canada* (Admissibility Report), Inter-Am. C. H. R., Petition 592–07, Report No. 105/09, October 30, 2009.

25. Indian and Northern Affairs Canada, *First Nation and Inuit Community Well-Being: Describing Historical Trends (1981–2006)* (Strategic Research and Analysis Directorate, April 2010).

26. *See* UN Committee on Economic, Social and Cultural Rights, Concluding Observations of the Committee on Economic, Social and Cultural Rights: Canada, UN Doc E/C.12/1/Add.31, Para. 18 (December 10, 1998).

27. IACHR, Report No. 105/09, *supra* at paras. 35–38 (2009) (footnotes omitted). I serve as lead counsel on the case.

28. *Report by the Special Rapporteur on the situation of human rights and fundamental freedoms of indigenous people, James Anaya Addendum Situation of indigenous peoples in Australia,* A/HRC/15/37/Add.4 June 2010, para. 32.

29. *Id.* at para. 50.

30. [1992] H.C.A. 23 (High Court of Australia).

31. [2002] H.C.A. 58 (High Court of Australia).

32. *Id.* quoting *Members of the Yorta Yorta Aboriginal Community v. Victoria* [1998], FCA 1606 at para. 129.

33. 432 U.S. 191 (1978).

34. Amnesty International, *Maze of Injustice: The Failure to Protect Indigenous Women from Sexual Violence in the USA* (2006).

35. *Id.* at 2–4.

36. Deloria, *supra* at 30.

37. *Worcester v. Georgia,* 31 U.S. 515 (1832).

38. *See* sources cited, *supra* note 8.

# BIBLIOGRAPHY

I consulted numerous books, articles, and other sources in the course of researching and writing this book over a ten-year period. The following is by no means an exhaustive list of all the works I found helpful or that influenced my thinking on the idea of the savage in the history of the West, but it does reflect those sources I either quoted directly or relied on extensively throughout my research, as indicated in the notes accompanying each chapter.

Aeschylus. *Persians and Other Plays.* Translated by Christopher Collard. Oxford, UK: Oxford University Press, 2008.

Aldhouse-Green, Miranda Jane, ed. *The Celtic World.* New York: Routledge, 1995.

Allen, Stephen. *Celtic Warrior: 300 BC–AD 100.* Illustrated by Wayne Reynolds. Oxford, UK: Osprey, 2001.

Allport, Gordon. *The Nature of Prejudice.* Reading, MA: Addison-Wesley, 1954, 1979.

American Psychiatric Association. *Diagnostic and Statistical Manual of Mental Disorders,* 4th ed., Text Revision. Arlington, VA: Author, 2000.

Anderson, Perry. *Lineages of the Absolutist State.* London, UK: Verso, 1974.

Anderson, Perry. *Passages from Antiquity to Feudalism.* London, UK: Verso, 1974.

Arber, Edward, ed. *The First Three English Books on America.* Birmingham, UK: Author, 1885.

Aristophanes. "The Birds." In *Aristophanes II.* Translated by Benjamin Bickley Rogers. London, UK: William Heinemann, 1927.

Aristotle. *The Politics of Aristotle.* Translated by Ernest Barker. Oxford, UK: Clarendon Press, 1948.

Bakaoukas, Michael. "Ancient Greek Cultural 'Proto-Racism': Were the Ancient Greeks Racists?" 1 *ERCES Online Quarterly Review* (2004).

Balsdon, J. P. V. D. *Romans & Aliens.* Chapel Hill, NC: University of North Carolina Press, 1979.

Beard, Mary, and Michael Crawford. *Rome in the Late Republic.* Ithaca, NY: Cornell University Press, 1985.

Berkhofer, Robert F., Jr. *The White Man's Indian: Images of the American Indian from Columbus to the Present.* New York: Vintage Books, 1978.

Bernal, Martin. *Black Athena: The Afroasiatic Roots of Classical Civilization,* Vol. 1. London, UK: Free Association Press, 1987.

Bernheimer, Richard. *Wild Men in the Middle Ages: A Study in Art, Sentiment, and Demonology.* Cambridge, MA: Harvard University Press, 1952.

Blickman, Daniel R. "Lucretius, Epicurus, and Prehistory," 92 *Harvard Studies in Classical Philology* 157 (1989).

Blumm, Michael C. "Native Fishing Rights and Environmental Protection in North America and New Zealand: A Comparative Analysis of Profits A Prendre and Habitat Servitudes," 8 *Wisconsin International Law Journal* 1 (1989).

Bontier, Pierre, and Jean Le Verrier. *The Canarian, or, Book of the Conquest and Conversion of the Canarians in the Year 1402.* Translated by Richard Henry Major. London, UK: Hakluyt Society, 1872; New York: Franklin, 1971.

Brady, Thomas A., Heiko Augustinius Oberman, and James D. Tracy, eds. *Handbook of European History, 1400–1600: Late Middle Ages, Renaissance, and Reformation.* Leiden, the Netherlands: Brill, 1995.

Braudel, Fernand. *The Structures of Everyday Life: The Limits of the Possible.* Translated by Sian Reynolds. Berkeley, CA: University of California Press, 1981.

Bridges, Emma, Edith Hall, and P. J. Rhodes, eds. *Cultural Responses to the Persian Wars: Antiquity to the Third Millennium.* Oxford, UK: Oxford University Press, 2007.

Brown, G. Baldwin. *The Fine Arts: A Manual* (4th ed.). New York: Charles Scribner's Sons, 1916.

Brown, Peter. *The Rise of Western Christendom* (2nd ed.). Malden, MA: Blackwell, 2003.

Bryson, Gladys. *Man and Society: The Scottish Inquiry of the Eighteenth Century.* Princeton, NJ: Princeton University Press, 1945.

Bulfinch, Thomas. *Bulfinch's Mythology.* New York: Thomas Y. Crowell, 1913.

Burkert, Walter. *Greek Religion.* Cambridge, MA: Wiley-Blackwell, 1991.

Burkert, Walter. *Structure and History in Greek Mythology and Ritual.* Berkeley, CA: University of California Press, 1982.

Byfield, Ted. *Darkness Descends: A.D. 350 to 565, The Fall of the Western Roman Empire.* Edmonton, Alberta: Christian History Project, 2003.

Byron, Lord George Gordon. *Childe Harold's Pilgrimage: Canto the Fourth.* London, UK: John Murray, 1818.

Caesar, Julius. *The Gallic Wars.* Translated by W. A. McDevitte and W. S. Bohn. New York: Harper and Brothers, 1896.

Calcani, Giuliana, et al. *Apollodorus of Damascus and Trajan's Column: From Tradition to Project.* Rome, Italy: L'Erma di Bretschneider, 2003.

Campbell, Joseph. *The Hero with a Thousand Faces.* Princeton, NJ: Princeton University Press, 1949.

Cassani, Silvia, ed. *Pompeii: A Guide to the Site (English).* Naples, Italy: Electa, 2002.

Champion, Craige B., ed. *Roman Imperialism: Readings and Sources.* Malden, MA: Blackwell, 2004.

Cheung. Alex T. *Idol Food in Corinth: Jewish Background and Pauline Legacy.* Sheffield, UK: Sheffield Academic Press, 1999.

Cicero, Marcus Tullius. *Cicero's Brutus: Or a History of Famous Orators.* Translated by Edward Jones. London, UK: B. White, 1776.

Cicero, Marcius Tullius. *Selected Works.* Translated by Michael Grant. Harmondsworth, UK: Penguin Books, 1971.

Clark, Kenneth B., and Mamie P. Clark. "Racial Identification and Preference among Negro Children," in *Readings in Social Psychology,* ed. E. L. Hartley. New York: Holt, Reinhart, and Winston, 1947.

Cochrane, Charles Norris. *Christianity and Classical Culture: A Study of Thought and Action from Augustus to Augustine.* Indianapolis, IN: Liberty Fund, 2003.

Cole, Thomas. *Democritus and the Sources of Greek Anthropology.* London, UK: American Philological Association, 1967.

Coleman, John E. "Ancient Greek Ethnocentrism," in *Greeks and Barbarians: Essays on the Interaction of Greeks and Non-Greeks*, ed. John E. Coleman and Clark A. Walz. Bethesda, MD: CDL Press, 1997.

Columbus, Christopher. *The Journal of Christopher Columbus*, ed. L. A. Vigneras. London, UK: Hakluyt Society, 1960.

Commager, Henry Steele, ed., *Documents of American History* (8th ed.). New York: Appleton-Century-Crofts, 1968.

Connelly, Joan Breton. *Portrait of a Priestess: Women and Ritual in Ancient Greece*. Princeton, NJ: Princeton University Press, 2007.

Cotterill, H. B. *Ancient Greece*. Hertfordshire, UK: Oracle, 1996.

Curtius, Ernst Robert. *European Literature and the Latin Middle Ages*. Princeton, NJ: Princeton University Press, 1991.

Davies, J. K. *Democracy and Classical Greece* (2nd ed.). Cambridge, MA: Harvard University Press, 1993.

Davies, Merryl Wyn, Ashis Nandy, and Ziauddin Sardar. *Barbaric Others: A Manifesto on Western Racism*. London, UK: Pluto Press, 1993.

Davis, William Stearns, ed. *Readings in Ancient History: Illustrative Extracts from the Sources*, Vol. 2. Norwood, MA: Norwood Press, 1913.

Deloria, Vine, Jr. *Spirit and Reason: The Vine Deloria, Jr. Reader*, eds. Barbara Deloria, Kristen Foehner, and Sam Scinta. Golden, CO: Fulcrum, 1999.

Devine, Patricia G., et al. "Prejudice With and Without Compunction," 60 *Journal of Personality and Social Psychology* 817 (1991).

Dickason, Olive Patricia. *The Myth of the Savage and the Beginnings of French Colonialism in the Americas*. Edmonton, Alberta: University of Alberta Press, 1984.

Dobbs, E. R. *The Greeks and the Irrational*. Berkeley, CA: University of California Press, 1951.

Dougherty, Carol. *The Raft of Odysseus: The Ethnographic Imagination of Homer's Odyssey*. Oxford, UK: Oxford University Press, 2001.

Dougherty, Carol, and Leslie Kurke, eds. *Cultural Poetics in Archaic Greece: Cult, Performance, Politics*. New York: Oxford University Press, 1998.

Drinnon, Richard. *Facing West: The Metaphysics of Indian-Hating and Empire-Building*. Minneapolis, MN: University of Minnesota Press, 1980.

Dudley, Edward, and Maximilian E. Novak. *The Wild Man Within: An Image in Western Thought from the Renaissance to Romanticism*. Pittsburgh, PA: University of Pittsburgh Press, 1972.

Dunnett, Walter M. "Scholarship and Spirituality," 31 *Journal for the Evangelical Study of the Old Testament* 1 (1998).

Ehler, Sidney Z., and John B. Morrall. *Church and State Through the Centuries*. New York: Biblo and Tannen, 1967.

Erdmann, Carl. *The Origin of the Idea of Crusade*. Translated by M. W. Baldwin and W. Goffart. Princeton, NJ: Princeton University Press, 1977.

Euripides. *Ten Plays*. Translated by Moses Hadas and John McLean. New York: Bantam Books, 1960.

Euripides. *Three Great Plays of Euripides:* Medea, Hippolytus, Helen. Translated by Rex Warner. New York: Mentor Books, 1958.

Finkelberg, Margalit. "Homer as a Foundational Text," in *Homer, the Bible, and Beyond: Literary and Religious Canons in the Ancient World*, eds. Margalit Finkelberg and Guy G. Stroumsa. Leiden, the Netherlands: Brill, 2003.

Fleming, William. *Arts and Ideas* (3rd ed.). New York: Holt, Rinehart, and Winston, 1968.

Fletcher, Richard. *The Barbarian Conversion: From Paganism to Christianity*. New York: Holt, 1998.

Foxhall, Lin. "Cargoes of the Heart's Desire: The Character of Trade in the Archaic Mediterranean World," in *Archaic Greece: New Approaches and New Evidence*, eds. Nick Fisher and Hans van Wees. London, UK: Classical Press of Wales, 1998.

Freeman, Kathleen. *Ancilla to the Pre-Socratic Philosophers*. Cambridge, MA: Harvard University Press, 1983.

Gallagher, Clarence. "The Imperial Ecclesiastical Lawgivers," in *The First Christian Theologians: An Introduction to Theology in the Early Church*, ed. G. R. Evans. Malden, MA: Blackwell, 2004.

Gay, Peter. *The Enlightenment: The Rise of Modern Paganism*. New York: W. W. Norton, 1966.

Gentili, Alberico. *De jure belli libri tres*. Translated by John C. Rolfe. New York: Oceana, 1964.

Gerlach, Don R. *Philip Schuyler and the American Revolution in New York, 1733–1777*. Lincoln, NE: University of Nebraska Press, 1964.

Getches, David H., Charles F. Wilkinson, Robert A. Williams, Jr., and Matthew L. M. Fletcher. *Cases and Materials on Federal Indian Law* (6th ed.). St. Paul, MN: West, 2011.

Giamatti, A. Barltett. *The Earthly Paradise and the Renaissance Epic*. Princeton, NJ: Princeton University Press, 1966.

Gill, James E. "Theriophily in Antiquity: A Supplementary Account," 30 *Journal of the History of Ideas* 401 (1969).

Glenn, Cheryl. *Unspoken: A Rhetoric of Silence*. Carbondale, IL: Southern Illinois University Press, 2004.

Grant, Michael. *History of Rome*. New York: Quality Paperback Book Club, 1978.

Grindle, Gilbert. *The Destruction of Paganism in the Roman Empire*. Oxford, UK: Blackwell, 1892.

Grotius, Hugo. *The Law of War and Peace*, Book II. Roslyn, NY: Walter J. Black, 1949.

Gummere, Richard M. *The American Colonial Mind and the Classical Tradition: Essays in Comparative Culture*. Cambridge, MA: Harvard University Press, 1963.

Guthrie, W. K. C. *A History of Greek Philosophy*, Vol. 3: *The Fifth-Century Enlightenment*. Cambridge, UK: Cambridge University Press, 1969.

Hakluyt, Richard. *The Principle Navigations, Voyages, Traffiques and Discoveries of the English Nation*. Glasgow, Scotland: J. MacLehose and Sons, 1904.

Hall, Edith. *Inventing the Barbarian: Greek Self-Definition Through Tragedy*. Oxford, UK: Clarendon Press, 1989.

Hall, Jonathan M. *Ethnic Identity in Greek Antiquity*. Cambridge, MA: Harvard University Press, 1997.

Hejduk, Julia. "Jupiter's Aeneid: Fama and Imperium," 28 *Classical Antiquity* 279 (2009).

Herodotus. *The Histories*. Translated by Aubrey De Sélincourt and John Marincola. New York: Penguin Books, 1996.

Hesiod. *The Works and Days, Theogony, the Shield of Herakles*. Translated by Richard Lattimore. Ann Arbor, MI: University of Michigan Press, 1959.

Homer. *The Iliad: Books 1–12*. Translated by A. T. Murray. Loeb Classical Library No. 170. Cambridge, MA: Harvard University Press, 1924.

Homer. *The Iliad*. Translated by W. H. D. Rouse. New York: Signet Classic, 1966.

Homer. *The Odyssey: Books 1–12*. Translated by A. T. Murray. Loeb Classical Library No. 104. Cambridge, MA: Harvard University Press, 1919.

Homer. *The Odyssey*. Translated by W. H. D. Rouse. New York: Signet Classic, 1937.

Hulme, Peter. "Tales of Distinction: European Ethnography and the Caribbean," in *Implicit Understandings: Observing, Reporting, and Reflecting on Encounters Between Europeans and Other People in the Early Modern Era*, ed. Stewart B. Schwartz. Cambridge, UK: Cambridge University Press, 1994.

Hyde, Charles Cheney. *International Law Chiefly as Interpreted and Applied by the United States*. Boston, MA: Little, Brown, 1945.

Isaac, Benjamin. *The Invention of Racism in Classical Antiquity*. Princeton, NJ: Princeton University Press, 2006.

Jaeger, Werner. *Paideia: The Ideals of Greek Culture*, Vol. 1 (2nd ed.). Translated by Gilbert Highet. New York: Oxford University Press, 1945.

Jahoda, Gustav. *Images of Savages: Ancient Roots of Modern Prejudice in Western Culture*. London, UK: Routledge, 1999.

Janko, Richard. *Homer, Hesiod and the Hymns: Diachronic Development in Epic Diction*. Cambridge, UK: Cambridge University Press, 1982.

Jefferson, Thomas. *The Writings of Thomas Jefferson*, Vol. 2, eds. Andrew A. Lipscomb and Albert Ellery Bergh. Washington, DC: Jefferson Memorial Association, 1904.

Johnson, Sarah Iles. *Religions of the Ancient World: A Guide*. Cambridge, MA: Harvard University Press, 2004.

Johnson, Steve. "Skills, Socrates and the Sophists: Learning from History," 46 *British Journal of Educational Studies* 201 (1998).

Joint Congressional Committee on Inaugural Ceremonies, ed. *Inaugural Addresses of the Presidents of the United States: From George Washington, 1789 to George H. W. Bush, 1989*. New York: Cosimo, 2008.

Jones, W. R. "The Image of the Barbarian in Medieval Europe," 13 *Comparative Studies in Society and History* 376 (1971).

Jung, C. G. *Psyche and Symbol*, ed. Violet S. de Laszlo. Garden City, NY: Anchor Books, 1958.

Juvenal. *The Sixteen Satires*. Translated by Peter Green. Harmondsworth, UK: Penguin Books, 1974.

Katz, Phyllis A. "The Acquisition of Racial Attitudes in Children," in *Towards the Elimination of Racism*, ed. Phyllis A. Katz. New York: Pergamon Press, 1976.

Kerferd, G. B. "The First Greek Sophists," 64 *Classical Review* 8 (1950).

Kingsbury, Susan Myra, ed. *The Records of the Virginia Company of London*, Vol. 3. Washington, DC: Government Printing Office, 1933.

Knight, Virginia. *The Renewal of Epic: Responses to Homer in the Argonautica of Apollonius*. Leiden, the Netherlands: Brill, 1995.

Kors, Alan Charles, and Edward Peters. *Witchcraft in Europe, 400–1700: A Documentary History* (rev. ed.). Philadelphia, PA: University of Pennsylvania Press, 2001.

Levi, Adolfo. "The Ethical and Social Thought of Protagoras," 49 *Mind* 284 (1940).

Levin, Harry. *The Myth of the Golden Age in the Renaissance*. Oxford, UK: Oxford University Press, 1972.

Lippmann, Walter. *Public Opinion*. New York: Harcourt, Brace, 1922.

Lissarrague, François. "The Athenian Image of the Foreigner," in *Greeks and Barbarians*, ed. Thomas Harrison. New York: Routledge, 2002.

Lloyd, G. E. R. *Polarity and Analogy: Two Types of Argumentation in Early Greek Thought*. Indianapolis, IN: Hackett, 1966.

Löbbermann, Dorothea. "Fashion/ing Statements: Reading Homeless Bodies in Contemporary Fiction," 5.1 *Expositions* 62 (2011).

Locke, John. *Two Treatises on Government*, ed. Peter Laslett. New York: New American Library, 1965.

Long, Timothy. "Pherecrates' 'Savages': A Footnote to the Greek Attitude on the Noble Savage," 71 *Classical World* 381 (1978).

Lovejoy, Arthur O. *Essays in the History of Ideas*. Baltimore, MD: Johns Hopkins University Press, 1948.

Lovejoy, Arthur O. "The Supposed Primitivism of Rousseau's *Discourse on Inequality*," 21 *Modern Philology* 165 (1923).

Lovejoy, Arthur O., and George Boas. *Primitivism and Related Ideas in Antiquity*. Baltimore, MD: Johns Hopkins University Press, 1935.

Lucretius. *On the Nature of the Universe*. Translated by Ronald Latham. Baltimore, MD: Penguin Books, 1951.

Lyons, Claire L., and John K. Papadopoulos. *The Archaeology of Colonialism*. Los Angeles, CA: Getty Research Institute, 2002.

MacMullen, Ramsay. *Christianizing the Roman Empire: A.D. 100–400*. New Haven, CT: Yale University Press, 1984.

Major, Richard Henry, trans. and ed. *Select Letters of Christopher Columbus, with Other Original Documents Relating to His Four Voyages to the New World*. London, UK: Hakluyt Society, 1847; New York: Corinth Books, 1961.

Malkin, Irad. "Postcolonial Concepts and Ancient Greek Colonization," 65 *Modern Language Quarterly* 341 (2004).

Malkin, Irad. *The Returns of Odysseus: Colonization and Ethnicity*. Berkeley, CA: University of California Press, 1998.

Mayor, Adrienne. *The First Fossil Hunters: Paleontology in Greek and Roman Times*. Princeton, NJ: Princeton University Press, 2000.

Mayr-Harting, Henry. "Charlemagne, the Saxons, and the Imperial Coronation of 800," 111 *English Historical Review* 1113 (1996).

McNeal, Richard A. "Protagoras the Historian," 25 *History and Theory* 299 (1986).

Meek, Ronald L. *Social Science and the Ignoble Savage*. Cambridge, UK: Cambridge University Press, 1976.

Moffatt, James, trans. *The New Testament: A New Translation*. New York: Association, 1919.

Mohr, Walter H. *Federal Indian Relations, 1784–1788*. Philadelphia, PA: University of Pennsylvania Press, 1933.

Montaigne, Michel Eyquem de. *The Essays of Michel Eyquem de Montaigne*, ed. W. Carew Hazlitt. Translated by Charles Cotton. Chicago, IL: Encyclopaedia Britannica, 1952.

Montesquieu, Baron de. *The Spirit of the Laws*, Vol. 1. Translated by Thomas Nugent. New York: Hafner, 1949.

Montiglio, Silvia. "Wandering Philosophers in Classical Greece," 120 *Journal of Hellenic Studies* 86 (2000).

Morison, Samuel Eliot. *The European Discovery of America: The Southern Voyages, A.D. 1492–1616*. New York: Oxford University Press, 1974.

Motto, Anna Lydia. "The Idea of Progress in Senecan Thought," 79 *Classical Journal* 225 (1984).

Muldoon, James, ed. *The Expansion of Europe: The First Phase*. Philadelphia, PA: University of Pennsylvania Press, 1977.

Mullett, Charles F. "Classical Influences on the American Revolution," 35 *Classical Journal* 92 (1939).

Munro, Dana Carleton, ed. *Urban and the Crusaders*. Philadelphia, PA: Department of History of the University of Pennsylvania, 1901.

Nagy, Gregory. *Homeric Questions*. Austin, TX: University of Texas Press, 1996.

Nielsen, Donald A. "Natural Law and Civilizations: Images of 'Nature,' Intracivilizational Polarities, and the Emergence of Hetorodox Ideals," 52 *Sociological Analysis* 55 (1991).

Nippel, Wilfred. "The Construction of the 'Other,'" in *Greeks and Barbarians*, ed. Thomas Harrison. New York: Routledge, 2002.

Nussbaum, Arthur. *A Concise History of the Law of Nations* (rev. ed.). New York: Macmillan, 1954.

Oberg, Michael Leroy. *Dominion and Civility: English Imperialism and Native America.* Ithaca, NY: Cornell University Press, 2004.

Oppenheim, Lassa. *International Law: Peace* (3rd ed.), ed. Ronald F. Roxburgh. London, UK: Longmans, Greens, 1920.

O'Regan, Daphne. *Rhetoric, Comedy and the Violence of Language in Aristophanes' Clouds.* Oxford, UK: Oxford University Press, 1992.

Osborne, Robin. "Early Greek Colonization?: The Nature of Greek Settlement in the West," in *Archaic Greece: New Approaches and New Evidence*, eds. Nick Fisher and Hans van Wees. London, UK: Classical Press of Wales, 1998.

Ovid. *The Metamorphoses.* Translated by Mary M. Innes. Harmondsworth, UK: Penguin Books, 1955.

Ovid. *Tristia Ex Ponto.* Translated by A. L. Wheeler. Cambridge, MA: Harvard University Press, 1924.

Parry, Milman. *The Making of Homeric Verse: The Collected Papers of Milman Parry*, ed. Adam Parry. Oxford, UK: Oxford University Press, 1971.

Pater, Walter. *The Renaissance.* Cleveland, OH: Meridian Books, 1961.

Pearce, Roy Harvey. *The Savages of America: A Study of the Indian and the Idea of Civilization* (rev. ed.). Baltimore, MD: Johns Hopkins Press, 1965.

Pelling, Christopher. "East Is East and West Is West—Or Are They? National Stereotypes in Herodotus," 1 *Histos* 51 (1997).

Penrose, Maryly Barton. *Indian Affairs Papers: American Revolution.* Franklin Park, NJ: Liberty Bell Associates, 1981.

Pentikäinen, Juha. *Kalevala Mythology.* Translated by Ritva Poom. Bloomington, IN: Indiana University Press, 1999.

Plato. *The Laws.* Translated by A. E. Taylor. London, UK: Dent & Sons, 1960.

Plato. *Plato in Twelve Volumes.* Translated by R. G. Bury. Cambridge, MA: Harvard University Press, 1967.

Plato. *Protagoras.* Translated by Benjamin Jowett. Rockville, MD: Serenity, 1999.

Plato. *Symposium.* Translated by Benjamin Jowett. Upper Saddle River, NJ: Prentice-Hall, 1956.

Pocock, J. G. A. *The Machiavellian Moment: Florentine Political Thought and the Atlantic Republican Tradition.* Princeton, NJ: Princeton University Press, 1975.

Pocock, J. G. A. "What Do We Mean by Europe?" 21 *Wilson Quarterly* 12 (1997).

Porter, H. C. *The Inconstant Savage: England and the North American Indian, 1500–1660.* London, UK: Duckworth, 1979.

Prucha, Francis Paul. *American Indian Treaties: The History of a Political Anomaly.* Berkeley, CA: University of California Press, 1994.

Prucha, Francis Paul, ed. *Documents of United States Indian Policy* (2nd ed.). Lincoln, NE: University of Nebraska Press, 1990.

Quinn, David B., ed. *The Voyages and Colonizing Enterprises of Sir Humphrey Gilbert* (2 vols.). London, UK: Haklyut Society, 1940.

Raaflaub, Kurt A. "A Historian's Headache: How to Read 'Homeric Society'?" in *Archaic Greece: New Approaches and New Evidence*, eds. Nick Fisher and Hans van Wees. London, UK: Duckworth, 1998.

Raaflaub, Kurt A., ed. *War and Peace in the Ancient World.* Malden, MA: Blackwell, 2007.

Rabelais, François. *The Works of Francis Rabelais,* Vol. 1. Translated by Sir Thomas Urquhart and Peter Anthony Motteux. London, UK: Lackington, Allen, 1807.

Reckford, Kenneth J. "Some Appearances of the Golden Age," 54 *Classical Journal* 79 (1958).

Reynolds, Henry. *The Law of the Land.* Victoria, BC: Penguin Books, 1992.

Romm, James S. *The Edges of the Earth in Ancient Thought: Geography, Exploration, and Fiction.* Princeton, NJ: Princeton University Press, 1992.

Ronis, David L., et al. "Attitudes, Decisions, and Habits as Determinants of Repeated Behavior," in *Attitude, Structure and Function,* eds. Anthony R. Pratkanis, Steven J. Breckler, and Anthony G. Greenwald. Hillsdale, NJ: Lawrence Erlbaum, 1989.

Ross, James Bruce, and Mary Martin McLaughlin, eds. *The Portable Renaissance Reader.* New York: Viking Press, 1953.

Rostovtzeff, M. *Greece,* ed. Elias J. Bickerman. Translated by J. D. Duff. London, UK: Oxford University Press, 1963.

Rostovtzeff, M. *Rome,* ed. Elias J. Bickerman. Translated by J. D. Duff. London, UK: Oxford University Press, 1960.

Rousseau, Jean-Jacques. *The Social Contract and Discourses* (rev. ed.), eds. J. H. Brumfitt and J. C. Hall. Translated by G. D. H. Cole. London, UK: Everyman, 1973.

Said, Edward W. *Orientalism.* New York: Vintage Books, 1979.

Sanders, Ronald. *Lost Tribes and Promised Lands: The Origins of American Racism.* New York: HarperPerennial, 1992.

Sassi, Maria Michela. *The Science of Man in Ancient Greece.* Translated by Paul Tucker. Chicago, IL: University of Chicago Press, 2001.

Sayre, Farrand. "Greek Cynicism," 6 *Journal of the History of Ideas* 113 (1945).

Schiappa, Edward. "Sophistic Rhetoric: Oasis or Mirage?" 10 *Rhetoric Review* 5 (1991).

Scobie, Alex, "The Origins of 'Centaurs,'" 89 *Folklore* 142 (1978).

Servi, Katerina. *Greek Mythology.* Athens, Greece: Ekdotike Athenon S. A., 2006.

Shakar, Alex. *The Savage Girl.* New York: HarperCollins, 2001.

Shear, Ione Mylonas. *Tales of Heroes: The Origins of the Homeric Texts.* New York: Aristide D. Caratzas, 2000.

Sheehan, Bernard W. *Savagism and Civility: Indians and Englishmen in Colonial Virginia.* Cambridge, UK: Cambridge University Press, 1980.

Sheehan, Bernard W. *Seeds of Extinction: Jeffersonian Philanthropy and the American Indian.* Chapel Hill, NC: University of North Carolina Press, 1973.

Shelley, Percy Bysshe. *Hellas: A Lyrical Drama,* ed. Thomas J. Wise. London, UK: Reeves and Turner, 1886.

Shepherd, William. *The Life of Poggio Bracciolini.* Liverpool, UK: J. McCreery, 1802.

Sidebottom, Harry. "Roman Imperialism: The Changed Outward Trajectory of the Roman Empire," 54.3 *Historia* 315 (2005).

Slotkin, Richard. *Regeneration Through Violence: They Mythology of the American Frontier, 1600–1860.* New York: HarperPerennial, 1973.

Sowerby, Robin. *The Greeks: An Introduction to Their Culture.* London, UK: Routledge, 1995.

Spariosu, Mihai I. *God of Many Names: Play, Poetry, and Power in Hellenic Thought from Homer to Aristotle.* Durham, NC: Duke University Press, 1991.

Stephens, Walter. *Demon Lovers: Witchcraft, Sex, and the Crisis of Belief.* Chicago, IL: University of Chicago Press, 2002.

Suetonius. *The Twelve Caesars.* Translated by Robert Graves. London, UK: Penguin Books, 2003.

Summers, Montague. *The History of Witchcraft and Demonology*. Whitefish, MT: Kessinger, 2003.

Tacitus. *The Agricola and the Germania*. Translated by H. Mattingly and S. A. Handford. Harmondsworth, UK: Penguin Books, 1970.

Tamanaha, Brian Z. *On the Rule of Law: History, Politics, Theory*. Cambridge, UK: Cambridge University Press, 2004.

Tarbell, Frank B. "Centauromachy and Amazonomachy in Greek Art: The Reasons for Their Popularity," 24 *American Journal of Archaeology* 226 (1920).

Tarbell, Frank B. *A History of Greek Art*. New York: Macmillan, 1907.

Taylor, E. G. R., ed. *The Original Writings and Correspondence of the Two Richard Hakluyts* (2 vols.). London, UK: Hakluyt Society, 1935.

Taylor, Margaret E. "Primitivism in Virgil," 76 *American Journal of Philology* 261 (1955).

Taylor, Margaret E. "Progress and Primitivism in Lucretius," 68 *American Journal of Philology* 180 (1947).

Tertullian. *Tertullian's Treatise on the Incarnation*. Edited and translated by Ernest Evans. London, UK: SPCK, 1956.

Thucydides. *The Peloponnesian War*. New York: Modern Library, 1951.

Tierney, Brian. *The Crisis of Church and State: 1050–1300*. Upper Saddle River, NJ: Prentice-Hall, 1964.

Todorov, Tzvetan. *The Conquest of America: The Question of the Other*. Translated by Richard Howard. Norman, OK: University of Oklahoma Press, 1999.

Todorov, Tzvetan. "Voyagers and Natives," in *Renaissance Characters*, ed. Eugenio Garin. Chicago, IL: University of Chicago Press, 1991.

Tsetskhladze, Gocha R., ed. *Ancient Greeks West and East*. Leiden, the Netherlands: Brill, 1999.

Van der Vliet, E. C. L. "The Romans and Us: Strabo's 'Geography' and the Construction of Ethnicity," 56 *Mnemosyne* 257 (2003).

Waddell, Helen. *The Wandering Scholars* (6th ed.). Harmondsworth, UK: Penguin Books, 1954.

Wallerstein, Immanuel. *The Modern World-System I: Capitalist Agriculture and the Origins of the European World-Economy in the Sixteenth Century*. Orlando, FL: Academic Press, 1974.

Washington, George. *The Writings of George Washington* (14 vols.), ed. Worthington Chauncey Ford. New York: G. P. Putnam's Sons, 1889.

Waterhouse, Edward. "A Declaration of the State of the Colony and Affairs in Virginia. With a Relation of the Barbarous Massacre in the Time of Peace and League, Treacherously Executed by the Native Infidels upon the English, the 22 of March Last. Together with the Names of those Massacred," in *The Records of the Virginia Company of London*, Vol. 3, ed. Susan Myra Kingsbury. Washington, DC: Government Printing Office, 1933.

Westlake, John. *Chapters on the Principles of International Law*. Cambridge, UK: Cambridge University Press, 1894.

White, Hayden. "The Forms of Wildness: Archaeology of an Idea," in *The Wild Man Within: An Image in Western Thought from the Renaissance to Romanticism*, eds. Edward Dudley and Maximilian E. Novak. Pittsburgh, PA: University of Pittsburgh Press, 1972.

White, Mary E. "Greek Colonization," 21 *Journal of Economic History* 443 (1961).

Williams, Robert A., Jr. *The American Indian in Western Legal Thought: The Discourses of Conquest*. New York: Oxford University Press, 1990.

Williams, Robert A., Jr. "Encounters on the Frontiers of International Human Rights Law: Redefining the Terms of Indigenous Peoples' Survival in the World," 1990 *Duke Law Journal* 660 (1990).

Williams, Robert A., Jr. *Like a Loaded Weapon: The Rehnquist Court, Indian Rights, and the Legal History of Racism in America.* Minneapolis, MN: University of Minnesota Press, 2005.

Xenophon. *Xenophon in Seven Volumes,* ed. E. C. Marchant. Cambridge, MA: Harvard University Press, 1923.

# INDEX

CPSIA information can be obtained at www.ICGtesting.com
Printed in the USA
LVOW09*1948190215

427614LV00004B/25/P